P9-ELO-223

I probably knew Payne as well as anybody on Tour, but it wasn't until after his death that I realized how far-reaching his life really was. I always knew he loved people, but I didn't know how generous he was with his time, how gracious and charitable he was to others. He was incredibly compassionate to me when I was sick; he was the first guy to call me and was always there when I needed him.

Paul Azinger, PGA Tour Player

Payne was a passionate person—someone who understood passion at all levels—in his personal life, in his spiritual life, and in his quest to be the greatest golfer in the world. He played with passion, and he lived with passion.

Hal Sutton, PGA Tour Player

Payne Stewart assured himself a prominent place in the history of the game with a career that ended much too tragically and much too soon. He established an impressive record as a player and contributed so much more through his outgoing personality and generous spirit.

Arnold Palmer, PGA Tour Player

He was a great player, but he was huge as a person. He was a friend who always tried to help.

Sergio Garcia, PGA Tour Player

Payne was an extraordinary person with extraordinary flair, and he went out on top—on top of his game and on top of life.

Mark O'Meara, PGA Tour Player

The loss of Payne Stewart was a tremendous one for the golfing world and for me personally. I always loved Payne's loose and relaxed swing. His performance at the U.S. Open last year was truly fantastic. Payne was a devoted family man and a man of strong faith. He was a great champion who truly respected the game, and he will be sorely missed by anyone who ever knew him or had the pleasure of watching him play.

Jack Nicklaus, PGA Tour Player

Payne Stewart's story is an inspiration to anyone who appreciates the spirit of a competitor. Early in his career he kept falling short of victory, but he had more inside than his critics could imagine, and with hard work he proved himself to be a true champion.

Tiger Woods, PGA Tour Player

Payne Stewart was a leader on the Tour, a leader to the players, and a great example of a father.

Davis Love III, PGA Tour Player

Payne touched people's lives more than he ever realized. Payne got every single thing that he could out of life. If there's anybody who went to heaven a happy man, it was Payne Stewart.

Clay Walker, Recording Artist

He was a super guy that I know is with the Lord. Seeing him with that W.W.J.D. bracelet on at the U.S. Open inspired me. That picture of him clutching the trophy says, "Complete."

Paul Stankowski, PGA Tour Player

We all wished we had Payne's personality. He was the center of attention at parties, mostly because he had a gift of making people feel good about themselves. He was a wonderful husband, father, and friend. It was my privilege to have known him.

Todd Woodbridge, Professional Tennis Player

Payne Stewart inspired me. Watching him, I learned about being gracious in defeat and celebrating victory. I learned about being a good and faithful husband and an involved and caring father. I learned about loving my fellowman and about loving and worshiping my God. Ultimately, he taught me the importance of leaving a legacy. I am blessed to have known Payne.

Michael W. Smith, Recording Artist

Payne was a great man in all ways—husband, father, friend, and golfer. He was a wonderful sportsman and it was a great honor to have known him.

Donald Trump, The Trump Organization

Not only was I lucky to have been able to play golf with Payne Stewart, I was even more blessed to have known him.

Vince Gill, Recording Artist

When Payne was around, everything around him was better. It didn't matter whether it was a golf course or a monastery, he could light it up. Hopefully, his flame will never go out.

Will McDonough, Columnist, Boston Globe

Payne was a person you felt like you had known forever.

David Duval, PGA Tour Player

I'll never forget him. Payne welcomed me with open arms when I came to America. He played a big part in my career. He was an all-round gentleman.

Jesper Parnevik, PGA Tour Player

I remember Payne as somebody who wanted to uphold the principles of the game of golf—act in a professional manner, be courteous, play to win, but be gracious whether you win or lose. Payne didn't hold anything back. Payne enjoyed life, and he wanted to make sure everyone around him did too.

Lee Janzen, PGA Tour Player

He was one of the guys who was significant in making the PGA Tour what it is today.

Nick Price, PGA Tour Player

How do you celebrate the life of the greatest "celebrator of life" that you've ever known?

Chuck Cook, Golf Instructor

Some people light up a room. Payne electrified the entire house. He was a man who cherished his wife and children and looked for ways to express his love meaningfully. He was uncommonly loyal to his family, friends, business associates, and fans. His growing faith in Christ encouraged me. I was always proud to call him my boss, and I feel blessed to have been counted as one of his friends.

Gloria Baker, Personal Assistant, Payne Stewart Enterprises

Payne Stewart was a great man. He wasn't just a golfer; Payne was a leader.

Ward Carroll, Commander, United States Navy

Payne Stewart was the epitome of a happy and talented champion who possessed a warm smile and a swing of pure elegance. We all loved him.

Ben Crenshaw, PGA Tour Player

Payne's life drove a message home to me that I have precious little time to spend with my kids. Because of Payne, I'm going to devote more time to my family.

Glenn Frey, Recording Artist, The Eagles

Payne was a great friend both personally and professionally. When he entered a room, his energy, enthusiasm, and charisma put a smile on everyone's face. He loved life more than any person I've ever known. His absence has left a void in the lives of all who knew him.

Kel Devlin, Nike Golf Sportsmarketing Director

Payne Stewart was a true professional, he related to the "everyman"; not just the golf fan, but people everywhere.

Dr. Richard Coop, Sports Psychologist

It was fascinating to see the transition in Payne over the years as to how he prioritized life. That's what it's all about. . . . We're only here for a short time; and Payne has left something that will live forever.

Ken Venturi, CBS Golf Commentator

Payne Stewart was devoted to his faith, family, and friends. He was a supremely confident man who displayed wit, humility, compassion, and unbridled generosity. He was truly a great friend and I miss him every day.

Joe T. Ford, Chairman and CEO, ALLTEL Corporation

Payne enjoyed life to its fullest. Payne respected people and appreciated his life and what he had accomplished.

John Cook, PGA Tour Player

I've been a great admirer of Payne and the way he handled himself in golf. He's one of the reasons that golf is so popular with young people today. He was a true sportsman.

Clint Eastwood, Actor, Part Owner of
Pebble Beach Golf Links

Payne's death brought more people toward God than he ever could have done in his life. That is a good thing. Not having Payne with us is a bad thing.

Rocco Mediate, PGA Tour Player

Because of Payne's death, his life touched even more people because of the things that mattered to him most—his passion for the game, his faith, and his family.

Amy Grant, Recording Artist

Payne Stewart was one of the first guys to welcome me to the PGA Tour; he was very much a gentleman in every way.

Casey Martin, PGA Tour Player

He had such a great sense of humor; it was impossible not to like Payne.

Frank Lickliter II, PGA Tour Player

He was a guy that my kids looked up to, and I looked up to, and a guy who I was proud to know as a friend.

John Elway, former NFL Quarterback

PAYNE
STEWART

PAYNE
STEWART

The Authorized Biography

TRACEY STEWART
WITH KEN ABRAHAM

WALKER & COMPANY
New York

Large Print edition published by arrangement with Broadman & Holman Publishers, 2000

First Large Print Edition published in the United States of America in 2000 by Walker Publishing Company, Inc.

Library of Congress Cataloging-in-Publication Data
Stewart, Tracey, 1959–
    Payne Stewart : the authorized biography / Tracey Stewart with Ken Abraham.—Large Print ed.
    p. cm.
    ISBN 0-8027-2767-0
    1. Stewart, Payne, 1957–1999. 2. Golfers—United States— Biography. I. Abraham, Ken. II. Title.

GV964.S84 S83 2000
796.352'092—dc21
[B]
                                                          00-043426

Scripture versions used in this book include NASB, the New American Standard Bible, © the Lockman Foundation, 1960, 1962, 1963, 1968, 1971, 1972, 1973, 1975, 1977; used by permission; NIV, the Holy Bible, New International Version, copyright © 1973, 1978, 1984 by International Bible Society; and the King James Version.

Scripture used in chapter 27 is taken from *Handbook to Prayer*, by Kenneth Boa, from the devotional for Day 18.

Printed in the United States of America

10 9 8 7 6 5 4 3 2 1

To Chelsea and Aaron

May this book be a permanent reminder
of your wonderful father and how much
he loved you both. May you both
live with a similar sense of love, joy,
adventure, and enthusiasm for life.

I love you,
Mum

Let me begin by thanking all those who have helped me write this book. To name each of you would be a daunting task, so let me simply express my gratitude. I am also grateful for all the cards, notes, and letters our family received. I have been unable to write and thank each of you for caring, and sharing our grief with us. I have been sustained not only by my faith and the support of family and friends, but also through the fans of the great game of golf. Wanting to reach out and thank you, I pulled out the scrapbooks and the old date books . . . and, as if you were sitting on the sofa with me, I am sharing with you my life with Payne . . . as we saw it, as we experienced it. I couldn't write each of you, so I picked up my pen and wrote this book. This way I could not only thank you, but also share with you a little of Payne.

Tracey Stewart

CONTENTS

I always felt that golf was what the Lord intended me to do.

He gave me a gift, a talent.

PAYNE STEWART

FOREWORD

P ayne Stewart's life will be a perpetual challenge to me—a challenge to live life more
fully each day, to draw closer to God, to love
my family and friends, and to align my priorities accordingly.

Payne Stewart knew what courage was all
about; he overcame fear and came back from
the brink of defeat to win again. We need
heroes like Payne today.

Shortly after the tragic accident in which
Payne died, a friend sensed my sadness at our
loss and tried to help me sort it all out. "Calling
this 'death,'" she said, "is not honorable and is
not respectful." She preferred to express
Payne's passing as "going home." Indeed, that

is exactly what Payne did—he went home, leaving behind a trail of love, laughter, loud and funny stories, fond remembrances, gracious defeats, and incredible victories. He left behind a model of faith, pointing the way that we can follow.

Had Payne known that he was about to leave us, he would have questioned departing just when so much in his life was so right. But more than that, he would have been grateful for having the deep love of his family, for receiving the respect and honors that were bestowed on him during his life, and for knowing that he had made a difference in this world. Most of all, he would be thankful for the source of his strength—his relationship with God.

May Payne's life inspire you to love more, smile more, hope more; to be humble while performing bold acts; and to be brave, strong, and courageous in standing for what is right. A devoted son, committed husband, dedicated father, and great friend, Payne Stewart is now with his heavenly Father, and yet, in many ways, he is still with us. This very special man gave us his best—and calls for ours.

Mike Hicks, Caddy

PAYNE
STEWART

1

The Greatest
Open Ever

T his could be it. I leaned forward in my chair, eyes glued to my husband's image on the television screen, anxiously watching and waiting, hanging on the commentators' every word. This could be the critical shot of the 1999 U.S. Open. Payne's caddy, Mike Hicks, handed him his putter as he approached the sixteenth green at Pinehurst No. 2.

The U.S. Open is held each year at one of the most challenging golf courses in America. The mid-June tournament spans a four-day period, beginning on Thursday and ending on Father's Day. Open to both professional golfers and any amateurs who can survive the sieve of sectional qualifying rounds conducted at various locations across the nation, the U.S. Open is truly America's tournament. Nearly seven thousand golfers vie for a spot in the prestigious field each year, hoping to capture the prized silver trophy. Of that number, fewer than 160 men earn the right to tee it up in the Open.

One of the most difficult golf tournaments in the world, separating the good golfer from the truly great, the U.S. Open is "designed to identify the best golfer in the world," according to former United States Golf Association president Sandy Tatum. The players, however, don't always see it that way. Over the years, several have been heard mumbling, both privately and publicly, that the Open is designed more to humiliate them. Indeed, Ben Crenshaw, 1999 Ryder Cup captain, describes the U.S. Open as the "hardest test in golf."

For the 1999 Open, North Carolina's famed Pinehurst No. 2 golf course was configured by the USGA to play as a 7,175-yard par 70. Adding difficulty to an already tough course, USGA officials decided that two of Pinehurst's par-5 holes, number 8 and the hazard-strewn number 16, would be played as long par 4s. The chilly, damp weather that settled over North Carolina that weekend added yet another dimension of difficulty to Pinehurst's treacherous greens.

Payne had taken the lead during Friday's

second round, and at the end of play on Saturday, still clung to a one-shot advantage over Phil Mickelson. But as Sunday's final round commenced, Payne's position at the top of the leaderboard was jeopardized as Mickelson, Tiger Woods, Vijay Singh, and David Duval mounted separate charges. Payne started the day playing well and rode a two-shot lead going into the ninth hole. As the round progressed, Duval dropped off, but Tiger Woods and Vijay Singh still lurked just below the top names on the leaderboard. Then, Payne began to struggle. Between holes 9 and 12, Payne missed four greens in a row, settling for bogeys at 10 and 12, which allowed Phil Mickelson to snatch the lead. Fighting back at the thirteenth, Payne sank his putt for birdie, pulling even with Mickelson again.

Meanwhile, Tiger Woods, playing in the group ahead of Payne and Phil, sank a difficult putt at 14 to draw within two strokes. The leaderboard was getting crowded at the top. On 16, Woods drained another sensational putt, dropping him to even par, only one stroke behind the leaders. Making matters worse, Payne narrowly missed his putt for par on 15 and now trailed Phil Mickelson by one stroke as they approached the sixteenth hole. Payne shut his eyes, shaking off the wayward putt and gathering himself for the final push to the finish.

Mickelson had played flawlessly all day long, sinking difficult putts, hitting incredible shots, and making virtually no mental mistakes. He had not bogeyed a single hole throughout the round. His steady play was especially remarkable considering that on this Father's Day, back home in Scottsdale, Arizona, his wife was due to deliver their first child. Phil knew that at any moment he might receive a phone call telling him that Amy was on her way to the hospital. Given a choice between contending in the Open and being at home for the birth of their baby, Phil had announced in advance that he'd walk away from Pinehurst to be with Amy. It was a decision Payne understood and heartily endorsed.

But the distractions of imminent fatherhood did nothing to diminish Phil's competitive edge. If anything, it inspired him all the more! Thinking about what it might mean to win the U.S. Open on Father's Day, he had mused, "It could be a cool story for my daughter to read about when she gets older."

The weather remained unseasonably cool and wet for June in North Carolina; and though the rain held off, by late Sunday afternoon a fine mist permeated the air. No matter what the weather, the par-4 sixteenth at Pinehurst was treacherous, a hole that only three players had managed to hit in regulation during Sunday's final round. It looked as though 16 might be Payne's waterloo as well. He missed the green on his approach and then made matters even worse by hitting a poor chip shot, leaving himself a monstrous 25-foot putt for par.

Payne chewed his gum pensively as he strode onto the green. Concentration creased his brow, yet he seemed amazingly calm and composed. He leaned over, went through his normal pre-putt routine, then took a smooth, even, pendulum stroke and rolled the putt in as though it were a 3-footer! As the crowd roared its approval, Payne nonchalantly raised his right arm and pointed his index finger skyward in a brief acknowledgment, as though saying, "Thank you very much, but I still have a lot of work to do."

Concerning his performance on 16, Payne later said, "I was kind of disappointed in my chip shot. It was obviously horrible. But then I got myself right back into it and said, 'OK, you gotta stand up here, read the line, and make the putt.' And I did it. It gave me a lot of belief that I still had a chance to win the golf tournament."

When Payne sank that extremely difficult putt, it notched up the pressure on Phil

Mickelson, who proceeded to miss a tough 8-footer for par. Suddenly, the two were tied again. Up ahead on the seventeenth green, Tiger Woods's putt spun around the left side of the cup and lipped out. He would have to birdie the last hole to have a chance to win.

At 17, a 191-yard par 3, both Payne and Phil nearly knocked the flag over, sticking their tee shots close enough possibly to make birdie. Payne's ball was about four feet from the cup, and Phil had a 6-footer. Phil missed his putt and had to settle for par. Before Payne lined up his putt on 17, a male voice in the broadcast booth could be heard on the air, saying ever-so-faintly, "Payne's gonna win." Payne made his 4-foot birdie putt and had a one-stroke lead.

After Payne made his birdie, I reluctantly pulled myself away from the television screen in our rented house where I had been watching every shot. I hurried outside to the car. Win or lose, I wanted to be there when Payne finished. Ripping out of the driveway, I roared toward the golf course, trying to locate a radio station that might be carrying the tournament. Fortunately, traffic was light, and I soon raced into the players' parking area near the clubhouse and ran to the eighteenth green.

Thousands of spectators lined the fairways and crowded around the eighteenth green to watch the national championship come to a close. People were sitting on the clubhouse roof; several were perched precariously in nearby trees; everyone strained for any advantage to their view. I quickly made my way out toward the green.

About the same time, in the group up ahead on the eighteenth green, Tiger Woods lined up his putt, a 30-footer that could put him back at even par and possibly keep him in contention. Woods stroked the putt as purely as he had any shot all day. The ball beelined across the green toward the hole but then rolled past, missing the cup by inches. Tiger doubled over in agony as he watched the ball dribble to a stop, possibly dashing his hopes of a championship. He shut his eyes and for a few moments seemed frozen in time, his face grimacing with disappointment. So close, yet so far away.

In the meantime, Payne had teed off on 18. He connected with the shot squarely and thought he had hit it well enough to be safe, though he couldn't see where the ball had landed. He was wrong. His drive had hit the first cut of deep rough, and instead of squirting through and landing in perfect position on the fairway, as so many similar tee shots had done that day, Payne's shot got hung up in the thick, wet grass. The ball bounced first to the left and then jogged back to the right, diving straight into the high grass just six inches off the fairway, in horrible position. After Payne hit his tee shot on 18, the chimes at the nearby Pinehurst chapel began to play. NBC-TV golf analyst Mark Rolfing noticed the sound and exclaimed, "They're playing 'Angels We Have Heard on High'!" The chimes must have struck a soothing chord with Payne.

When Payne trekked down the fairway and found his ball tucked in the rough, he was surprised and a bit disappointed. But Payne loved to hit the tough shots, and this one challenged him.

When Phil's drive landed in the heart of the fairway, Payne's one-stroke lead was once again in jeopardy. As he considered his predicament—178 yards out and in the thick rough—to Payne there was only one option. All week long he had stuck to his game plan whenever he was in trouble. He had learned from experience that when you're in trouble at the U.S. Open, you lay up and try to make par with your short game. He called this "taking your medicine," and he wasn't about to change the game plan that had helped him to lead after more rounds than anyone in the history of the U.S. Open.

Payne took his medicine and hit a 9-iron, landing well short of the bunker. It cost him a stroke, but it gave him a chance—what he knew might well be his last chance—to win the tournament.

"I hit the ball well all week," Payne said later, "and my wedge game had been particularly sharp. So when I drove it in the rough, I took my medicine and got into position to hit a wedge onto the green. Even though I was in the rough, I felt confident I could save par."

From the center of the fairway, Phil Mickelson saw an opportunity. With Payne forced to lay up, Phil felt free to attack the green. He launched an aggressive second shot, which rolled to a stop within twenty feet of the pin.

By now, I had made my way through the clubhouse and outside to an area restricted to players, family, USGA officials, and media; but I was still stuck in a crowd, three or four people deep, behind several taller spectators. I stood on my tiptoes, stretching to see Payne's next shot. "Where's Payne?" I asked a USGA official who was standing nearby. He eyed me curiously, as though he might recognize me, but I didn't give him any further hint concerning my identity.

"He's in the fairway," the official replied matter-of-factly. "He had to lay up."

My heart sank. If the round ended in a tie, that would mean an eighteen-hole play-off on

9

Monday. Oh, no! I thought. Not another play-off! Payne's track record in play-offs was a lackluster three wins and six losses.

I whispered a quick prayer, "Lord, please be with him and help him to be the best he can be." I didn't pray for Payne to win because he and I had long since learned that there were more important things in life than winning golf tournaments. I did, however, pray, "Help him, Lord, to make the best effort he can and to bring glory to you."

Payne and his caddy, Mike Hicks, surveyed the situation and talked over the next shot. Mike, a thirty-eight-year-old native of North Carolina, had caddied for Payne off and on for more than eleven years; and even though Payne had tremendous confidence in Mike's knowledge of the golf course and in his own ability, he still wasn't satisfied. He paced off the full distance—about seventy-seven yards to the green—and then back, looking over the approach, the formidable bunker in front of the green, and the pin placement. Payne knew he had only one shot. He could not afford to misjudge the distance, the speed of the green, or anything else. If he didn't get the ball close enough to leave himself with a makable putt, the tournament would be up for grabs again.

Lining up over his ball, Payne hit a carefully placed wedge shot onto the green, leaving

10

himself a nasty 15-foot putt for par. It was makable, but by no means a sure thing, especially under these conditions, at the end of the tournament, when one spike mark could send the ball veering off course. Payne knew that possibility only too well because that is exactly what had happened to him on the eighteenth green at the previous year's U.S. Open at the Olympic Club in San Francisco.

2

An
Unforgettable
Finish

P ayne had led the pack for three days at the 1998 Open. But during the final round, on Father's Day, he had allowed a four-shot lead to slip away. Almost as if it were a replay of the 1993 U.S. Open at Baltusrol, Lee Janzen came from seven shots behind and overtook him. Needing to sink a difficult 25-foot putt on the eighteenth green at Olympic to force a play-off, Payne gave it his best shot but missed the cup by a few inches. Lee Janzen, a tough competitor, especially on difficult courses, returned home with his second U.S. Open trophy.

Such dramatic turnarounds are not unusual during golf's four major tournaments: the Masters, the U.S. Open, the British Open, and the PGA Championship. These four events are known as "majors," even though the field of players competing against one another is basically the same as in other tournaments. Still, the majors have become the standard by which a professional golfer's career is measured. A fabulous player can win a dozen tournaments, and millions of dollars, but if he never wins a "major," he does not attain golf greatness. Thus the most ominous and despised tag in golf, "The Best Player Never to Have Won a Major," has been an albatross around the necks of numerous golf superstars.

Payne had finally removed the albatross from his own neck in 1989, when he won the PGA Championship. He'd won his second major—the U.S. Open—in 1991, but the 1998 Open loss hurt nonetheless. Payne's disappointment, though he handled it well, was very real. After his 1991 U.S. Open triumph, he had won only twice since on the PGA Tour, and by 1999, at forty-two years of age, Payne knew that his opportunities for keeping pace with the young lions on the golf course were growing slimmer. Payne passionately wanted to win at least one more major tournament in his career.

As he approached the 1999 tour season, Payne had only two main golfing goals: to win another major and to make the Ryder Cup team.

Both objectives could be accomplished by a victory at Pinehurst. That's why I was surprised when, after he played poorly and missed the cut at the FedEx St. Jude Classic in Memphis the week before the U.S. Open, Payne called home and said, "I'm going to stay here a few days." Payne always looked forward to staying with our friends, Mark and Vicki Hopkins in Memphis. Payne had grown-up with Mark and Vicki in Springfield, and we both had developed a close friendship with them, taking numerous vacations together over the years.

Payne's mother had traveled from Springfield, Missouri, to spend time with him while he was in Memphis, so it made sense that he would want to stay in town to visit with her as well. Also, Payne's golf coach, Chuck Cook, and his wife, Lana, were flying in to Memphis so Chuck and Payne could work together before going on to Pinehurst for the U.S. Open. However, from my point of view, remaining in Memphis after missing the cut seemed like a waste of time, and I told Payne so.

"Well, Mom is here, so I'm just gonna stay till Sunday," he said tersely. I could tell that he was still peeved that he had missed the cut.

"I understand," I said, "but I think you'd be better off to get over to Pinehurst and start preparing for the Open. Remember the goals you set. It's a major and one of your goals is to win a major. You really need to think about that."

At first, Payne wasn't overjoyed to hear my opinion on the matter. He insisted on staying in Memphis. A few hours later, though, he called back. "You know, love, you're right. I'm going to go on over to Pinehurst as soon as Chuck and Lana get here."

"Good idea," I replied.

That was so typical of Payne. He adamantly insisted on making up his own mind, but he was always open to advice and quick to take suggestions—once he'd had a chance to think them through. Nobody on earth could tell Payne Stewart what to do, but once he saw the light and took ownership of an idea, he was always willing to change.

Payne, Chuck, and Lana arrived at Pinehurst on Saturday afternoon, June 12, and moved into the house we had rented for the week of the tournament, about five minutes away from the clubhouse. Dr. Richard Coop, a sports psychologist with whom Payne had been working since 1988, had noticed that Payne seemed to play better whenever we stayed in private housing during major tournaments, rather than in hotels. We had rented a home during both of the majors Payne had won previ-

15

ously. Getting away from the crowds allowed him to escape the constant and often frenetic pace of the professional golf circuit. We could relax and talk about anything—anything other than golf—and the brief respite allowed Payne to concentrate better when he returned to the links.

Chuck and Payne began their preparation immediately. On Saturday evening, they walked the course to become familiar with its intricacies. Payne carried his 7-, 8-, and 9-irons, his wedges, and a putter as they played all sorts of shots, chipping to the greens and putting from various locations. They followed the same routine on Sunday. On Monday and Tuesday, Payne played practice rounds. He took part of Wednesday as a practice day, working on the driving range but not going out on the course. He took the rest of the day off.

By the time I arrived in Pinehurst on Wednesday, Payne was in a good frame of mind. He felt well-prepared to play the Open, and although he had not played Pinehurst No. 2 many times before in actual competition, he genuinely liked the golf course. He was bubbling with confidence.

Aaron, our ten-year-old, was staying with the family of one of his friends back in Orlando, and thirteen-year-old Chelsea was attending a girls' basketball camp in Tallahassee. That allowed Payne and me to relax even more. After Chuck and Lana moved to their hotel room, it was just the two of us at the house. Rather than going out to restaurants, we ate all our meals at the house. Payne enjoyed helping with the cooking, and together we prepared simple, healthy meals of grilled chicken and lots of fruits and vegetables. There'd be no fancy cuisine or newfangled diets at our "training table." For variety, we had spaghetti one night—Payne loved spaghetti— and steak another. Lana and Chuck joined us one night for dinner. Otherwise, we kept to ourselves and tried to maintain a sense of normalcy amidst the hype and hoopla of a major championship.

Many professional athletes become superstitious when something is working well for them. For example, when a baseball team is on a winning streak, some of the guys will wear the same socks or T-shirt every game. Some players establish certain routines and refuse to deviate from them as long as they are winning. They might get up at exactly the same time and eat the same foods at the same time and place. The logic behind these superstitions is: If the wheel is rolling, don't mess it up by doing something different.

Interestingly, perhaps, pro golfers are generally not given to such superstitions. Nevertheless, when Payne got off to a good start by shooting an opening round 68 on Thursday, I remembered that we had enjoyed some mangoes as part of our fruit-and-muffin breakfast that morning. That evening, I made a point of going to the grocery store and stocking up on mangoes for the rest of the week. Mangoes became our signature fruit at breakfast every morning of the tournament.

On Friday, Payne played well again. As I had done on Thursday, I walked the course, keeping about half a hole ahead of Payne so I could watch where his shots landed. Chuck Cook followed Payne on Thursday and Friday as well. Although Payne and I rarely talked during a round unless there was some specific reason to do so, he wanted me to be there as often as possible. He claimed to know exactly where I was on the course at all times. Sometimes friends or fans would distract me from watching him, and Payne always let me know later that he had noticed. "Who was that person you were talking to?" he'd ask with a mischievous grin.

"Aren't you supposed to be concentrating on your golf?" I'd tease in return.

"I am, but I always know where you are on the course," Payne said.

Payne's confidence grew even stronger after he shot another great round on Friday, shooting 69 and leading the tournament after two tough days of competition. By Saturday, the crowds at Pinehurst were so huge I knew I wouldn't even be able to see Payne's shots. I told him, "I think I'm going to watch the round on television today. It's so hard to see out there with so many people. I'll be there, though, when you get done."

Payne understood perfectly.

Because Payne was leading the tournament, NBC focused its cameras on him for almost every one of his shots on the back nine during the third round. I stayed glued to the television most of the afternoon. Payne played well enough to remain atop the leaderboard on Saturday, but something was wrong. He was having trouble sinking his putts. As the afternoon slipped away, so did Payne's lead.

I peered intently at the television screen, following Payne's every move. I rarely played golf—tennis is more my game—but I had watched Payne play week in and week out for twenty years, so I knew his game well. I could usually tell if he needed to make an adjustment. As I watched on television, I noticed that Payne was moving his head ever so slightly on his putts, forward and upward, as though he were trying to watch the ball go into the hole. The slight head motion had already cost him several strokes. I watched helplessly as one putt after another curled around the cup and lipped out. "Oh, Payne!" I cried aloud to the television screen. "Keep your head down!" He ended up shooting a 72, his worst round of the tournament. Though he was still one stroke ahead of Phil Mickelson, and several strokes ahead of the pack, it wasn't a comfortable lead to sleep on.

At the conclusion of his round, I headed to the press tent, where I figured Payne would be answering questions about his round. Sure enough, because he was still leading the tournament, as soon as he had signed his scorecard he'd been whisked straightaway to the media tent. When I arrived, a press conference had already begun, so I slipped in at the back of the tent and waited. When the reporters finally had their fill, I stood at the entrance until Payne saw me and came over. "I'm going to go hit some balls," he said.

"OK, I'll go with you," I said. "You need to spend some time on the putting green too." Payne nodded in agreement. "You need to keep your head down," I continued quietly.

Payne looked surprised. "Really?"

"Yes. When you're putting, you are trying

to watch the ball go in, rather than keeping your head down."

Payne and I walked over to the driving range. While most "weekend" golfers take time to hit balls at the range before a round, loosening up and establishing their swing routines, many amateur players are surprised to discover how much work the pros put in at the range after a round. The golfers whose names are most often seen atop the leaderboard are usually the same players you'll find in the practice areas after they've played their rounds on the course.

Payne often did his best practice work after a round. Rehearsing the good shots, and making minor adjustments to avoid the poor ones, he was committed to practicing after each round of the 1999 U.S. Open. At the Olympic Club in 1998, by the time he'd finished with his media interviews, the sun was usually beginning to set over the Pacific Ocean. Consequently, Payne hadn't been able to get to the practice areas after his rounds, and he later had said on many occasions that he regretted that situation.

He was not about to make the same mistake. So even though it was nearly dusk and a chill swept across "Maniac Hill," as the Pinehurst practice area is known, Payne pulled on his glove and went to work. I watched as he hit one golf ball after another on the driving range, working on his irons for more than half an hour. Then we walked over to the putting green near the clubhouse, and he spent another forty-five minutes working on his putts. He forced himself to keep his head still and not look up until the ball was well away from the putter. He got to the point where he was literally putting with his eyes closed and hitting the center of the cup almost every stroke. I stayed right there with him and watched as he concentrated on keeping his head still during each shot.

"Is that better?" he asked after a while.

"Yes, much better. It looks great."

It was nearly dark by the time we got back to the house. I prepared a simple dinner while Payne showered and then responded to the barrage of phone messages stored in his cellular phone's voice mail. He was always good about returning phone calls, and it seemed that half the world had his "private" cell phone number.

Because Chelsea was at basketball camp, we couldn't talk to her, but Payne made a point of calling Aaron at his friend's home.

"Aaron, I'm leading the U.S. Open again," Payne said enthusiastically to our ten-year-old son.

Aaron was unimpressed. "That's great, Dad," he replied. "Guess what! Conner got a long-board skateboard!"

Payne laughed. Unwittingly, our kids had a marvelous way of keeping Payne's feet on the ground, and he loved them all the more for it. Although they were always encouraging to their father, to them being a professional golfer was no big deal. That's just what their dad did for a living. Some of their friends' parents were doctors, lawyers, dentists, and schoolteachers. It just so happened that their father made his living hitting a small white ball into a 4-inch hole in the ground. They expected him to do it well; after all, he was . . . Dad. That he was one of the greatest players ever to walk the links hadn't yet sunk in to them.

After dinner and his phone calls, Payne settled back to watch the Stanley Cup hockey finals. We stayed up late to make it easier to sleep in a bit on Sunday morning. Because Payne had a late tee time on Sunday, the last thing he wanted to do was wake up at sunrise and pace around impatiently until it was time to get ready.

We slept as late as we could and then enjoyed a leisurely Sunday morning. We had our usual breakfast, including our mangoes, and then Payne got ready to play the final round of the U.S. Open. As part of his normal pre-round routine, he pressed his own clothes, including his plus fours—the knickers that had become an indelible part of his golf persona. Prior to the birth of our daughter, Chelsea, in 1985, I had always pressed the clothes that Payne would wear on the course. But after our children were born, Payne began doing his own ironing during tournaments. He refused to have his clothes sent out to a dry cleaner or to have anyone else press them. He was fastidious about getting every crease just right. Sometimes, if I was running late, he even pressed my clothes!

With the television blaring and Payne on his cell phone answering calls from friends, family members, and other well-wishers, I went to take a shower. When I came out of the bedroom, I was shocked to see that Payne's eyes were puffy. He looked like he had been crying.

"Luv'ie, what's wrong?" I asked as I crossed the room toward him. Payne wiped his eyes with his knuckle and motioned toward the television. "NBC just ran a Father's Day segment," he replied emotionally.

"So?"

"It was about my dad and me." Payne had been unaware that NBC had planned to broadcast a segment concerning Bill Stewart—Payne's dad, who had died of cancer in 1985—and his influence upon Payne's life and career. Payne had simply been tuning in to watch the early tournament coverage. As he watched the video of himself and his dad, tears flooded his eyes.

Rather than being disconcerted, however, Payne drew strength from the piece. It inspired him to want to play his best Father's Day round ever.

As the time neared to leave for the golf course, Payne dressed in navy blue knickers with a matching tam-o'-shanter hat; white kneesocks and white golf shoes; and a red-and-blue-striped shirt, highlighted by his Payne Stewart clothing line logo. Red, white, and blue. It was, after all, the U.S. Open. Because of the damp, chilly weather, Payne also donned a navy blue rain jacket. On his wrist he wore a dark green wristband, given to him by our son, Aaron, which bore the letters W.W.J.D., for "What Would Jesus Do?"

About two hours before his tee time, I drove Payne to the course. I slowly pulled the white courtesy car to a stop at the base of the circular drive, just past the famed Pinehurst No. 2 clubhouse. I looked across at Payne and tried to encourage him with some words of wisdom before he left to play the final round of the U.S. Open Championship.

"Just go out there and trust yourself," I said to him. "Believe in your heart that you can do it!"

He looked over at me, and with his little mischievous grin he said, "I've got a big heart, love." I laughed, we kissed good-bye and said "I love you" to each other.

The "big heart" that Payne was referring to was a diagnosis he had received in 1994 after a routine EKG in a fitness examination prior to the Los Angeles Open. The doctors discovered that Payne had a bundle-branch block in his heart, an anomaly that meant his heart did not squeeze blood normally and that the beat was not as strong as it should have been. This condition caused Payne's heart to be enlarged.

To keep the situation in check, Payne was advised to take Avapro medication on a daily basis, work out at least five days a week, and limit his consumption of alcohol. The doctors predicted that he would probably need a pacemaker later in life. Rather than worrying about his condition, Payne always made jokes about having a big heart anytime someone mentioned that he had "heart," "courage," or "intestinal fortitude." As he bounded out of the car toward the clubhouse, that big heart was about to be put to the test.

Arriving two hours early was a standard

part of Payne's pre-tournament routine. He was obsessed with being on time. "In my line of work, I can't afford to be late," he reminded me frequently. "If I'm late for work, we don't get paid!"

I, on the other hand, was frequently late. If there was one area in which Payne wished (and prayed!) for my improvement, it was the matter of punctuality. Every year, he asked me to make a New Year's resolution that I would attempt to be on time. I made the resolutions, but my follow-through was less than Payne desired. He never gave up hope though!

After I dropped Payne off at the Pinehurst clubhouse, I returned to our rental home and switched on the television to watch the tournament coverage. Payne, as always, went to the fitness trailer, where he did some stretching exercises to loosen up his neck, back, and shoulders, all of which he had injured at one time or another during his twenty-year career. He usually had a massage at the fitness trailer. Only then, after his body was limber, was he ready to head to the range.

Mike Hicks had Payne's clubs in his designated position on the driving range, but when Payne got ready to hit balls, he felt the sleeves of the rain jacket tugging at his arms. The sleeves were restricting Payne's long, fluid swing, yet because of the weather, he needed the warmth the rain gear provided.

"Get me a pair of scissors, Mike," Payne asked his caddy. Mike found a pair in the pro shop, and Payne proceeded to cut the sleeves off the rain jacket, trimming the garment so that it covered his shoulders and about three inches down his arm, transforming the rain jacket into golf's first "muscle man" look. It didn't look bad! Although Payne was internationally known for his sartorial splendor on the golf course, he was not concerned about appearances today. All that mattered was playing his best. That was Payne though. His attitude was, "If there's a problem, let me fix it." And he usually did.

Coming into the 1999 Open, Phil Mickelson had never won a major, though at twenty-nine years of age, he had already won thirteen times on the PGA Tour. Now, as he approached the green on the final hole of the tournament, he faced a 20-foot birdie putt that could lead to his name being inscribed on the silver championship trophy. Phil's putt was uphill, with a slight right-to-left break. If he made it, Payne would be forced to make his putt just to stay even and send the tournament to a Monday play-off. If Phil missed it, he still had a chance to win because of the difficulty of Payne's putt.

Phil Mickelson is one of the finest putters on the PGA Tour. With his calm demeanor, he rarely gets flustered, regardless of the pressure. To the millions of people watching on television, Phil appeared poised to do what he had done all day—sink another spectacular putt. The thousands of people squeezed around Pinehurst's eighteenth green collectively held their breath as Phil stroked the ball well, then stood expressionless while the ball traversed the twenty feet toward the cup. For a moment, it looked as though the putt was in, but then it rolled off and stopped a few inches to the right of the hole. Payne chewed his gum rhythmically as he watched Phil tap in for par.

Now it was Payne's turn. If he missed the putt yet left the ball close to the hole, he could tap in and live to play another day. But this putt was extremely risky on the notoriously fast U.S. Open greens. Payne would never forget his frustration during the second round of the 1998 U.S. Open, when his 8-foot birdie putt on Olympic's eighteenth green slipped past the cup by inches; and then, because of the outrageous hole location selected by USGA officials, kept rolling . . . and rolling . . . and rolling. By the time Payne's ball had stopped, it was a full twenty-five feet away. His possible birdie had turned into a three-putt bogey. Payne had been leading the tournament by three strokes. He ended up losing by one.

Now, one year later, Payne faced a dicey 15-foot uphill putt with a left-to-right break that would decide the winner of the 1999 U.S. Open. Nobody—least of all, Payne—took the line on the eighteenth green for granted. Many in the crowd were already assuming that we'd be coming back on Monday for a play-off.

Payne slowly went through his usual preputt routine, crouching low, eyeing every undulation in the putting surface, lining up the putt. Finally he stood, pulled the putter back evenly, and brought it forward firmly but smoothly, aiming just to the left inside edge of the cup. The blade connected with the ball momentarily, sending it on a slight banana route toward the hole. Payne did not move his head.

Neither did Phil Mickelson. He watched from the side of the green, knowing that he had done his best and there was nothing further he could do. The tournament was out of his hands.

From my vantage point off the green, I could not see the hole. I saw Payne's ball rolling, as if in slow motion, across the green, bumping over the spike marks, each one a potential land mine that could knock the ball off course; but the ball kept rolling. On line, curving slightly, bending, the ball seemed suspended in time, the Titleist logo turning over and over, still rolling . . . and then, suddenly, the ball disappeared.

The huge crowd at Pinehurst exploded! It was one of the loudest—and best—responses from a gallery that I'd ever heard. Payne had won the 1999 U.S. Open!

In a moment that has since become immortalized in golfing lore, Payne instinctively punched the air with his right arm and fist, his leg extended like a baseball pitcher who had just thrown a game-winning pitch. With that spontaneous gesture, Payne released four days' worth of pent-up emotion as he bellowed from deep within himself. He had shown virtually no emotion throughout the entire day, not even after sinking the incredible putt on 16, but now it all came gushing out.

"You beauty!" Payne shouted, as Mike Hicks ran across the green and leaped into his arms. Payne seemed to catch his caddy in midair with one arm, as Mike patted Payne on the back and congratulated him.

They attempted to smack hands in a high-five . . . but missed. Payne picked his ball out of the cup, kissed it, and slid it into his pocket. This was one ball he'd want to keep.

As the crowd continued to cheer, Payne quickly looked for Phil Mickelson. More than anyone, Payne knew the disappointment that Phil felt at that moment, but he also knew the exhilaration that Phil was about to experience. As the two men met, Payne reached out and literally held Phil's face in his hands. The words Payne spoke to his competitor and colleague had little to do with golf championships, winning or losing majors, or silver trophies. Payne had something far more important on his mind.

"You and Amy are going to have a baby, Phil . . . and there's nothing like being a father!"

Phil nodded appreciatively, hardly knowing how to respond. Later, Phil would marvel at Payne's magnanimous comments. "Payne wasn't thinking about himself at the time of his greatest triumph, and that showed a lot of class; that showed the type of individual Payne Stewart was."

On the side of the green, I pushed to the front of the crowd gathered inside the roped-off area where the players exit the green. Roger Maltbie, a greenside announcer for NBC and an old friend of Payne's and mine, spotted me and we hugged. We were both too choked up to speak. The crowd noise was so loud, it's doubtful that we could have heard each other anyhow. But it didn't matter. Words were unnecessary. Tears of happiness flowed freely from Roger's eyes, and I was crying too. Awash in an incredible sense of relief, tears of joy seemed the only appropriate response.

Payne was walking toward me. Because of the throng of people, he didn't see me at first and nearly walked right past.

"Payne!" I called out to him.

He pulled me close and we embraced on the green. With my head buried in his shoulder, I heard him say in my ear, "I did it. I kept my head down. All day . . . all day, I did it. I kept my head down."

Through my tears I said, "I know you did, and I'm so proud of you!"

That's all we had time to say before the USGA officials guided Payne down the stairs to sign his scorecard. Several minutes later, we walked back out on the green for the trophy presentation. Dan Hicks of NBC threw an arm around Payne and steadied a microphone in front of his face.

"You want me to talk?" Payne quipped.

"How do you begin, Payne," Dan said with a smile, "to put this championship—the

33

moment you just realized a few moments ago—
into perspective, not only winning the Open for
the second time, but in the storybook fashion
you just pulled off?"

"Well, first of all, I have to give thanks to
the Lord. If it weren't for the faith that I have in
him, I wouldn't have been able to have had the
faith that I had in myself on the golf course. So,
'Thank you, Lord!'"

The crowd roared its approval in the background.

Dan gulped hard at Payne's response, but
it didn't seem to throw him off. He immediately
steered the conversation back to golf. "Payne,
the resiliency you showed today on the golf
course, making all the big, great putts, after last
year . . . we know the scars are still there, and
to win it coming off that year . . ."

"Well, all I know to say is . . . whoooooo!"
Payne let out a yell that would have made his
Ozark Mountain childhood friends proud. The
crowd loved it and joined with Payne in celebrating.

"You said that experience made you
tougher," Dan continued, "and there were
numerous times on the golf course today when
you had to dig deep."

"Well, I could never give up out there . . .
Phil played unbelievably . . ." Payne turned

34

toward Phil Mickelson and said, "You'll win yours. I know Amy's at home, and I'd like to express to Phil and Amy that being a parent is a special thing. I'm glad that he made the commitment, that whether he got the beep today or not, he was going to be there with his wife . . . and that's very special. There's nothing like being a parent."

When Dan asked him to express his feelings, the ever-gracious Phil Mickelson returned kind words toward Payne. "I had a great time today," he said. "I know the outcome wasn't what I had hoped for, but I thought that the putts Payne made on 16 and 18 showed what a great champion he is, and I think he represents the United States exceptionally well as our champion."

The crowd responded again with an enormous ovation, expressing appreciation for both Payne's and Phil's classy and heartfelt comments. What we didn't know at the time was that Phil's wife, Amy, had spent Saturday night in the hospital and would give birth to their first baby, a darling little girl they named Amanda, on Monday. Had Payne missed his putt on Pinehurst's eighteenth green, the tournament would have gone to a Monday play-off, and Phil might have missed that special time with his family.

✦ ✦ ✦

Many people were amazed at how Payne handled losing the 1998 U.S. Open and winning the 1999 Open with equal measures of grace. Members of the press, and some of his fellow competitors, were intrigued. Something was different about Payne Stewart. Oh, sure, he was still Payne—spontaneous, outspoken, extremely confident, and always wearing his emotions on his sleeve. He still loved a good party, and he'd still tell you what he thought about a subject if you asked him—or even if you didn't. He still worked hard, played hard, and loved passionately. Yet people who knew Payne well recognized that he had changed somehow for the better, if that were possible. He possessed a deeper, unusual sense of peace . . . a peace that hadn't always been there.

3

Growing Up in Springfield

P ayne always said that his ability to play golf was a God-given gift—that it was in his genes. Indeed, golf reigned supreme in the Stewart family even before Payne was born. A neighbor gave Payne's father, William Louis Stewart, his first set of golf clubs when Bill was just a boy growing up in Springfield, Missouri, a sprawling community in the foothills of the Ozark Mountains. Of Scottish heritage and an all-around athlete, Payne's father played football, basketball, and golf in high school. But his passion was golf. He learned the basics of the game from his high school coach, but he taught himself to play well. Soon he was competing in amateur golf tournaments all over Missouri and winning!

Bill attended Southwest Missouri State Teacher's College (now a university), located in Springfield, where he lettered in football, basketball, and golf. There, he found himself in a competition of a different sort. In addition to his athletic abilities, the tall, lanky, extremely likable fellow with the slightly receding hairline was one of the best ballroom dancers on campus. Graceful and fluid on his feet, Bill made it a rule to dance with as many of the campus coeds as possible at the school's social events. "It was only the fair and polite thing to do," he liked to say, only half joking. But it was Bee Payne, an attractive young woman from Joplin, of Scottish-English descent, whom he walked back to the dormitory after the dance.

While Bill was intent on capturing birdies on the golf course, Bee was intent on catching him! Her outgoing, quick-witted personality was attractive to Bill, and before long they struck up a steady dating relationship—if that's what you'd call a courtship that took place largely from tee to green. Bee didn't play golf before she met Bill, but she quickly realized that if she wanted to see him, taking up the game was the way to his heart. "I had to court him on the golf course!" she recalls.

Bill patiently taught Bee the game, sometimes positioning her in a sand trap and letting her swat at her ball until she got it out of the bunker. A fun-loving, gregarious, quick-to-laugh fellow himself, Bill was all business on the course. He took his golf seriously. "He told me I laughed too much," Bee remembers. "I told him that I could really do well at this game if I just didn't have to hit that little ball!"

Bee and Bill married on December 20, 1942. Bill had notions of pursuing a career in professional golf, but when Bee became pregnant with their first daughter, Susan, he felt that he needed a more stable income. Bill had a medical deferment which kept him out of the war, so he and Bee worked for the Army Corps of Engineers during World War II. The money on the pro golf tour following the war was hardly enough to support a single fellow, much less a married couple with a new baby. For the sake of his family, Bill took a job as a salesman and developed a strong clientele. But of those days Bee says, "Selling was his occupation; golf was his avocation. It's what he really loved to do."

Daughter Lora came along six years later. Like Susan before her, Lora was not given a middle name. "When the girls get married, they'll probably drop a name anyhow," Bee said, "so there's no use in giving them middle names. Let them keep their last name if they

39

want. That way they will always be a Stewart-hyphen-somebody." Bill tried to teach Susan and Lora to golf, but the girls weren't interested. They went along to the golf course, had lots of fun, and even helped tug Dad's pull-cart carrying the golf bag, but they never acquired a genuine desire to play the game themselves.

Bill continued to excel on the course. He became an accomplished amateur, winning the Missouri State Amateur Championship in 1953. He qualified at the sectional level for the U.S. Open, and in 1955 he competed in the first two rounds of the Open at the Olympic Club in San Francisco. He shot an 83 on Thursday and an 89 on Friday and missed the cut, but he still dreamed of a day when the Stewart name would be atop the leaderboard at the most prestigious golf tournament in America.

Two years later, Bill and Bee had a baby boy who would one day grow up to fulfill Bill's dream. William Payne Stewart was born January 30, 1957. He was named William after Dad and Payne in honor of his mother's maiden name. As though it were a preview of coming attractions, Bill Stewart again won the state amateur title that year.

Bill had taken a job as a traveling salesman for Leggett & Platt, selling mattresses, box springs, and other bedding products. He was good at his job, and he and Bee were frugal in their lifestyle. Soon they were able to provide a comfortable living environment for their family. A month after Payne's birth, the Stewarts moved to a new, one-story, ranch-style home on Link Street (where else would a future golf legend live?) in Springfield.

Rambunctious even as a toddler, Payne was bursting with energy and inquisitive about everything. Once, while visiting some friends who owned a farm, Payne fearlessly approached a large cow to pet it. The cow bucked its head, smacking Payne in the face and knocking out several of his front teeth.

Bill saw athletic ability in Payne early on. While his young son was still in a high chair, Bill began tossing a ball to him. By the time Payne was three, he was hitting golf balls in the backyard, with the long club shaft and grip tucked beneath his arm. Bill had a set of adult clubs cut down to size for Payne, and at four years of age, Payne started whacking balls with Mom and Dad on the fairways of Springfield's Hickory Hills Country Club. "He walked along with us," recalls Bee, "and we'd let him hit his own ball as much as he wanted. He'd hit it and then run after it and couldn't wait to hit it again. We didn't force him to play; he just loved doing it."

Bee also encouraged Payne to play football as a young boy. Although he liked the game, he didn't want to go out for the school team, preferring instead to play with the kids in the neighborhood. Nevertheless, to please his mother, he tried out for the team. On the first day of practice, Payne broke his arm and was out for the season. Instead of coddling him, Bee teased her boy, "You did that on purpose, didn't you, just so you wouldn't have to play."

"Yeah, I did!" Payne retorted. Of course, he hadn't, but Mom's cajoling took some of the pain out of his injury.

Payne grew up in a loving family, an environment with lots of laughter, hugs, and kisses, a home in which expressions of emotion were not only acceptable but expected and modeled by Bee and Bill. "We were always lovin' on one another, and I was never afraid to hug and kiss my father," Payne often said later. "Even as an adult."

The Stewarts attended Grace United Methodist Church in Springfield, or the "Smethodist" church, as young Payne pronounced it through the gap in his front teeth. Even if Bill or Bee did not make it to church, they always saw to it that Payne and his sisters were in Sunday school, where they were taught the great stories of the Bible and learned biblical principles of ethics and morality from the time they were old enough to walk. All the Stewart children were active in the church youth group.

When Payne was in fifth grade, his friend Erwin Busiek's dad, a local doctor, brought a batch of Gideon New Testaments to school and passed them out to the class. Payne later wrote Dr. Busiek a thank-you note:

Dear Dr. Busiek,

I want to thank you for the Testaments, and thank you for taking time to bring some Testaments over and giving them to us.

How come the Testaments don't have pictures in them?

I like the Testaments. They are easy to read in bed. They are real nice Testaments. Thank you.

Your friend,
Payne Stewart
December 1, 1967
Greenwood 5th Grade
Springfield, Missouri

Besides love of family and love of God, the Stewart family's love for their country was another cornerstone in their home. "Bill and I loved America," said Bee, who was actively involved in politics. Although equally fervent in his patriotism and respect for the United States, Bill spent most of his spare time on the golf course rather than in the political arena. Nevertheless, every Memorial Day and Fourth of July holiday found the Stewarts at Hickory Hills Golf Course for the golf tournament, picnic, and fireworks display honoring America. As a youngster, rather than having a lemonade stand like other kids, Payne and some of his friends had a fireworks stand along the side of the road where they sold small firecrackers, sparklers, and other fireworks.

Because Bill's job required that he spend a great deal of time away from home making sales calls during the week, he frequently delegated the job of disciplining the kids to Bee. "Now, you make them mow the yard. Make them do their homework." Even when Bill was home, he put the onus of punishing the kids on Bee because he was too much of a softie when it came to correcting them.

That's not to say that the Stewart kids got

away with much. Once, as a toddler, Payne got in trouble for throwing rocks at the cars that passed in front of the family's home on Link Street. When he hit a woman's vehicle, she slammed on the brakes, stopped the car, grabbed Payne, and brought him to Bee. When Bee discovered what Payne had done, she assured the woman that he would never do such a thing again. Then she went out back, cut a small branch off a tree, and gave Payne a "good switchin'," swatting him on the back of the legs. The switch, or a flyswatter, was a common and dreaded method of punishment for Payne's or his sisters' mischief.

Even if they did get away with something, Payne could never keep a secret; he'd always tell on his big sisters. Shortly after Susan turned sixteen and got her driver's license, Bill bought a brand-new, white Pontiac. While Bill was away at a weeklong furniture convention in Chicago, Bee let Susan drive Lora to their piano lessons. Susan's lesson was first, so while she waited for Lora, she decided to drive up the street to get a doughnut. Upon her return, she hit a parked car.

Susan called her mom, fretting and crying, "Oh, Mother, I've had a wreck! Daddy's gonna kill me! I've wrecked his new car!"

When Bee discovered that the accident

was merely a fender-bender and that nobody had been hurt, she calmed Susan and they devised an intricate plan to break the news to Dad. The night Bill got home they prepared an especially nice dinner, complete with a beautifully set table in the dining room. Susan's stomach was churning as she waited for just the right moment to tell her dad the bad news. She didn't have to wait long. Bill Stewart had barely sat down when five-year-old Payne ran to his elbow and in his high-pitched voice practically shouted, "Guess what, Dad? Susan wrecked your car!"

"I wanted to hit him!" recalls Susan, "but at least now I didn't have to worry about telling Dad." Typical of Bill Stewart's kindhearted attitude, he didn't get angry; he simply wanted to know why the accident had happened and talked to Susan about how it could be prevented in the future.

The Link Street neighborhood was filled with kids and bustled with constant activity. There were few fences in those days, and the kids played freely in the neighborhood backyards. As a boy, Payne was slight of build, but he liked to play with some of the older kids, who sometimes picked on him and called him a "pain" in the neck. Once, Lora watched from the living room window as some bigger boys dropped Payne into a hole the telephone company had dug for some new poles they were installing. She raced outside, screaming at the bullies, "What are you doing? Let him out of there!" Most of the bullies ran off, but Lora latched onto one of the boys and made him pull Payne out of the pit. "We were always watching out for one another," she remembers.

When Payne was old enough to read, he began taking piano lessons along with his sisters. Payne loved music, the louder the better, but he was much too fidgety to spend long hours practicing scales. Years later, when he was diagnosed with attention deficit disorder, Bee better understood what a miracle it was that he'd sat still long enough to learn the rudiments of piano.

Payne attended school at Greenwood, remaining in the program from kindergarten through high school. The Greenwood schools, associated with Southwest Missouri State University, were semiprivate laboratory schools that admitted only fifteen boys and fifteen girls in each new class. In Springfield, it was considered a privilege to attend the Greenwood schools; but the flip side of that privilege was that some people thought the school was populated by an elitist group, even though admission was not based on wealth, status, or position but simply determined by the birthdays of the students and the space available at the school. The Stewarts placed a premium on higher education—both Bee and Bill held degrees—and all three Stewart siblings would go on to college. Nevertheless, Bill Stewart didn't demand academic excellence from Payne as long as he did his best and made decent grades. Bill certainly wanted Payne to attend a school with a strong golf program. Greenwood fit the bill.

Like his father, Payne was a natural, an all-around athlete. In grade school, he played Little League baseball—he was a pitcher for his team, the Bumblebees, much to Queen Bee's delight—and he played basketball on the Backeroos, sponsored by the Sertoma Boys Clubs. His team won the local basketball championship. In fifth grade, Payne won the Springfield Punt, Pass, and Kick contest.

"Payne really thought he was something when he won that contest," Bee recalls. "He was so full of himself, a real braggadocio. I had to remind him that he was not that good, that there were other boys who could play well too. That wasn't good enough for Payne. He wanted to be the best."

The entire Stewart family attended Payne's games, with Bee, Susan, and Lora serving as Payne's personal cheering section.

Despite their enthusiasm, they couldn't compare with Payne's biggest fan, his dad. Bill loudly communicated his encouragement to Payne and freely offered his opinions to the referees concerning their calls. His voice could be heard all over the gymnasium during Payne's basketball games. Once, Bill's vociferous riding of the referees from three rows up in the bleachers cost Payne's eighth-grade basketball team a technical foul.

The way Payne told the story, his father "knew officiating and he was getting all over the referees. They were young guys, and when they'd finally had just about enough, one of the refs stopped the game and called a technical foul. Our coach jumped up and yelled, 'What? A technical? On who?'

"The ref pointed to the stands and said, 'That man up there in the orange sweater!' I looked up and there was my father. I wanted to crawl under the bench." Almost thirty years later, Payne himself would nearly be ejected from one of Aaron's baseball games for similar behavior. Like father, like son.

Although Bill Stewart traveled a lot for his work, he made a special effort to be a part of his children's lives. After a long, tiring week on the road, he'd often come home and find his kids out in the yard playing ball or some other game.

Weary or not, without a moment's hesitation, he was right out there with them. He constantly shuffled his work schedule to accommodate baseball, basketball, and football games and piano recitals. He missed few major events in his family's life. The only thing that competed with his love for his wife and children was his love for golf. It was an example that Payne would emulate.

Family picnics and vacations inevitably revolved around a golf tournament somewhere across the nation. "We got to see a lot of pretty country," recalls Lora, "but we were bored stiff by all that golf."

The Stewart children even received golf gifts as Christmas and birthday presents. Bill won numerous tournaments where he received gift certificates as prizes, so he bought many of his gifts for Bee and the kids at the pro shops. New clubs got handed down from Bee to Susan to Lora, and then Payne played with them.

To Bill's delight, Payne's love for the game of golf soon rivaled his own. Payne wanted to learn and Bill was a good teacher. Everything Payne learned about golf in those days he learned from his dad, but he also had a God-given ability that, once set in motion, seemed almost self-perpetuating. It was as though he were born to play golf. Payne had a natural, fluid motion to his golf swing. It was as pure a swing as anyone around Hickory Hills had ever seen. Only one other fellow could match it—the boy's father.

Not only did Bill teach Payne how to play golf; he taught him an appreciation for the game's etiquette and traditions. He encouraged him to compete fiercely but also to be gracious in defeat. "You don't have to enjoy not winning," Bill told Payne, "but you should know how to conduct yourself as a gentleman, even if you play poorly." Once, Payne's father saw him throw a club in anger, ruining the club's shaft. Bill Stewart reprimanded Payne by not allowing him to play golf for a month, plus he had to pay for a new shaft on the golf club. At the time, Payne was earning a dollar a week mowing lawns, and he received a weekly allowance of fifty cents. "It took me nearly a month to pay for that shaft," Payne recalled.

Bill Stewart loved to teach golf, especially to Payne but also to anyone with whom he happened to be playing. He gave so many impromptu lessons and free golf tips that Sam Reynolds, the club pro at Hickory Hills, put up a sign at the course, "Bill Stewart: Teaching Pro."

Bill also taught Payne to dance. Bill had taught his daughters to dance by letting them stand on his feet while he swished them around the living room to the sounds of big-band music, and he did the same with Payne. Fortunately for Bill, he taught Payne to dance before the boy experienced a teenage growth spurt that didn't stop until his feet had reached a size twelve. Bill's dance lessons also included instruction on etiquette. "When you sit at a table and there are eight or ten ladies, you always dance with each of them at least once," Payne's father instructed him.

Always curious about how things were made or how they worked, Payne once removed the fine finish from his mother's Hogan 3-wood, just to see what the persimmon wood grain looked like below the surface. Another time, he spray-painted Bill Stewart's putter blue to see if he could improve its appearance. "What did you do that for?" asked his perplexed father.

"I just thought the change might be good," Payne replied.

Payne was always interested in learning something new, but he preferred learning it experientially rather than simply reading about it in a book. As a boy, he learned how to cook, how to sew, and how to iron his own clothes. One day he came to Bee, crying.

"What's wrong, Payne?" Bee asked.

Payne held up a new nylon jacket that he had attempted to iron. The hot iron had seared through the fabric in an instant, leaving a perfect impression on the jacket and ruining the iron at the same time.

One of the most exciting days in Payne's young life was the day Jack Nicklaus came to town for an exhibition at Hickory Hills. At the conclusion of his clinic, Nicklaus putted his ball over to the edge of the eighteenth green, where a passel of young boys scrambled for it. Payne didn't get the ball, but from that day forward, Jack Nicklaus was his hero. "Someday, I'm gonna play with Jack," he said without a trace of doubt.

During his freshman year at Greenwood, Payne "went out" for the golf team, although his making the team was a foregone conclusion for anybody who knew Payne's game. By junior high, he had already won several local tournaments in his age group.

Bill Stewart had a talk with Paul Mullins, Greenwood's football coach and assistant basketball coach, who had also inherited the golf coaching job by default. "I want you to make him toe the line, but don't touch his golf swing," Bill cautioned the coach. Bill knew that

Payne's golf swing was close to perfect; he didn't want anyone—not even the coach—tampering with Payne's natural talent. Coach Mullins had known Payne since he had enrolled in elementary school. "He was fun," Coach Mullins recalls. "An easy kid to like."

Mullins is modest concerning his contributions to Payne's game. "I was the golf coach," he says, "but all I did was schedule the matches and take Payne to and from the matches. Bill did all of Payne's coaching back then. As far as my coaching him in golf, there wasn't much to it. He already knew how to play the game before he ever got to me." Indeed, Bill Stewart was Payne's personal coach, and Bill's number-one assistant was Bee. When Bill had to leave town for business, he gave Bee a series of drills for Payne to do while he was gone.

"Lay out two towels on the ground, about eighteen inches apart. Then you stand behind Payne, and make sure he hits the ball right straight between the two towels," Bill instructed. Payne's success on the golf course was never in question to Bill Stewart. It was only a matter of time. In many ways, Bill was reliving his own life vicariously through his son. His own golf aspirations now lay distinctly within reach through Payne.

Throughout his freshman year, Payne shot

par, or a few strokes over, in all his matches. To Paul Mullins, Payne's short game was his strong point: his ability to hit the greens and to get up and down when he got in trouble. His drives were consistently in the fairway, though not impressively long, because his upper body strength had not yet developed fully. The worst score Mullins remembers Payne ever hitting was a 41 on the front nine in a match in which he was the first to tee off early in the morning, while it was still foggy and damp. The greens had not yet been mowed or rolled and were still covered with dew. Payne's putting was severely affected. Payne was nonetheless disgusted with himself because he was 6-over par. In his mind, he should have shot par.

By the end of Payne's freshman year, he and his father had established a definite plan. Payne was going to play golf professionally. He told Coach Mullins, "I'm going to be a pro golfer. Don't worry about trying to get me basketball or football scholarships; I'm going to play golf. I'm going to go to college somewhere in the South so I can play year-round."

When Payne was fifteen, Bill Stewart took him to the U.S. Open sectional qualifying competition. Bill knew that his son had little chance of qualifying, but the U.S. Open held special significance to Bill Stewart and he conveyed that importance to Payne. "When you sign your name to enter the U.S. Open, always sign William Payne Stewart," he said. "It's our national championship, so you should sign your full name."

Meanwhile, Payne's academic performance was not keeping pace with his athletic ability. When he turned sixteen and wanted to get his driver's license, Bee seized the opportunity. "Before you can get your license, you must have a B average," she told him. Not only did Payne pull up his grades, he also memorized the driver's manual and didn't miss a single question on the test.

Bee knew a good thing when she saw it. She told Payne, "Honey, you did so great on your test, and I am so proud of you. Now, if you want to drive the car, you'll have to make the honor roll at school."

Payne went back to school with a new motivation. He studied like mad and couldn't wait until the grading period ended and report cards came out. Every time he received a test grade from his teachers, he brought the paper home to show his mom how well he was progressing. He made the honor roll, and Bee allowed him to drive the family car.

One of the reasons Payne wanted to drive was his newfound interest in girls. A good-looking fellow, well-liked in school, Payne had no problem getting dates. He dated a wide variety of girls and had a few long-term high school romances, but no pretty young lady could compete with Ben Hogan, the name on Payne's new golf clubs.

In high school, Payne excelled in several sports. He had good hands and a strong arm, which was a good thing, since running was not his forte. He was the quarterback on the football team and the point man on the basketball team. He enjoyed calling the plays and telling the other guys what to do, and he was good at it. He received the Springfield Quarterback Club Award for Outstanding Senior Back in 1974. Payne loved the team competition, which he would later relish in golf, as well, when he participated in some of the most exciting Ryder Cup matches the world had ever seen.

4

Degrees of
Education

P ayne was Bill Stewart's "ace in the hole."
Literally. Bill won more than a few dollars
betting on his son's golfing ability. The
"pigeons" flocked freely around Hickory Hills
Country Club, where golfers were willing to
lay down some money in hopes of beating
Payne. Most of them went home with lighter
wallets. It wasn't the money that mattered so
much to Bill; it was the competition.
Meanwhile, Payne was learning a principle that
would serve him well in the years to come: If
you play well, you get paid. If you don't, you
go home with nothing.

Bill and Payne frequently engaged in
fierce competition against each other to see

who could win a few dollars. Sometimes Payne skinned his father, and sometimes his father returned the favor. Occasionally, Bill and Payne even got snippy with one another in their desire to win. But even though Bill was hard on Payne, correcting him as they played, father and son always maintained their cool and all was forgiven after the round.

As Payne drew closer to his high school graduation, Bill Stewart began to explore where his son might find the best college scholarship offers. In those days, the recruiting of high school players by college golf coaches was extremely limited. Usually, the players contacted the college and laid out their high school golf achievements in hopes of securing some sort of offer. Several of Payne's friends in Springfield planned to attend Southern Methodist University, a highly regarded school in Dallas, Texas. When SMU offered Payne the best scholarship help of any of the colleges and universities that Bill Stewart had contacted, the choice was simple: Payne would attend SMU on a golf scholarship that covered his tuition; Mom and Dad would pay for housing and meals.

One day, shortly before Payne departed for college, he and his father were driving out to the golf course when Bill proffered what he felt was important advice for his son. "Don't let those college girls tell you they're pregnant," he said seriously. That was about as close as Bill and Payne ever got to a discussion of "the birds and the bees."

Everyone told Payne that college would be the best time of his life, so along with his roommates, Lamar Haynes and Barry Snyder, Payne set out to prove them right. Payne first met Lamar in 1975, one week before classes began at SMU, at the U.S. Amateur Golf Championship in Richmond, Virginia, where they were competing. Lamar was from Shreveport, Louisiana, and had grown up playing with Hal Sutton, another future PGA Tour star. Payne and Lamar hit it off instantly, especially when they discovered that they'd be playing on the same team at SMU.

Barry Snyder was the most studious of the three friends. The son of a Jewish business family in Pittsburgh, Barry was a decent golfer but not good enough to be on the SMU team, which played against such golf powerhouses as the University of Texas and Oklahoma State. Nevertheless, Barry and Lamar were friends, and before long, Lamar, Barry, and Payne moved in together. They became like brothers.

Payne majored in business with an emphasis on real estate, but he spent most of his time in college living it up, partying, and having a good time. He acquired a taste for alcohol and cigarettes and let his hair grow long and shaggy, much to his father's dismay. Payne preferred long, lazy afternoons on the lakes around Dallas to late evenings in the college library. It wasn't that he lacked academic ability; he was simply more interested in playing golf and pursuing his primary major: "party management."

Barry's father was a part owner in the Texas Rangers, the Major League Baseball team in nearby Arlington, so when the Rangers were in town, Payne, Barry, and Lamar were in the stands. Payne was an enthusiastic fan, loudly offering his opinions on everything from the players' performances to the umpires' calls. Barry Snyder quipped, "It was amazing how much more enthusiastic Payne got after having a couple of beers."

Barry, too, was majoring in business, but he recognized from the start that Payne's heart was not in accounting. He often teased Payne, "Thank God you can play golf because if you had to rely on selling real estate to make your living, you'd be starving!"

Payne's father visited campus often, and as proud as he was of his son, he disapproved of Payne's penchant for partying. He was particularly disappointed that Payne had developed a habit of smoking. "I thought you were a leader, not a follower," Bill chided him. Although his father's words hurt him, Payne continued to party, and his grades suffered accordingly. He was having such a good time at one point that Bee decided she'd better go down to Dallas to straighten him out a bit. Bill and Bee's main concern wasn't that Payne might become ineligible for the golf team if he didn't improve his grades; they wanted him to graduate with his class. After Bee's visit, Payne enrolled in summer school and brought his grades back up to an acceptable level.

One of the skills Payne learned at SMU had nothing to do with business or golf. On the long trips back and forth from Springfield to Dallas, Payne taught himself to play the harmonica while driving down the highway in his Volkswagen. Lora's husband, Jim Thomas— "Mr. T," as he was known to the family—and Steve Cash, a musician with the Ozark Mountain Daredevils, a local rock-a-billy group, helped Payne with the basics, and Payne took it from there.

During his senior year, Payne became captain of the golf team, replacing his friend Charlie Adams, who had graduated. Payne played well that fall but did not win a tournament. At that time, Payne was known more for his long drives off the tee, rather than being the "feel" player with the exquisite touch around the greens that he would later develop.

When Payne came home for Christmas break, Bill Stewart asked him, "Now that you are going to graduate in May, what are you going to do for a living?"

"I'm going to play golf," Payne replied, surprised that his father would even ask such a question.

"What makes you think you can do that?" Bill pressed. "You haven't won anything yet. You haven't done anything in college but have fun!"

Payne went back and won three tournaments before graduation, including the 1979 Co-Championship of the Southwest Conference (an event in which he tied for first with Fred Couples, another future PGA Tour star). One of Payne's incentives to win the Southwest Conference title was that the winner of the tournament was granted the privilege of playing in the nearby PGA Tour event, the Colonial, in Fort Worth. Since Fred Couples and Payne had tied, they had a play-off to see which of them would earn the berth in the professional tournament. Payne beat Fred on the first hole of the play-off.

Characteristically upbeat, Payne approached his father, "Dad, my college graduation ceremonies are being held the same weekend as the Colonial, so I guess we won't be going to graduation."

"We'll see," his father replied flatly. "If you make the cut, then I guess we'll play."

Payne attended his SMU graduation ceremony that Sunday.

He earned his degree in business in May 1979. His parents were thrilled that he had completed his studies in only four years, a rare achievement among college golfers at that time. Many guys on college golf teams took much longer to get through school, and some left college without a degree at all. Besides pleasing his parents, earning his degree convinced Payne that he could do anything he set his mind to.

During the summer after his graduation, Payne played in several amateur golf tournaments and won the Missouri State Amateur title. Not to be outdone, his father won the Missouri Senior Amateur title the same year.

That fall, Payne played in the PGA Tour Qualifying School, attempting to earn his PGA Tour card, which would allow him to compete with the best pros. The Tour card is similar to a license that indicates a person is qualified to play on the PGA Tour. A golfer—even a great golfer—doesn't get a slot at a PGA Tour event simply by calling up and requesting to play. He either must win a recognized amateur championship, or he must qualify. In the early 1980s, the PGA Tour held two Qualifying Schools per year, six months apart, for aspiring golfers who hoped to gain a spot on the Tour. Nowadays, Q School is conducted only once each year, in three stages.

The name "Qualifying School" is somewhat misleading, because there is no real PGA Tour training school—other than the proverbial "School of Hard Knocks." Up-and-coming players do not major in golf in college (although one might think so by looking at some of their GPAs) the way young artists, for example, can attend art school or emerging musicians can hone their craft in a school of music. Q School is basically a series of rounds authorized by the PGA Tour, designed to weed out the poorer players and allow those with true potential to rise to the top.

Each year, depending on the attrition rate, the PGA Tour allows a small number of new golfers to join the Tour—usually about twenty to thirty spots open per year. To earn one of those coveted spots, a player must rank high at the Q School tournament. Many in the field are young kids, fresh out of college golf programs.

Other competitors are old guys who have always dreamed of teeing it up with the "big boys." Some are local pros or instructors, and some are just trying out, hoping to win bragging rights at their local clubs. Regardless of their experience level, duffer or pro, only the top players in the Q School tournament earn their cards and the privilege of competing on the PGA Tour.

In 1979, the top twenty-five finishers in the Q School were granted a Tour card. Unfortunately, Payne was not among them. Now he was in a quandary. He had earned his degree in business but really didn't care to pursue a career in that field. He had planned to make his living playing golf, but now he had nowhere to play professionally, and he had no income.

He decided to get a job while he awaited his next shot at Q School, which was not scheduled until June of the following year. Payne took a job at a JCPenney store, working in the sporting goods department for an hourly minimum wage and a commission on whatever he sold. He had worked less than three days for JCPenney when Jay Hayes, a member of Hickory Hills Country Club, offered him another job. Jay ran a store known as Ed V's Clothing Company, in Springfield. "If you come to work for me," Jay convinced Payne, "you'll make more money."

Payne quit his job at Penney's and went to work at Ed V's for the same hourly wage he had been making. Instead of working as a salesman, with the possibility of earning commissions, now he was employed as a stock boy and general handyman, whose main responsibilities included cleaning the rest rooms and painting the walls. He hadn't exactly taken a step up in the world. The only advantage, as far as Payne was concerned, was that his job at the clothing company allowed him flexible hours to play golf. If he worked mornings, he'd play golf in the afternoon. If he worked evenings, he was at Hickory Hills in the morning.

At the golf course, Payne frequently played some of his partners for money— "pigeons," as Payne referred to them, who were willing to put their money on the line to test their skills against the state amateur champ. Payne recalled, "One day, I plucked the pigeons pretty good for about three hundred dollars, and then I went in and got my check for two weeks' work at the clothing store. The check was for $83.75."

"Jay-Leo, I can't work for you anymore," Payne soon told his boss.

"Why not?"

"This isn't where I belong," Payne answered. "I belong out on the golf course." Payne left his job that day, more determined than ever to make his living playing golf. But where?

About that time, Perry Leslie, a former PGA Tour player in Springfield, gave Payne some information about the Asian Golf Tour, a series of eleven tournaments played throughout Southeast Asia, Indonesia, and India. The tournaments paid relatively small monetary prizes compared to the PGA Tour, but they were better than nothing.

Bill Stewart and five other men formed a limited partnership with Payne to sponsor him on the Asian Tour. Each man put up some money to help cover Payne's travel expenses and tournament entry fees. Payne agreed to pay the sponsors back by giving them a percentage of his winnings. Although the sponsors hoped to make some money, most of them got involved because they knew Bill Stewart's integrity and they knew Payne's ability to play the game. They wanted to see Payne succeed. Most of his sponsors had high hopes that their hometown boy would make good and put Springfield on the golf world's map—and Payne fulfilled their hopes.

At the time Payne decided to join the

Asian Tour in 1979, only a few "mini-tours" were in operation in the United States. The mini-tours were golf's equivalent to the minor leagues in professional baseball—they were beyond college competition but not quite to the PGA Tour level. Nevertheless, the competition on the mini-tours was intense, and there was real money to be made. But it also cost real money to enter the U.S. mini-tour events.

Mini-tours in California, for example, 72-hole events conducted by the National Golfers Association, cost a minimum of $800 to $1,000 per event to enter. Mini-tour events in Florida on the "Goosie Tour" averaged about $450 and were usually two 36-hole events per week at separate venues. The prize money in those days was around $3,000. Some of the guys playing in Florida had been on the circuit for so long that they knew every blade of grass on each course on a first-name basis, and they were tough to beat.

Payne's choice was between paying higher entry fees to play on the U.S. mini-tours or going overseas to play, where the entry fees were only about $100 per week, and the first-place prize money was usually $10,000 for each event. Since he was a Missouri State Amateur Champion, his acceptance on the Asian Tour was assured.

In February 1980, Payne packed his bags and set out to play on the eleven-week Asian circuit, along with thirty other young American golfers, one of whom was Terry Anton. Terry was to Payne what a match might be in a firecracker factory. They were dangerous together. Terry and Payne had met previously in 1978 at the Houston International, a college tournament. Terry recalls, "I thought Payne was incredibly cocky. He just acted as though he were 'Joe It.' Unfortunately, so did I!"

Despite their egos, Terry and Payne hit it off as friends almost immediately. Having grown up in a military family, Terry's patriotic roots ran deep. He and Payne could have been poster children for the John Wayne–loving, flag-waving, God-bless-America crowd. Terry also possessed a needle-sharp sense of humor similar to Payne's. Each was funny in his own way, but put them together and they became a comedy team, rife with one-liners, sarcastic jabs, hilarious stories, and outlandish attempts to "get" one another. Each guy's irrepressible and irreverent sense of humor fed off the other.

They also respected each other on the links. Terry had played his college golf in Florida on a top-five team. Shortly after college, however, he was involved in a head-on auto accident that nearly ended his life, not to mention his golf career. Like Payne, Terry had failed to get his PGA Tour card, so they played in various small-scale golf events prior to playing together in Asia. Payne noticed that Terry seemed to walk on his toes with his heels barely touching the ground as he walked up a fairway, so as Payne was prone to do with many of his friends, he gave Terry a nickname. Payne called him "Tiptoe," and the name stuck.

Terry set the tone when he donned a Star Wars Yoda mask as the guys deplaned in Manila for the first stop on the tour. "These American golfers are very strange," one of the tour hosts was overheard saying. For the remainder of the tour, at every airport, as the golfers deplaned and were greeted by their hosts, Terry wore the Yoda mask.

After the first few weeks of the trip, Payne and Terry became roommates, sharing the expenses of their hotel rooms. Most of the hotel rooms had no televisions, so in the evenings, the guys usually went out on the town. One night in Thailand, Terry and Payne returned to the room and began their usual games of testosterone-based one-upmanship.

"Oh, I could whup you anytime," Payne drawled.

"No, you can't. Don't even say that, or I'll have to kick your behind," Terry retorted.

"Ha, let's see it!"

With that, Terry tackled Payne right there between the double beds. They wrestled around the room, banging into the furniture, crashing into the walls, and flipping each other onto the beds. Terry grabbed Payne and pushed his feet up over his head, flipping Payne off the bed, onto the floor. He landed facedown in the corner, with his feet up in the air, against the wall. Terry leaped off the bed like a baboon and landed on the back of Payne's thighs. He grabbed Payne's hands and pulled them behind his back as he bounced up and down on Payne's legs, yelling loudly, "Say uncle! Say uncle or I'll never let you up!"

Reluctantly, Payne mumbled, "Uncle." When Payne got up, he huffed, "You'd have never gotten me if it hadn't been for that wall."

"Oh, yeah, well just remember this. When you become a rich and famous golfer, I can always say that I knew you when you were nothing, and I pinned you in Thailand!"

Over the years, Terry and Payne relived that wrestling match many times, and Terry always reminded Payne that he had pinned him.

Terry spared no efforts when it came to pulling something on Payne. Knowing how patriotic Payne was, Terry decided to test his true colors. Toward the end of the Asian Tour, they were in Taiwan on their way to Seoul, Korea. Terry's older brother was stationed in Seoul as a captain in charge of the U.S. special security force. Terry called his brother and said, "I'm coming in with about twenty-five or thirty professional golfers. Can you set it up for me to be arrested at the airport when we arrive in Seoul?"

"Can I what?" Terry's brother asked, as he burst out laughing. "Are you out of your mind?"

"No, I just want to pull a joke on my friend, Payne Stewart," Terry replied. "I want you to have me arrested on charges of espionage." Terry talked his brother into participating in the practical joke on Payne.

Sure enough, as soon as Payne and Terry arrived in Korea and got off the airplane, several military officers approached the golf professionals, and one of the officers blocked Terry's path. "Excuse me, are you Terrance Anton?"

"Yes, I am," Terry answered, as he looked furtively at Payne, who was walking next to him.

"May I see your passport?"

"Sure, what's the matter?" Terry asked, with feigned fear in his voice.

"Sir, I have a warrant for your arrest."

"On what charges?"

"Espionage against the government of the United States of America."

Payne instinctively took a step backward and stared at Terry in abject horror. The expression on his face said, "I can't believe it. You're a spy!"

The officers handcuffed Terry, confiscated his suitcase and golf clubs, and took them through customs. They put Terry in the back seat of a military squad car and whisked him away with the red lights flashing. Payne stood there, paralyzed with disbelief.

The officers took Terry to see his brother, and everyone had a good laugh over the fact that they had fooled Payne. Meanwhile, Payne was left to fret about his friend's whereabouts. When Terry returned to the hotel later that afternoon, he went up to the room he was to share with Payne. But Payne didn't want anything to do with him!

"Get out of here!" Payne shrieked. "You're a spy!"

"Payne, if I were a spy, would they have released me?"

"I don't know, man; I don't know if I want anything to do with you anymore."

"Hey, come on, man. You've been with me every step of the way. You know I'm not a spy.

Tell you what. I heard about a really great place in town; let's go out there tonight."

"I ain't goin' anywhere with you!" Payne roared.

"Come on, let's go." Terry said, as he nudged Payne toward the door.

They went out that night to one of the seedy sections in the underbelly of Seoul. The place Terry led them to was a dark, crowded, smoke-filled club, teeming with military guys. As the music blared, Terry and Payne picked their way toward a table in the back, when Terry suddenly tripped over a hulk of a man who was sitting with his legs stretched out in the aisle. "Hey, watch it, Fatso!" Terry lashed out.

The big lug lurched to his feet and glared down at Terry. "Are you talking to me, punk?"

"Yeah, I am!" Terry answered boldly. "What? Are you deaf too?"

The man shoved Terry, and Terry pushed him right back. "Do you want some of me?" the giant asked.

"Do you mean do I want to go toe to toe, punch for punch?" Terry said with obvious derision in his voice.

"Yeah!" the hulk roared.

"No, I don't, 'cause I'd dance circles around you," Terry said as he sidestepped the larger man.

"But my buddy here does!" Terry stepped behind Payne and pointed at him.

"Oh, really! So you're a tough guy, huh?" the hulk poked his finger into Payne's chest. "So you want to go one on one with me?"

"No, no, no," Payne stammered. "There must be some mistake."

From behind him, Payne heard Terry laughing hysterically. He whirled around and boomed, "What's so funny?"

Terry was holding his sides as he said, "Payne, I'd like you to meet my brother, Bill." The hulk extended his hand and grinned. "Payne, how're ya doin'? Captain Bill Anton. I'm mighty glad to meet you."

During their stay in Seoul, Payne wanted to get some clothes made at one of the Korean tailoring shops, known for their fine quality and reasonable prices. Captain Anton said, "I'll set you up with the tailor who does all of my stuff. This guy is awesome. Just tell the guy that you are my brother."

Payne found the tailor's shop and did as Bill instructed. "Hi, my name is Terry Anton," Payne lied to the tailor, "and I'd like to have some clothes made. Captain Bill Anton is my brother."

"Oh, yes, Captain Anton, very good customer. How can I help you?"

Payne ordered all sorts of clothing: sport coats, slacks, and other items. When he picked up the clothes, he looked inside the sport coats. Embroidered on the inside pocket of all the coats was the name Terry Anton. Payne looked at the slacks, and sure enough, Terry Anton was on them as well. As a special favor to Captain Anton, the tailor had embroidered Terry's name on every item of clothing Payne had purchased.

Besides his Yoda mask, Terry also carried with him a realistic-looking, three-foot-long, green rubber snake, complete with red mouth and fangs. A naive young golfer in the room adjoining Terry and Payne's looked like Ernie on My Three Sons. He was away from home for the first time and was experiencing extreme culture shock. One night, Terry and Payne and several of the other American golfers were having a drink in this young man's room while he was in the shower. As "Ernie" was lathering his hair, they quietly opened the door to the bathroom and slipped the rubber snake in the back end of the tub. Then the guys took seats and waited for the show.

They didn't have to wait long. In a matter of seconds, they heard screaming in the shower. With shampoo still in his hair, "Ernie" bounded out of the bathroom, stark naked, screaming, "There's a snake in the bathtub!" He was so scared that he ran out of the room and down the hall before he realized he didn't have any clothes on. Meanwhile, Payne, Terry, and the other guys were roaring with laughter.

Sometimes the jokes weren't so funny. The day before a tournament in Thailand, Payne decided to throw a glass of ice water on Terry while he was under a hot shower. He whipped the glass around the shower curtain and smashed the glass into Terry's knee. The flimsy glass exploded and blood squirted all over Payne's hand. "Oh, Tip," Payne cried. "Are you OK? I'm sorry, man. I was just trying to get you with the water. Is your knee all right?"

"Payne, I'm not bleeding," Terry said. "It's your hand that's bleeding." Payne looked down and discovered that he had slit his right hand between the forefinger and thumb, precisely where the shaft of his golf club would lie in his grip. The guys didn't trust the local doctors, so they cleaned the wound and bandaged it themselves. The next day, Payne made his tee time at the Rose Garden Golf Course; in fact, he played all week with his hand bandaged, finishing second in the tournament.

Although Payne loved to party, he was not wild and lascivious, even though he thought of himself as quite the ladies' man. Wherever he went, a flock of young women followed, but just beneath the surface of his bombastic, self-confident personality lurked a pervasive insecurity. Beyond that, his Methodist upbringing no doubt had instilled within him a sense of morality that kept him from straying too far from the straight and narrow path.

Payne's mischief in those days often leaned toward the juvenile. One of his favorite pranks on the Asian Tour involved an ingenious handheld rubber device known as the "Handy Gasser," developed by an ex-golf pro from Oklahoma. Far better than a whoopie cushion, the Handy Gasser produced an extremely realistic sound that simulated flatulence. Payne and Terry each had one of these toys and were fond of using them while riding in crowded elevators or in the equally crowded Southeast Asian taxi cabs.

Payne's first experience with the Handy Gasser had been at a Los Angeles nightclub, prior to his embarking on the Asian Tour. Payne, Terry, and another friend spotted three pretty young women on the dance floor who were being entertained by a local "Joe Disco," dressed in his best John Travolta look-alike black outfit. "It looks like the local talent is already taken," Payne said, nodding toward the women.

"I'll handle that," Terry replied. Before

Payne could say another word, Terry walked up behind Joe Disco and squeezed the Handy Gasser. At the same time, he sprayed a shot of pressurized sulfa spray—which he also carried with him—hitting the fellow in the back of the jacket. Joe Disco whirled around to see what had happened, and as he did, the sulfa smell whirled with him, nearly knocking the young ladies over. "How disgusting!" one of the women shrieked, as the trio hurried to the opposite side of the dance floor. Payne, Terry, and their buddy moved in and enjoyed a delightful, fun-filled evening with the ladies.

Payne found the Handy Gasser especially amusing while playing in pro-ams. Often, while his partner bent over to place a tee in the ground or to mark his ball, Payne let go with his favorite toy. "Hey! Watch it, there, bud," he'd say, pretending to be repulsed.

Besides giving vent to Payne's mischievous side, the Asian Tour provided him an opportunity to see the gross inequities and abject poverty of many parts of the world. It was truly an education for him. He had never before imagined such poverty as he saw in India. In the Philippines, he saw the opulence displayed by Ferdinand and Imelda Marcos and felt the restrictions of their despotic regime. Traveling in Thailand and other places throughout Southeast Asia, he often heard the American government denigrated. Payne was unaccustomed to hearing the United States spoken of in derisive terms, and it made him uncomfortable. It also fired his patriotic passions. He gained a new perspective on life and a new appreciation for his homeland.

Indeed, as he often said, he received his degree from SMU but his education from the Asian Tour. Six weeks into the tour, Payne's eyes were about to be opened in another way.

5

Love at
First Sight

Queensland, Australia, is around the world from Springfield, Missouri, . . . in more ways than one. I was born on June 27, 1959, in Rockhampton, the last of Norm and Shirley Ferguson's four children—joining my older brother, Michael, and my two sisters, Deidre and Andrea. Mum and Dad named me Anastasia Theresa, but from the earliest time I can remember, everyone called me Tracey.

My mother was a committed homemaker, though she also worked outside our home during my growing-up years. My father was a policeman, similar to a state trooper in the United States. His position required periodic transfers to rural towns. Consequently, my siblings and I spent most of our early years in various country towns.

In 1967, our family moved from Rockhampton to Innisfail, a sugarcane farming community in far north Queensland. When my dad wasn't working, his favorite pastime was playing golf. A scratch golfer, he passed along his love for the game to Michael, who also developed a real knack for playing.

Outside the home, one of the main influences in Innisfail was the Catholic church, which Mum and Dad attended occasionally. Although my parents weren't greatly involved in the church and didn't talk a lot about God in our home, they highly esteemed the teachings and values taught by the church. They made sure we Ferguson children were in services every week. Not surprisingly, they enrolled us in the Sacred Heart Convent School, a parochial school adjoining the church.

Upon finishing high school, Michael moved to Brisbane, the capital of Queensland. There, he signed on for a three-year golf apprenticeship with Charlie Earp before turning professional. Michael then played on the Australian Tour and soon rose in the ranks, becoming one of Australia's top pro golfers. Another young man who came through that same apprenticeship program did OK for himself too—a fellow named Greg Norman.

About the time I entered high school, Dad was transferred again and our family moved to Mt. Isa, a small, rural mining town in the Australian outback. In Australia, a high school student's required courses are completed by the end of tenth grade, at age fifteen, unless the student intends to continue along an academic path. After high school, I had planned to further my education, but I was offered a job at Mt. Isa Mines, a copper mining company that was the heart of the town. The job paid $80 a week, which was big money for a young woman just out of school, so I took it. The mining company trained me to be a tracer, a draftsperson who worked with maps and blueprints, so I became known as "Tracey the tracer." I started working for the mines at age fifteen and stayed there for three years. Being an independent sort, I bought my own clothes, my own car, and saved a bit of money as well.

Eventually, the small-town atmosphere began wearing on me, or perhaps it was just my sense of adventure that was awakening. At eighteen, I decided to move to London to join some friends I had met through my job at the mines. I worked in England for about six months and then took a break to travel around

Europe. While I relished being on my own and enjoyed the people in Europe, I had no desire to stay in London. The English weather was too damp, dreary, and depressing for me. Accustomed as I was to the gorgeous, lush landscapes and the Hawaiian-like beaches of Australia, I soon grew homesick and a bit bored in Great Britain. I returned to Australia and took another job.

For a while, I worked for Greg Norman's father, who was the boss at Mt. Isa Mines in Brisbane. Our families had a lot in common, as the Norman family had also lived in Mt. Isa, and Greg and my brother, Michael, both did their apprenticeships at Royal Queensland Golf Club.

Next, I did some temporary work on Australia's Gold Coast while sorting through what I wanted to do with the rest of my life. I was twenty years old, free spirited, happy-go-lucky, fun loving, and spontaneous, so when Michael and his wife, Sandra, invited me to join them for a three-week stint of golf tournaments on the Asian Tour, through Malaysia, Singapore, and Jakarta, Indonesia, it was too good an offer to pass up. I thought, Great! A three-week holiday coming up. It's sure to be an adventure! In my wildest dreams, I never could have imagined just how much of an adventure was about to begin.

Our first stop was in Kuala Lumpur, Malaysia, at the Royal Selangor Golf Course, for the 1980 Malaysian Open. We traveled with Wayne Grady, a well-known Australian player, and a contingent of four other Australian golfers who went everywhere together. On Tuesday night, we attended a cocktail party at the golf course as part of the pro-am festivities for the upcoming tournament. I had barely stepped inside the clubhouse when my eyes were drawn to a rakish blond fellow all the way across the room.

He was the most beautiful man I had ever seen (or have ever seen since!). Tall and slender—he looked to be about six-foot-one, 170 pounds—about twenty-three years of age, unspeakably handsome, with slightly disheveled sandy-blond hair and dancing blue eyes; he was gorgeous, definitely what nowadays we'd call a "hunk."

Dressed in a casual, hot-pink golf shirt, he seemed extremely confident as he moved among the contestants and their guests, eating and drinking something with everyone to whom he spoke. I soon realized that he was part of a group of young golfers who seemed determined to make dinner out of the tiny hors d'oeuvres being served at the party. It was great fun to watch him manipulate his way in front of another tray of food while never missing a word of conversation. What I didn't know at the time was that these guys were on an extremely tight budget and were strapped for cash. It was hors d'oeuvres or nothing for dinner that night!

The handsome fellow and I made eye contact occasionally, but we did not speak to each other. "Who is that guy?" I asked Michael when I was certain we were out of earshot. I nodded discreetly toward the handsome one.

"Oh, I don't know. Just some American guy," Michael replied. "I don't know his name."

I couldn't sleep that night. I kept thinking about the blond guy I had seen at the party. I didn't know anything about him; I didn't even know his name! But I couldn't get him out of my mind.

Over the next few days, this same fellow and I had a few chance encounters at the golf course. We played "eye games" in which he'd look at me, I'd look at him, then one or both of us would look away. Neither of us was yet willing to break the sound barrier by initiating a conversation. On Friday, Sandra and I were walking to the pro shop, and there he was again. We didn't speak, but I knew that he had noticed me. Sandra and I walked on to the pro shop and went inside. We were in the front part of the store, looking at some potential gifts to purchase, when I saw the American outside the window looking in at me. I was determined to stare him out this time, but he became embarrassed and ran away!

A few minutes later, just as I was getting into the car to leave the country club with my Australian friends, one of the American golfers "semi-introduced" the blond fellow to me. He said something that sounded like, "This is Pain Stewart." At least, that's what I thought he had said, but I couldn't quite make out the name. It didn't matter; I was ducking into the car, so I quickly replied, "Hi! . . . Bye!" and I got in the car without saying another word.

The members of our group were already in the car waiting for me. "Ahhh, you finally met him. What's his name?" one of them asked.

"Well, I don't know," I answered honestly. "It starts with a P. It must be Paul or Pete Stewart or something like that. But it sounded like the guy said he was a pain."

Nikki Reed, our host, who was working as a volunteer at the golf course during the tournament, knew the players' names. Nikki laughed and said, "It must be Payne Stewart, P-A-Y-N-E."

"Payne?" I repeated quizzically.

Michael couldn't resist. "Payne? Payne! What's that all about? What kind of name is Payne?"

I ignored Michael's feigned sarcasm and mulled the name over in my mind. Payne. Payne Stewart.

On Saturday morning, I was sitting in the clubhouse with my brother. Michael said, "I'm going to go practice, but I'll see you later. Sandra should be along any time now."

"Oh, don't worry about me," I replied. "I'll be fine."

Michael left and within minutes, Gaylord Burroughs, the fellow who had attempted to introduce me to Payne Stewart the previous evening, came over and sat down at my table. "You know," he said, "there are a few of the American guys who would like to ask you out." He spoke loudly, as if he were speaking so others in the room could hear.

"Oh, really?" I replied, playing along.

"Well, yeah, one of them is that guy who is sitting right over there!" He pointed to a table next to us. I looked over and there was Payne Stewart, sitting at the table, smiling broadly at me, listening to our conversation. He waved impishly at me, and I couldn't keep from smiling.

Payne came over to the table and after Gaylord had introduced us properly, he sat down. Within minutes, Gaylord made a hasty departure, although Payne and I hardly noticed.

We talked for a while, before Payne had to

leave to prepare for his round that afternoon. I had been watching Michael play all week, and I thought it might be interesting to watch the American play for a while. After following Michael for a few holes, I slipped away and ended up following Payne almost all the way around the course.

After his round—I'm not sure how Payne played or what he shot—we went back out on the golf course and fed some bananas to the wild monkeys that populated the trees in the rough alongside the fairways. Payne and I hit it off immediately. We walked and talked and laughed . . . and clicked. It was an interesting "first date."

That night, Payne and I went out to dinner at The Ship restaurant, one of the nicer eateries in the area. We talked about everything and anything, even the names we imagined for our first children, if either of us ever decided to marry. When it came time to pay the bill, Payne pulled out a credit card, but the restaurant wouldn't accept it.

"No problem," Payne said. "Here, let's use this one," he smiled as he thumbed through a series of plastic cards, obviously trying to impress me with his extensive credit line. Payne handed another credit card to the waiter, and we continued talking.

Soon the waiter returned with a look of chagrin on his face. "I'm quite sorry, sir, but that card is unacceptable as well." Embarrassed now, Payne fumbled around until he found another card that he was absolutely sure would accept the charges.

In a matter of minutes, the waiter was back. The look on his face said it all. Payne appeared nonplussed. "Well, hey," he said in a mixture of a Texan and Midwestern drawl, "we'll just pay cash then." Payne peeked into his slim wallet and pulled out some bills to cover the meal. He didn't have a lot of money, but fortunately he had enough to pay for our meal. We laughed our way out of the restaurant.

From that night on, we were inseparable, a true case of "love at first sight." In fact, although I did not learn of it for some time, the night Payne saw me at the pro-am party, he had told two of his American buddies, "That's the woman I'm going to marry!" Payne and the group of about thirty American golfers, between the ages of twenty-one and thirty, were just past the midpoint in an eleven-country golf tour that had begun in the Philippines. In the years that followed, he often needled me, "One of the reasons I was so attracted to you was that I hadn't seen a blonde-haired woman in more than six weeks!"

The golf tour moved from Malaysia to Singapore, where Payne and I went out for dinner almost every night after he played his round. Payne's roommate, Terry Anton, went along with us most evenings. Terry and Payne were hilarious together. We laughed a lot, and then Terry always disappeared shortly after dinner, leaving Payne and me to develop further our relationship.

For three solid weeks, Payne and I enjoyed each other's company in a lover's fantasy world, traveling from one exotic place to the next. We didn't have much money, but we didn't need a lot. We just had fun being together. We ate as inexpensively as possible, and we talked incessantly. Most of all, we both knew that we had found something wonderfully special; we were soul mates, and we were falling in love.

At the end of the Asian Tour, we had to say good-bye, knowing that we would not see each other for another six months, when Payne planned to return to Australia to play the Tour in my homeland. We both wanted to continue the relationship, so we promised to keep in touch by phone and mail; but we made no other pledges to each other. We were realists . . . and the reality was that we lived on opposite sides of the world.

Nevertheless, when I returned home, I couldn't contain my excitement. "Oh, Mum, I met the most wonderful, beautiful, American man!"

Mum seemed genuinely happy for me, but she did express concern. "That's wonderful, Tracey. But aren't there any men in Australia?" It didn't take long, however, for Mum to realize that this fellow was different from anyone else I had ever dated.

Meanwhile, back home in America, Payne went to work trying to qualify for the PGA Tour. Ironically, it had been his near miss at the 1979 Q School that had brought him to Malaysia and had brought us together.

When Payne returned home, he lived with his parents in Springfield and played in some mini-tour events, making a bit of money here and there. He attempted to earn his Tour card at the fall Q School in 1980, but once again he missed qualifying. Discouraged, he went to Pittsburgh to visit Barry Snyder, one of his college roommates. While he was there, Payne had a talk with Barry's dad, whom he greatly respected. Merv Snyder suggested that Payne seek a new career. "You've tried to get your card twice now and missed. You've given it a good shot, Payne. Maybe it's time you tried something else. With your outgoing personality, you'd probably do very well in some sort of sales."

"Thanks, Merv," Payne replied gratefully, "but I'd like to give it one more try. If I don't make it, then I may have to consider some other options." Undaunted, Payne called me and said he was coming to Australia.

He had planned to play on the Australian Tour anyhow, during October and November, our summer months, so his arrival in Sydney was not a surprise. We had been communicating by phone and mail since we'd met in March, and our feelings for each other had continued to deepen. I was tremendously excited to see him again. By now, I had moved to Sydney with my friend, Helen Richmond, and I was earning good money as a tracer and draftsperson. I traveled with Payne to most of the tournaments in and around Sydney. I even caddied for him at The Lakes Golf Course in Sydney. "We make a good team," Payne said.

Mark O'Meara, another American golfer, was also playing in that tournament. He had won the U.S. Amateur Championship in 1979 by beating the defending champion, John Cook. Mark and Payne were the same age, and Payne noted that Mark had just received his PGA Tour card and was gearing up to go out on the Tour at the beginning of the year. Mark and his fiancée, Alicia, were planning to get married in December before the new golf season began.

While playing in Australia, Payne and I traveled up to my parents' home on the Gold Coast, and my folks fell in love with him too. Mum was impressed with his polite Midwestern manners, and Dad was delighted that I was actually dating a professional golfer—even though his career was in the fledgling stages. One night, Payne said, "I'd really like for you to come to America to spend Christmas with my family and me. I've told my mom and dad all about you, and they would love to meet you. You can stay at our house in Springfield. Will you come?" Payne had mentioned in letters and in our phone conversations that he was hoping I could visit with his family in the States over Christmas. We laughed about it because it seemed like such a dream.

He didn't need to ask me twice. Payne played in Australia for about a month, and when the Australian Tour dates were completed, he moved on to New Zealand to play for a couple of weeks. We made plans to meet in Los Angeles after he finished his tournaments in New Zealand.

Payne didn't feel that he was wasting his time playing the Asian or Australian Tours.

Quite the contrary, he often said that he was learning an important lesson during those days, namely that the game was not about having great form or a pretty swing—both of which Payne had—but it was about getting a little round ball in the hole in the least amount of strokes. Payne said, "You go over there on the Asian Tour, playing in a different country every week. It's like playing for a national open every week. I was watching guys that didn't have pretty swings, guys with unorthodox swings, guys that didn't do all the things that I had always been told you were supposed to do to play golf well, and I watched those same guys beat me week in and week out!

"One fellow from Thailand was about four-foot-eleven, and he wrapped his 56-inch driver all the way around his head when he swung, but he beat me! I thought, What does he know about this game that I don't? I realized then that the game wasn't about being perfect. It's about getting the job done. It's about getting the ball in the hole with the least amount of strokes. It's about figuring out how to do that your way. It isn't about the beauty of your golf swing. It's about the number you post at the end of the day."

Playing overseas also taught Payne a new meaning of the term "golf course hazards." At the Indian Open in New Delhi, one of the guys in Payne's group overshot the green. When he went to retrieve his ball, he was in for a big surprise. "Suddenly, he came running back toward us," Payne said, "and behind him was a king cobra, fully erect! The guy decided to take a stroke and drop a new ball. It made me appreciate playing in the U.S."

It was an exciting day when I met Payne at the Los Angeles International Airport. He had left his car, a late-model silver Pontiac Grand Prix, with a friend, so we picked up the car and set out on another adventure. Because it was my first trip to the United States, Payne wanted to show me the entire country on our way from Los Angeles to Springfield. We stopped at Disneyland, Las Vegas, and all sorts of places in between. It took us more than two weeks to get back to Payne's hometown.

I was a bit uneasy meeting Payne's family for the first time, but his parents and sisters were extremely kind and gracious, welcoming me and making me feel right at home. Payne's dad, however, frequently dropped subtle hints that I should not take Payne's and my relationship too seriously. He made a point of telling me about the many other girlfriends that Payne had, although I knew that Payne had never before invited anyone from a foreign country home to meet the family. Of course, I may have been the only girl he knew from a foreign country.

Bill Stewart was nice to me; but it was clear that he had a plan for Payne and he didn't want any woman to interfere with Payne's golf career. "He needs to concentrate on his golf," Bill Stewart said frequently. "Don't think you're anything special because Payne has plenty of other girlfriends too," Bill reminded me every way he could.

Despite Bill's attempts to discourage me, the family members could tell that Payne and I were in love. I was the only woman Payne had brought home for any length of time.

I spent more than six weeks in the States with Payne before I had to return home. Before I left, Payne asked me if I could meet him again in Asia in March. Because he had missed earning his Tour card, he planned to play the Asian Tour again in 1981. I went back to Australia and took a job from January to March, with my sole purpose simply to make enough money to pay for the next airfare to meet up with Payne again. I was willing to travel around the globe to see the man I loved and to share in his dream of making it as a professional golfer.

I met Payne at the Tour stop in Malaysia and accompanied him for three weeks on the

Asian Tour. During my second week in Asia, we attended another pro-am dinner in Singapore. We were at a table along with ten other people, pretending to be eating the monkey brains and other disgusting "delicacies" our hosts were serving. Payne nudged me and said, "Let's go to McDonalds to get something to eat when we get out of here!"

I agreed wholeheartedly. We sat at the table, just talking between the two of us about how much we were going to miss each other when I returned to Sydney, when suddenly Payne said, "You're just going to have to marry me."

I didn't say anything.

"Well?"

"Well, what?" I asked.

"Well, will you marry me?"

"Well, I don't know . . ." I feigned uncertainty. "I'll have to think about it."

"Wha—! Think about it?" Payne hooted. "If you have to think about it, don't worry about it! Just forget it!"

I laughed out loud. All ten of the other guests at our table were looking at us. It wasn't exactly the most romantic setting for a proposal of marriage. I clasped Payne's hand and said, "Yes, Payne. I will marry you."

"All right!" Payne let out an ecstatic

whoop that nearly scared the others at our table.

Payne hadn't purchased an engagement ring, but I had no doubt that he was serious about his proposal, especially when later that night, we called his parents and Payne told his mom and dad that we were getting married. Payne's mom was thrilled, but there was no response from Bill—at least none that we wanted to hear!

When I returned home and told my parents that Payne and I were engaged, my father's first response was, "Where's your ring?"

"I don't have one."

"Then you're not engaged," Dad said straightforwardly.

But we were nonetheless engaged, and Payne and I immediately started putting together our wedding arrangements.

While we were in Asia, Payne won his first golf tournaments on foreign soil, winning the Indian Open and the Indonesian Open. He received $10,000 cash in U.S. currency for each of the tournaments, and for the rest of the Tour, he carried a suitcase full of money as he traveled around Asia. When Payne returned to the United States, he divided the winnings with the sponsors who had helped get him started.

Payne finally earned his PGA Tour card in June of 1981, playing in the Q School held at the Walt Disney World courses that year. He and Terry Anton both shot 69s to earn their cards. Payne was like an excited puppy when he called me. "I made it, Tracey! We're on the PGA Tour."

I returned to the United States in July and again stayed with Payne's parents. Payne's mom, Bee, had an engagement party for us, but his father was not nearly so supportive. In truth, he was not at all happy about our marriage plans, and he was not quiet about his views. That is, when he talked to me at all. Frequently, Payne's dad simply ignored me, even when I was in the same room with him.

"Ask her what she thinks about this," Bill would say to Payne.

"Dad, she's sitting right here. You ask her yourself," Payne would answer.

It wasn't that Bill didn't like me. It wasn't a personal thing. No woman would have been good enough for his prize pupil on the links. He simply didn't think it was the right time for Payne to be getting married, just as he was beginning to experience some success in golf.

Because he had won the Indian Open and the Indonesian Open, Payne was invited to play in the prestigious British Open at Royal St. George's in England. While I remained at

101

his parents' home, Payne flew across the Atlantic. My brother, Michael, also qualified for the British Open that year, and the two of them came in dead last and next to last. Michael tied for fifty-third place, and Payne followed right on his heels, winning $1,031—almost enough to pay his plane fare.

As Payne set out to fulfill his dream of succeeding on the PGA Tour, his sponsors put up about $1,000 per week to cover his living expenses on the road, including food, gasoline, hotel accommodations, and tournament entry fees. Although he had his Tour card, the Monday qualifying system was still in place in those days, which meant that Payne had to qualify to play each week.

At the time, the top sixty players on the money list, as well as those who had won tournaments during the year, were exempt from having to qualify. The nonexempt players were known as "rabbits" because they were perpetually hopping from one tournament to the next, hoping to get into the tournament field and earn enough money to survive.

Today, the top 125 money winners from the previous year are exempt from having to qualify to play on the Tour. Those players are automatically invited to play in PGA Tour events. Their biggest decisions are which tournaments they want to play. When Payne joined the Tour, however, earning a card did not necessarily guarantee a spot in a tournament. It merely indicated that a player was one of the privileged few permitted to attempt to qualify each Monday.

The system spawned all sorts of insecurities among the young players, but at least it was a fair way of deciding who got to play each week. It was simple. If you played well on Monday, you got to play in the tournament. If you didn't play well on Monday, sorry, but it was down the road to the next stop on the Tour, where the nonexempt players could try again.

Payne's first check on the PGA Tour came at the Canon Greater Hartford Open, in Connecticut. He made a grand total of $715.50.

To save money, we frequently stayed with host families in their homes during the week of the tournament. We made some wonderful new friends, some of whom have remained close to us to this day. When we played the 1981 Buick Open in Michigan, Payne and I stayed with Patti Eister and her family. We hit it off so well with the Eisters that we returned to their home year after year.

Similarly, at the Memorial Tournament in Dublin, Ohio, Payne stayed with Terry and

Connie Bueter. He felt so comfortable staying in their home that every year he played the tournament he never considered staying anywhere else . . . even after we could afford hotel rooms.

6

Starting Out on the PGA Tour

S tarting out on the PGA Tour is a bit like learning to snow ski without using any poles—while competing in the Olympics! Each player is his own small business, an entrepreneur of sorts, banking on his ability to make a living playing the game. Back in the early 1980s, golf equipment companies and other advertisers did not pay megabuck endorsement fees to young, unproven players who were just coming out on Tour. Only the top players with bankable names—Palmer, Nicklaus, Trevino, and the like—received endorsement offers.

I knew that a career as a professional golfer could be like living in a roller-coaster car: one moment you're up; the next instant you're down. Everything could be purring along beautifully, and then suddenly, without warning, the bottom could fall out, or you could be jerked into twists and turns that threatened to throw you right off the ride! Nevertheless, I wasn't afraid to dream big dreams with Payne as we prepared to get married. We saw our life together as one great adventure. We weren't worried about making money or carving out a career. We were young and in love, and we were happy just to be together.

Certainly, I recognized that Payne had incredible potential as a golfer. He already possessed more skill than most people who ever pick up the clubs, and he was obsessed with improving. My brother, Michael, was also impressed with Payne's tremendous natural ability. "He's going to be a great golfer," Michael told me. My brother was making a comfortable living on the Australian Tour, so he had a good idea of what it might take to succeed on the PGA Tour. He assured me that Payne had the game to make it. I appreciated Michael's vote of confidence, but even without it, I knew in my heart that Payne would succeed on the PGA Tour. Still, nobody can say we married for money, because neither of us had much. In fact, on our wedding day, I had more money in the bank than Payne did!

We planned our wedding around Payne's golf schedule, working out a Tuesday wedding date in Southport, on the Gold Coast, right before Payne was to play in the Tweed Head Classic. Barry Snyder and Lamar Haynes, Payne's friends from college, were his best man and groomsman, and my sisters and my friend Helen were my bridesmaids. Our local Catholic church would not allow us to be married unless Payne attended catechism classes every week, which he could not do because of his schedule, so we were married on November 10, 1981, in the United Church instead.

Payne and his groomsmen wore powder blue tuxedos that I picked out because they matched Payne's eyes. About seventy people attended our modest wedding—small by American standards but rather the norm for Australian weddings. Our reception continued until about 2:00 a.m. with Payne and me being among the last ones to leave the party. Payne's reputation as a prankster made it inevitable that he should have to take some of his own medicine. Sure enough, during the reception, Michael, Barry, Lamar, and some of the other guys pulled Payne into a rest room, yanked his clothes off, and painted as much of his body as possible with Mercurochrome, staining his skin a reddish brown and getting Mercurochrome all over Payne's beautiful powder blue tux. The crimson color of the antiseptic caused Payne to look as though he were bleeding. We never did get that stuff out of his tux and ended up having to pay to replace the suit.

Worse yet, we later learned that there had been a fellow in one of the rest room stalls at the time of the ruckus with Payne. Hearing Payne's loud bellows as he struggled to free himself from the painters and seeing the red spattering the floor, the man in the stall thought something awful was happening. He remained sequestered until the noise died down and to this day probably has nightmares about that event.

Payne was scheduled to play in a pro-am the following morning at 7:00, but he called ahead of time and said, "I'm sorry; I won't be able to make it. It will be the first day of my married life." Instead, Payne and I went to my parents' home, about half an hour away, and did laundry. It was a mundane beginning for a great marriage, but at least we started out with clean clothes!

Payne participated in the Tweed Head Classic, but he didn't play very well. We played a few more tournaments and then went back to Sydney so I could gather my things before leaving my homeland to live with Payne in the

United States. On the way back to the States, we stopped in Tahiti for a weeklong honeymoon.

Back in the States, we hit the road in the silver Grand Prix and drove to California to catch the beginning of the West Coast swing of the PGA Tour. We went from tournament to tournament, with Payne attempting to win a spot in the Monday qualifying rounds. Each week, he fell short. Time after time he came so close, but a missed putt here, a bad chip there, a drive in the rough, and we were on our way to the next tournament site without earning a dollar. For twelve solid weeks, Payne failed to qualify, barely missing Monday after Monday.

I tried my best to encourage him. He was so close; we knew he would do it eventually. But the Tour's next stop was in Florida, and Payne still hadn't made it through a Monday qualifying round, much less a complete tournament.

"We'll get it next week," Payne said as we packed the car to head to the next tournament. "We'll work harder, and it will come around." To Payne and me, it wasn't just him out there on the course; it was us. It was always we will get it, we can do better, we will make it together. We were a team.

I never felt that I was sacrificing anything

109

to be with Payne. My whole life was committed to him and to helping him be the best he could be. If that meant submerging my career into his, so be it. I saw myself as his encourager and his helper. I soon recognized that he relied on me for honest opinions that he could trust. I watched him hour after hour on the golf course, lining up balls for him on the putting green, learning everything I could about his game and what it took for him to be the best at his craft.

Terry Anton still chuckles about the first time he saw Payne and me working on the putting green. I placed golf balls in a circle all the way around the hole, about ten feet away from the cup. As Payne putted around the circumference, I retrieved the balls and positioned them again, each time moving them in a little closer. The game was that he had to make every putt from each distance before I'd let him move in closer.

When Terry first saw us working on the putting green, it was about 11:00 A.M. That afternoon, Terry returned and found us still on the putting green at 1:30 P.M.

"What's goin' on?" he asked Payne.

"Man, she won't let me leave!" Payne said in mock dismay. "She says I have to make every putt from every distance before we can go. I have to make every one from ten feet, and if I miss one, I have to put that one back and try again until I make it. Then I have to make 'em from six feet, then three feet. We might be here all night! Tracey is serious about me becoming a good putter."

At first, Payne forced himself to practice—he wasn't wild about practicing—but gradually it became an ingrained part of the intense self-discipline that he would maintain throughout his career. I pushed him to practice during those times when he would've preferred to slack off. I knew that we wanted the same things—to see the dreams come true, to excel, and to win—so I did all I could to help motivate him.

I tried not to nag, but I didn't baby him or bow down to him as a spoiled brat either. Payne's personality was such that he took advice and correction well. He was humble in the face of criticism, even when it was unfounded. He especially took my opinions seriously because he knew that I loved him and wanted the best for him.

It wasn't until early March 1982 that Payne finally qualified on the Monday before the Doral-Ryder Open in Miami. The course, known for its Blue Monster water hazards, was a tough place to make it for the first time, and Payne missed the cut—the dividing line that determines the top seventy players in the tournament who will continue on after the first two rounds. The following week, the PGA Tour moved to the Bay Hill Club and Lodge in Orlando, but because the tournament was an invitational event, we didn't get to play. Finally, on March 8, 1982, at the Honda Inverrary Classic in Fort Lauderdale, Florida, Payne not only qualified on Monday; he made the Friday cut and finished the tournament tied for forty-second place, earning $1,322.28.

Four weeks after Inverrary, we went to Hattiesburg, Mississippi, for the Magnolia Classic, and Payne won his first PGA Tour tournament, pocketing a check for $13,500. At that time, Payne didn't have any advertising endorsements, but he did play a Titleist golf ball, so we also received a $10,000 bonus check from Titleist for winning a tournament while playing their ball. With $23,500 in our hands, we thought we were rich! The money counted on the PGA Tour official money list, but the victory did not count as an official PGA Tour win because it was played opposite (at the same time as) the Masters, in Augusta, Georgia. Nowadays, tournaments played opposite majors and other invitation-only tournaments are designated as official wins, the same as any other PGA Tour event.

At Hattiesburg, Payne established his practice of speaking openly with the media but not always in a manner to which the reporters were accustomed. Speaking facetiously in his postround interview, Payne deadpanned that "the Tour needs more blond-haired, blue-eyed guys." Payne was referring, of course, to the fact that the Tour seemed to breed blond-haired, blue-eyed players. Jack Nicklaus, the fabled Golden Bear, had been succeeded by Greg Norman and a bevy of other light-haired players who had joined the Tour. It would take a while before members of the media caught on to Payne's sense of humor—some never did.

Besides breaking into the win column, one of the best things to come out of our experience at Hattiesburg was our relationship with Paul and Toni Azinger. Paul and Toni were also newlyweds, just starting out on the PGA Tour. They were literally living in a camper, traveling from tournament to tournament as Paul also attempted to qualify on Mondays. When Paul heard Payne playfully jabbing the press, he thought, Who in the heck is this guy? A great player with a sharp, dry sense of humor himself, Paul knew that he had found a kindred spirit in Payne. Paul and Toni became two of our closest friends among the PGA Tour players.

Although Payne won the tournament at Hattiesburg, according to PGA standards, he still hadn't won an official event. That would soon change, along with another distinct aspect of Payne's game.

One day, out on the practice tee, Payne looked to his right and saw a fellow player wearing red slacks, white shoes, and a white Izod shirt with a red stripe and a tiny green alligator on the pocket. Payne looked down the range to his left and saw another pro wearing the exact same outfit. Then Payne looked at his own clothes. He, too, was wearing red golf slacks, white shoes, and a white Izod shirt, identical right down to the alligator. Right then and there, he decided he needed to do something about his wardrobe.

Payne recalled his dad's example when it came to the value of a distinct flare in fashion. Although Bill Stewart knew how to dress conservatively, he preferred not to. "My father was a salesman, and when he went on a sales call, he always wore a loud sport coat. My father said that if you stand out when you go to sell somebody something, they'll remember who you are, but if you come in dressed in a boring navy blue suit, you'll just be another person in the crowd."

Payne's father understood the power of a first impression; he just didn't understand stripes and plaids. His wild sport jackets were the subject of more than a few family discussions, especially when the slacks that he selected clashed with the coat. "My father didn't always get the colors just right, and sometimes his outfits really didn't match all that well," said Payne. "My sisters and I would give him a hard time about it. We'd say things like, 'Dad, you're really not going to go out dressed like that, are you?' But he never changed his clothes because we complained about them."

Pondering how to separate himself from the pack of Izod clones, Payne recalled Stewart Ginn and Roger Davis, two players he had met while playing on the Asian Tour who wore knickers and kneesocks. Payne liked the look; he felt that it looked classy and helped maintain a sense of golf's grand tradition.

Terry Anton, Payne's good friend and roommate on the Asian Tour, knew about Payne's appreciation for the traditional apparel. One day, when Terry and Payne were playing together, Terry showed up wearing a pair of knickers. Payne loved them! Terry told Payne about a guy in California who made some great-looking knickers. Payne was visiting friends in Dallas, getting ready to play in the

Byron Nelson Classic, when he decided to call the knickers designer.

Tim Barry owned a small, fledgling company, the T. Barry Knicker Company, in Palm Desert, California. Payne hoped that he might be able to work out some sort of cooperative deal in which Barry would supply him with knickers, and he in turn would commit to wearing them on tour. Payne gushed, "My name is Payne Stewart, and I'm on the PGA Tour."

"Great. What can I do for you, Mr. Stewart?" Tim Barry replied coolly, obviously unimpressed.

"Well, I'd like to wear your knickers out on Tour," said Payne. Little did Payne know that other players had already tried to hit up Tim Barry for an endorsement deal on his knickers, all to no avail. Barry wasn't interested in giving away his custom-made knickers for free, much less paying somebody to wear them!

Imagine Payne's surprise when Tim Barry said, "Here's what I'll do for you. You buy three pair of knickers, and I'll give you the fourth pair free." That was the best deal Payne could get.

"How fast can you get them here?" Payne asked.

"I can get them to you by the end of next week," Barry replied.

"OK, that's great. Let's do it."

The knickers arrived the following weekend, just in time for Payne to don a pair for the third round of the Atlanta Classic in May 1982. On Saturday morning, Payne picked out the first pair of knickers he would ever wear—a pale lavender. Making matters even more interesting, his playing partner that day was Lee Trevino. Lee's reputation as a quick-witted, sharp-tongued player was exceeded only by his reputation as an excellent ball-striker. When Lee saw Payne in those lavender knickers, he couldn't resist. He needled Payne all day long. "If you think Trevino didn't have a lot of fun with me . . ." Payne said later. "He wore me out!"

Despite Trevino's playful jibes, the spectators at the tournament responded positively. Women in the gallery especially approved of the knickers. They loved Payne's "new" look. So did the television producers. Their cameras followed Payne's every move, whether he was playing well or not. And his game was getting better with every round. He shot a 66 that first day he wore the knickers. Payne actually felt that putting on the knickers helped him mentally prepare for his round. "Clothes help your attitude," he said. "When I put my work clothes on, I get all fired up."

Of course, from some players, Payne's knickers drew nothing but snickers. Besides Lee Trevino, Fuzzy Zoeller and Hubert Green teased Payne constantly, although their poking fun was always lighthearted. Most of the players respected Payne for being bold enough to wear something different. Undoubtedly, had his golf game not spoken for itself, the knickers would not have drawn nearly the interest. In later years, Payne himself often said, "I don't think people would come out to watch a guy shoot an 80 in knickers."

The first event in which Payne wore the "plus fours," as the knickers were known more formally, in all four rounds was the 1982 Quad Cities Open in Moline, Illinois. To top off the knickers, Payne wore a traditional Scottish-style, tam-o'-shanter hat. "A golf hat or a visor just doesn't look right with knickers," he said. "It doesn't complete the outfit. I need a cap to accent the outfit." Maybe the knickers and the tam-o'-shanter had an effect, or maybe it was because his dad was at that tournament, but for whatever reason, Payne put his game all together and won the Quad Cities Open, his first official win on the PGA Tour! To Payne, it was a sign, an omen of good things to come, and the knickers and tam-o'-shanter became part of his trademark image.

At the Quad Cities Open, when Payne finished, his father joined him on the eighteenth green. Father and son embraced, and both Payne and his father cried for joy, unashamedly, in front of everybody. It was the beginning of a dream come true.

To this day, the 1982 Quad Cities Open holds bittersweet memories for me. It was our first official PGA Tour win, which gave Payne a two-year exemption on the PGA Tour. It was a milestone in his career. But although we could not imagine it at the time, it would also be the only championship that Payne's father would ever see him win. Moreover, in addition to the first place prize of $36,000, Payne received a Rolex watch as part of his championship prize package. On the back of the watch was engraved "1982 QCO Champion." It was the watch Payne was wearing on October 25, 1999, as he boarded a private jet heading for Dallas.

7

All the Right Moves

B y the end of the 1982 season in October, Payne had won enough money on the PGA Tour to repay the sponsors who had been supporting us since he had first earned his Tour card. Because Payne succeeded early on the Tour, we were able to give them back their original investment and a bit more. It was a win-win situation.

In November, we went back to Australia to play on the Tour there, and Payne won the Tweed Head Classic on our first wedding anniversary. Almost equally as significant to Payne, he got to play a practice round with his hero, Jack Nicklaus, at the Australian Open. Making it even more memorable, Payne and

Jack tied for second place in that tournament. From then on, any time Payne referred to the Golden Bear, he always called him by his first name—my friend, Jack—and over the years, Jack and Payne did indeed become good friends.

Payne was always open to trying new things, especially if they might help his golf game. While playing in Asia the previous year, Payne and our friend Terry Anton discovered a doctor who was a strong proponent of acupuncture to help relieve tension. By placing three tiny needles connected to pinhead-style studs in the left ear, a warming, relaxing sensation could be felt throughout the entire body whenever the pinheads were rubbed. Terry was so convinced that he had the Asian doctor place the needles in his ear. Payne was enthused but decided to wait until he returned to the States to have the acupuncture done.

After he arrived back home, Payne contacted his friend Hogan H'Doubler, a Springfield physician who knew about the process and implanted acupuncture needles in Payne's ear. Apparently, the needles really worked. When the stress of a tournament began to get to him, Payne simply reached up and rubbed his finger over one of the pinheads in his left ear. The pin's movement triggered a reaction in the brain that released serotonin—a natural tranquilizer—into the body. Whether the sensation was physical or psychological, the effect was the same. Payne relaxed and focused better on his game.

In the early 1980s, men with studs in their ears were not considered macho or medically progressive; they were considered gay. Payne took a great deal of ribbing from other players, who teased, "Excuse me, Sweetie . . ." Although he was convinced the needles helped, Payne couldn't explain why. But he didn't have to understand something to trust it. If he found something that worked, he'd go with it whether it made sense to other people or not. At the 1983 Masters, when someone asked Payne the purpose of the needles, Payne replied jokingly, "One is for temperament, one is for concentration, one is for anxiety, and I can't remember what the fourth one is for; memory, I think."

During the golf season Payne and I were on the road almost constantly. When we were not at a tournament location, we returned to his family's home in Missouri. We were usually home for no more than a few days at a time, so it made good financial sense for us to live with Payne's parents for the first eighteen months of our marriage. For the most part, we all got along quite well. Payne's father fully accepted me as his daughter-in-law. He now realized that rather than being a detriment to Payne's golf game, I actually influenced him positively, encouraging him to practice more rather than less. I worked with him and studied his game, trying to find every way possible that we could help him become a better player.

Still, no matter how much family members love one another, some stress is inevitable when parents and adult married children live together under the same roof. Bill and Bee Stewart were extremely kind to us, opening up their home and themselves, providing everything we needed, but Payne and I were newlyweds. We wanted a place we could call our own, a place where we could get away from the Tour and relax in a place that we had decorated, on furniture that we had picked. We wanted to sleep in our own bed, watch what we preferred to see on TV, listen to our own music—Payne always liked his Jimmy Buffett and Bruce Hornsby music loud—and have our friends over without worrying that we were imposing on Payne's parents. We decided to check on renting an apartment in Springfield.

Ever the pragmatist, Payne's father could not see the logic of us moving to an apartment when he and Bee had a comfortable home in which we could live. "Seems like a waste of money to me," he said. "Why do you need your own apartment? You're hardly ever here anyhow." Payne's family thought we were deserting them. Payne and I were convinced, however, that we needed our own space. We rented the apartment for about six months.

In 1983, Payne won the Walt Disney World Golf Classic in Orlando, Florida. The Disney check was the biggest that Payne had earned to date, $72,000. Because of that, we began to think more seriously about buying a home of our own. While we were in Florida, we stayed with our friends, Scott and Sally Hoch, and they encouraged us to consider moving to Orlando. Scott was an up-and-coming PGA Tour contender, so the Hochs understood the pluses and minuses of our sort of nomadic lifestyle. They assured us that Orlando was a great, growing city and a wonderful place to live.

Payne and I were quite impressed with the city. In fact, everything about Florida seemed conducive to our lifestyle. Florida's weather would allow Payne to practice year-round. Beyond that, Orlando has a large, modern airport, providing easy access to most of the East Coast tournaments. In contrast, living in Springfield required us to fly into St. Louis and take an Ozark Airlines shuttle flight home. We found ourselves spending most of our spare time in the St. Louis airport. All in all, a move to Orlando seemed to make sense. Payne and I could see only one drawback—we'd be a long distance from any family members.

Because my side of the family still resided in Australia, our move would not affect them, but we knew that Payne's family would not understand. They were happy living in Springfield; it was a wonderful community and it was home to them. Why would anyone ever want to live anywhere else?

Despite the disapproval of his parents, in January 1984 Payne and I bought a house and moved to Bay Hill Village, next to the Bay Hill Club and Lodge in Orlando. It was a lovely, new home, for which we paid around $180,000. Payne's father thought that was an outrageous amount of money for first-time homeowners to spend on a house. When Bill came to visit us in Orlando for the first time, he pouted during his first few days in our home. It wasn't that he didn't like our house or that he was not glad to be with us; he was simply upset that we had left Springfield. Because Payne had gotten his start in Springfield, his father thought he should remain there now that he was achieving some of his goals. Perhaps unconsciously, Bill lapsed back into giving me the silent treatment. He spoke to me only if absolutely necessary.

Finally, Payne and his father had a talk. "Look, Dad, this move is good for my career, and you should be happy for me." What Payne didn't say but easily could have was that the move was good for our marriage too. We had always enjoyed a great relationship. Payne always said, "Isn't it great that we can laugh so much together?" Now that we were truly on our own, our love for each other seemed to blossom even more. Something about cutting the strings that attached us to our Springfield family caused us to depend more on each other and, consequently, caused our marriage to flourish. Eventually, Bill came to accept our move, but I'm not certain that he ever approved of it, especially when Payne became known as one of Orlando's favorite sons.

Greg and Laura Norman, whom I had known from back home in Australia, now lived in Bay Hill Village, around the corner from Payne and me, so having a fellow Aussie in the neighborhood made me feel even more content about our move. Laura spoke often about her friends, Dixie and Robert Fraley, who also lived in the Village. Laura was not given to exaggeration, so when she described Dixie and Robert so warmly and enthusiastically, I knew they must be special people.

One day, I stopped by Laura's house and

126

Dixie was there. Laura introduced us, and I immediately understood why Laura was so impressed with Dixie. She was so personable. A slender, attractive woman whom I guessed to be in her late twenties, Dixie combined a down-home, country charm with an uptown subtle sophistication. She laughed easily, was bright, funny, and articulate; and there was something more to her that I couldn't quite comprehend. She cared; she exuded sincere concern and compassion; in a word, she was radiant. Genuine, unconditional love seemed to emanate from within her.

Not long after that, Payne and I dropped off some laundry at the Bay Hill Cleaners. I stayed in the car while Payne went inside. When I glanced out the window, I noticed Payne shaking hands with a fellow in the laundry. I didn't think much of it—Payne was always quick to meet new friends—but when he returned to the car, he told me that he had just met Robert Fraley, Dixie's husband.

Robert had been a star quarterback for Alabama's Crimson Tide, playing under the tutelage of their legendary coach, Paul "Bear" Bryant. Robert loved sports of all sorts, so he and Dixie owned a sports management company, Leader Enterprises, an agency that handled contracts and endorsement deals for sports celebrities. Known in Orlando as a man of integrity, Robert had played a key role in helping Bill Dupont bring the Orlando Magic basketball franchise to the city. Friendly and kind, Robert possessed a rare wisdom that went far beyond his years. He was a father figure, big brother, and best friend, all rolled into one person.

Dixie was particularly helpful to me in making the transition to Orlando, showing me around, making introductions for me, and helping me to get acclimated to my new lifestyle. She was so loving and giving, always ready to help in any way, with no strings attached. Payne and Dixie had similar personalities—spontaneous, outgoing, and always living on the edge, while Robert and I shared similar temperaments—more organized, reserved, and conservative. We enjoyed doing fun things together as couples, and Dixie and Robert became our closest friends. At almost every major triumph or crisis in our lives, Dixie and Robert were right there with us.

Payne had won tournaments in both of his first two years on the Tour, winning the Quad Cities Open in 1982 and the 1983 Walt Disney World Classic. We quickly got used to seeing his name atop the leaderboard. Over the next three seasons, Payne finished second in six PGA Tour events, as well as a second-place finish to Sandy Lyle in the 1985 British Open. The twenty-nine top-ten finishes he had during those three seasons helped our bank account grow, but Payne wasn't winning, and that wasn't satisfying to him or to me. Money was a poor substitute for victory. Payne had never played simply for the money; he had always played to win.

In May 1984, at the Colonial National Invitational, Payne was in the heat of the battle all the way, contending with Peter Jacobsen. On the last hole of the tournament, they were tied and Payne needed a par to win. Instead, he made bogey, and then Peter beat Payne in the play-off. A few months earlier, Peter had learned that his father had cancer. When Peter beat Payne at Colonial, Payne grabbed his hand and held onto it firmly as they shook hands on the green. "That one was for your dad," Payne said emotionally. Ordinarily one of the Tour's most quick-witted players, Peter nearly broke down crying right there on the green.

Peter recalls, "My father was on his deathbed, I thought. And Payne was so warm and so comforting to me, saying how happy he was that I had won the tournament—at his expense. Payne said, 'I hope your father is watching on TV, I hope your father is well, and that he lives for many years to come.' Which he did. My father lived another nine years."

A few weeks later, we received news that shook Payne like nothing I had ever seen: Bill Stewart—Payne's father, coach, role model, and the man he admired more than any other man on earth, the person who had influenced Payne's golf game and given him more coaching and encouragement than anyone else, the man he constantly strove to please in almost every area of his life—had been diagnosed with bone cancer. The technical term the doctors at the Mayo Clinic in Rochester, Minnesota, used to describe Bill's condition was multiple myeloma, a rapidly escalating, incurable disease.

At first, Payne couldn't believe it. Or wouldn't believe it. His father had always been the picture of health. He didn't drink, didn't smoke, wasn't overweight; his lifestyle was as straitlaced as anyone's could be. He walked the golf course rather than riding in a golf cart, frequently carrying his own clubs. How could he possibly have a deadly disease?

When we first got the news, Payne flew into motion, calling around, trying to get more information. There had to be some new method of treating bone cancer. His attitude was, "My father can beat this thing." But as the months went by, Bill's condition deteriorated, his once strong, vibrant body growing weaker by the day. Payne forced himself to face the reality that his father might not make it. He wouldn't talk much about it, but I could tell that his concern for his father never left his mind for long. When he went home to visit his dad, Payne found his father tired and relegated to his recliner but characteristically upbeat. Bill told Payne, "Don't worry about me. Get back out there on the Tour and win something."

Payne tried his best, but he couldn't keep focused. After he found out about his dad's cancer, the remainder of 1984 became a blur to him. His father was all he could think about. He played well enough, pulling in $288,795, then a PGA Tour record for the most money won without actually winning a tournament. Payne ended the season eleventh on the PGA money list, the main standard by which players were ranked at that time.

Almost as if God were giving us something to counteract the bad news, early in 1985 Payne and I were delighted to discover that I was pregnant with our first child. He couldn't wait to tell his dad that he, too, was going to be a father.

In February, back in Springfield, Payne was sitting up with his father before dawn. Bill

Stewart could hardly move by then, and the family's best efforts at keeping him comfortable were futile. Bill sat groggily in his recliner as Payne leaned down to his father's ear and softly said, "Dad, I've got a secret. Tracey is pregnant. I'm going to be a daddy."

The revelation roused Payne's father. His eyes welled with tears, and he tried to sit up straighter as he looked at Payne. In a voice not much louder than a whisper, the ever-practical father instructed his son, "Don't buy expensive baby furniture. It just wears out and you won't have it that long." Those were some of the last words that Payne heard his father speak. Two weeks later, Bill Stewart died, a mere nine months after being diagnosed with cancer.

Payne was devastated, but in an astonishing change of demeanor, he did not shed a tear at his father's funeral. It was extremely odd for Payne to react that way. He had never before been unwilling to express his emotions. He had cried when he won golf tournaments; he had cried after losing a few too. He had cried when I told him we were going to have a baby. Yet now the tears would not come.

Throughout the viewings and funeral proceedings, I frequently wrapped my arms around Payne and asked, "Are you OK?"

"I'm fine," he replied without emotion.

I held him tightly and tried to comfort him; there was nothing else I could do. His mother and sisters noticed his strange behavior and were equally puzzled and upset by it, but Payne was inconsolable. Years later, he told writer John Feinstein, "I wasn't sure if I was trying to be strong for everyone, or if I was in denial."

Most likely, it was both. Whatever the cause, Payne could not release his emotions. His father's death seemed so unfair to him. He didn't rant on about it or rail at God, but he frequently mentioned the injustice of this life, that often the good die far too young.

8

A Fresh
Start

Following the death of his father, Payne returned to his golf with even more passion. He had lost his mentor, friend, and coach, so Payne looked more to me for an honest reflection of how he was playing. It was easy to give him positive feedback; he was playing so well! We had only one problem—we weren't winning.

One tournament that was especially dear to Payne's heart was the Byron Nelson Golf Classic, played near Dallas. Payne had always admired Byron Nelson as a great golfer and as a person of integrity. As the years went by, Payne and I developed a close friendship with Byron and his wonderful wife, Peggy. Byron became a role model for Payne. Payne respected Byron for his talent and skill as a championship golfer, but even more because Byron is such a wise, caring, Christian gentleman. Payne loved Byron like a father and wanted so badly to win the tournament that was named after his friend.

A second reason why the Byron Nelson Golf Classic meant so much to Payne was that it was held in Las Colinas, Texas. Payne went to college at Southern Methodist University, in Dallas, so he always wanted to play well in front of his college friends.

It looked as though the 1985 Byron Nelson Classic was going to be Payne's breakthrough tournament. As he approached the eighteenth tee in the final round, Payne held a three-stroke lead over Bob Eastwood. At the same time, Bob was standing on the eighteenth green, lining up a 50-foot putt, almost a guaranteed two-putt or more. Just as Payne teed off, he heard a huge roar from the gallery around the green. Incredibly, Bob had holed his long putt for birdie! Suddenly, Payne's lead had dropped to two strokes, and he still had the final hole to play.

Payne's tee shot found the fairway bunker, which was bad enough. A really safe second shot would have been to lay up—to attempt to hit a good, solid, clean shot out of the bunker that would land somewhere short of the green in a good position. I knew Payne wouldn't settle for something that easy. A tougher shot, but still makable for Payne and still relatively safe, would be to aim for the largest part of the green. Just get the ball on the dance floor and then putt in for the victory. But Payne's inexperience surfaced. He was not about to play it safe. He knew that he had incredible shot-making ability and that he could put the ball right on the green, and maybe even right at the pin— from the bunker. He had made such sensational shots before.

Payne fired for the pin from the bunker. The crowd let out a collective "ooohhhhh!" as the ball lofted upward in the direction of the green, but it came up short. Instead of landing safely on the green, or even safely on the fairway, Payne's ball landed in a greenside bunker. He had gone from one bad spot to another.

Payne later acknowledged that he should have aimed for the fat part of the green, taken his par or even bogey, and walked away with the trophy. (It's always easy to second-guess a shot after the fact!) But at that moment, standing in the bunker, Payne felt that he could pull off any shot he wanted.

He climbed down in the bunker and

attempted to get some solid footing in the sand. As soon as Payne made his swing out of the greenside bunker, I knew we were in trouble. He hit the shot thin—which means he didn't get under the ball well enough to explode the sand beneath it, which would pop the ball up and out of the bunker and onto the green, and ideally toward the hole. Instead, he caught too much of the ball, sending it soaring over the hole, all the way across the green . . . and into another bunker on the other side of the green.

Payne was furious with himself. He hit his next shot onto the green and then two-putted for a double bogey. On one hole, he had gone from a three-stroke lead to a tie. Now it was play-off time.

When Bob Eastwood bogeyed the sudden-death hole, Payne still had a chance to win the tournament. But he was so distraught about his play on the previous hole that he double-bogeyed the play-off hole and gave the championship to Bob.

I had been following Payne on the course that day and had witnessed the entire debacle. As soon as the play-off was over, I made my way toward Payne. He was so devastated, he just took off walking by himself in the direction of the clubhouse. I caught up with him and tried to console him, but there wasn't much I could say that was going to help at that moment. We walked hand in hand in silence through the high grass and across a field. Words weren't necessary. Payne later told me that just my being there with him during the time it took us to walk back to the clubhouse gave him the courage to face his friends and the media.

The following month, at the U.S. Open at Oakland Hills Country Club in Birmingham, Michigan, Payne was in contention again. I knew that he had dreamed of winning a major and that he wanted to win the U.S. Open to satisfy himself and, in some way, as a special tribute to his father. Payne never forgot how important that tournament had been to his dad. Unfortunately, at Oakland Hills, Payne finished two shots behind the winner, Andy North. Another close one.

Rooting hard for Payne in the gallery that day was a young college golfer from Florida Southern who had played in the Open but had missed the cut. He was staying in the home of his roommate's family who lived right down the street from the golf course, so even though he was out of the competition himself, he'd stayed around to watch his heroes. The young man's biggest hero was Payne Stewart. During his senior year, his college team had even adopted Payne's tradition of wearing knickers during their tournaments. The idealistic young fellow hoped to meet Payne Stewart some-day—maybe even play with him. To dream of beating him twice in a U.S. Open would have been unimaginable. But in golf, as in faith, any-thing is possible. The young man's name was Lee Janzen.

In July, at the 1985 British Open, played at Royal St. Georges in Sandwich, England, Payne was in contention yet again. With the wind whipping around him and the internal pressure weighing heavy on him, Payne missed two short putts during the last round. Both putts were extremely makable, a 3-footer for par at one hole and an 18-inch birdie putt on another! Those missed putts came back to haunt him when Payne lost by one stroke to Scottish golfer Sandy Lyle, who got it up and down on the last hole for a bogey to win.

Despite the disappointing finishes, Payne and I were still excited about being out on the PGA Tour and living out our dreams together. As far as we could see, life could only get bet-ter. We had each other, we had material success, and we were expecting our first child.

Payne finished the 1985 PGA Tour sched-ule, and we prepared for the final stages of my pregnancy. Payne was excited about our having children; in fact, he was even more ready to start a family than I was. He'd have been delighted with four or five children, he loved them so much.

We didn't take any classes or have any other formal training to prepare us for natural childbirth, but Payne insisted on being in the birthing room along with me at Orlando Regional Medical Center on November 13, 1985. He didn't want to miss anything about the birth of our baby, and he was loving every minute of the process.

"What can I do? What can I do?" he cried while he held my hand.

Payne kept asking the doctor questions at every contraction. "What's happening now?" he wanted to know. "Oooooh, what's that? Oooooh, Tracey, have a look at this!"

"Ah-rrrhgh! Yuk! No thank you," I replied, doing my best to maintain some semblance of composure. Despite the contractions and the pain, giving birth was a glorious experience for me and an ecstatic experience for Payne. He cried when the doctors handed our baby—a girl—to him. We had not known the sex of our baby in advance, so we were delightfully surprised to have a daughter. We named her Chelsea, and Payne loved and cherished her from the moment he set eyes on her. We asked Robert and Dixie Fraley to be Chelsea's godparents, and they readily accepted, as they did again when our son, Aaron, was born in 1989.

Once we were home from the hospital, Payne relished his new role as father. He passed up playing in golf's "Silly Season," the special tournaments staged between the end of the official PGA Tour season in October and the beginning of the next year's Tour events in January. One week after Chelsea was born, we moved into our new home, just off the twelfth tee at the Bay Hill Club and Lodge. Payne loved to entertain, so he wanted a larger house; and with the baby we definitely needed more room than we'd had in our initial home in Bay Hill Village.

Payne helped with everything—changing diapers, rocking Chelsea in his arms, feeding her, and loving on her constantly. For some couples, the enormous responsibilities and the sheer amount of work involved in caring for a newborn sometimes create a strain in their relationship, but Chelsea's birth drew Payne and me even closer together. We recognized that in the same year that the Lord called Payne's father home, he had also blessed us with a precious new life.

Five weeks after Chelsea's birth, we

boarded a plane for Australia. We were determined to be together, regardless of the cost, sacrifice, or inconvenience. Traveling was certainly more of a feat with Chelsea. Besides Payne's golf clubs and clothes, we packed a stroller, diaper bag, and other child-care items, and lots of luggage. I took it as my job to get all those things organized and ready to go. Traveling in those days was a hassle, but it was worth it.

Fatherhood was good for Payne's golf game too. He went out in 1986 and had sixteen top-ten finishes, a PGA Tour record. Tiger Woods came close to reaching that mark in 1999 with fifteen top tens.

Payne always said, "Set your goals and aim for success, and the money will come with it. Aim to win, and the money will be a by-product." Sure enough, he was right. In 1986, Payne earned $535,389 and ranked third on the PGA Tour money list. In addition to the money he made on the golf course, Payne signed a deal with Head Sports Wear to provide him with his knickers and golf shirts in return for wearing their logo during tournaments.

By now, Payne had also begun wearing custom-made golf shoes with shiny "gold" tips around the front of the toes. The shoes, averaging about $400 per pair, were made by a Tampa shoe company called Fore Limited. We never struck an endorsement deal with the shoe company (although they provided their products to Payne without charge), but Payne wore them because he loved the look and the comfort of the shoe, and he felt that the gold tip and stylish trim completed his outfits perfectly.

Interestingly, about this same time, Payne began asking some tough questions about money. "How much is enough?" Payne asked me. "How much money will it take to make us happy?"

I didn't have an answer for him at the time, but over the years we learned that our time together was worth far more than money. Near the end of his career, Payne regularly turned down appearance fees of $50,000 to $100,000 per day, simply because he valued his time at home with our family.

Payne played incredibly well throughout the year in 1986, with several opportunities to bring home a championship. He had a one-shot lead with six holes to play on the final day of the U.S. Open at Shinnecock Hills, in Southhampton, New York. He was paired that afternoon with PGA Tour veteran Raymond Floyd, a burly fellow with a reputation for being one of the most intimidating men in golf, even when he wasn't in contention. When he was anywhere within striking distance on the last day of a tournament, Raymond turned into a glassy-eyed automaton. An extremely personable man off the course, Raymond focused intensely coming down the stretch of the 1986 Open.

Throughout the first twelve holes of that final round, Payne avoided Raymond's glare and stayed safely out of reach. Then on 13, Payne hit a beautiful, short chip for birdie that looked as though it was in, but the ball defied gravity, spun around the cup, and whipped back out. Worse still, it seemed as though the ball actually picked up speed by lipping out, and it rolled another six feet away from the hole.

Raymond birdied the hole. His heart pounding like a jackhammer, Payne missed the par putt, giving Floyd a one-stroke lead. Clearly rattled, Payne was mesmerized by Raymond's "get out of my way kid" look and played the remainder of the tournament in a daze. He dropped five spots on the leaderboard, finishing sixth in a tournament that he had been leading.

Payne later admitted, "I just sort of stepped back and watched Raymond. I got caught up watching Raymond and forgot what I was supposed to be doing." Floyd's notorious "look" hadn't escaped Payne's notice. "When I saw Raymond's eyes go big and wide and glaring, I thought, Man, look at him! From then on, instead of concentrating on my own shots, I was watching Raymond. I started trying to guide the ball instead of trusting my swing. Next thing I knew, the tournament was over and Raymond had won."

Payne took the loss at the 1986 Open hard. He kept reliving the missed chip at 13, wondering what might have been had he holed that shot or even had left it close. He was angry with himself for allowing Raymond Floyd's demeanor to intimidate him. Payne knew better than to worry about what his opponent was doing. Golf is very much an individual game. "Play your game; don't worry about anyone else," his father had taught him. Nobody can do it for you, but nobody can take it away from you, either—unless you allow them to do so, as he had allowed Raymond. Granted, Raymond played exceptionally well, but Payne felt that he had beaten himself. "I let it get away from me," he admitted.

Certain members of the media ripped into Payne after his collapse at the 1986 U.S. Open. Especially nettlesome to Payne, a few snide sportswriters took to calling him "Avis" because of his accumulation of second-place checks. The name stuck and even some of the caddies began using it. For the most part, Payne took the teasing good-naturedly, but that did not erase the frustration he felt at not winning.

Disappointed with himself, Payne moped his way through the Canadian Open two weeks later. He got off to a bad start by nearly hitting his first drive out of bounds. He three-putted the first green, and things went downhill from there. A few holes later he knocked a wedge shot completely over the green. He just wasn't concentrating. His body was on the course, but his mind and spirit were somewhere else. By the time he finished the first nine holes, it hurt for me to watch him.

I approached him at the turn, between the ninth green and the tenth tee, and said, "Look, if you don't want to be out here, let's quit and go home." My words shocked Payne back to reality, enough to play out the first two rounds, but he missed the cut on Friday night by several strokes. We headed home, with Payne pouting and feeling sorry for himself. As much as I loved him and empathized with him, I knew I could not allow him to wallow in his own self-imposed pit of despair.

"Why don't you quit if you're not happy," I cajoled him.

"Well, I thought that maybe I'd just take the rest of the year off," Payne sulked. "Maybe I could get another job."

"Oh, yeah? OK, what are you going to do?"

Payne thought about that for a minute. Yes, he had a business degree from SMU, but when it came right down to it, he was already doing what he was born to do. He was a golfer. We both burst out laughing about the same time, because the reality hit us: Golf was Payne's job. It was what he was good at. He didn't really want to do anything else.

Nevertheless, our conversation was a wake-up call for him. I encouraged Payne to talk with Harvie Ward, one of our Bay Hill neighbors. He was close to Payne's father's age and had achieved great success in amateur tournaments about the same time as Bill Stewart. Harvie was now the senior golf pro at Interlachen Country Club in Orlando. Resolutely, Payne visited Harvie at the golf course and hit some balls with him on the practice range. Harvie wasn't a Tour player's type of teacher, but he was a great encourager.

"The first thing I noticed about Harvie," said Payne, "was just how much he reminded me of my father. Like my dad, Harvie didn't try to change my swing. Instead, he helped me work on my attitude. He reminded me that I was a good player and that I was going to win a lot more golf tournaments, but I couldn't afford to beat myself."

For the next several years, Harvie served as Payne's informal golf coach, a role that Payne had previously permitted no other person besides his father to fill. But Payne recognized that Harvie was helping him, so whenever we came home to Orlando, he made it a point to hit balls with Harvie. Payne finished the 1986 season with several stellar performances, setting another record for the most money ever won without winning a tournament. He kept fine-tuning his game, and by 1987, he was ready to win again.

9

What It's All About

One of the fringe benefits of Payne's resplendent, color-coordinated golf outfits was that they distinguished him on the golf course. Spectators could easily recognize him from two fairways away, yet the clothes also allowed us the luxury of anonymity once we left the clubhouse and returned home. Out of his knickers and tam-o'-shanter caps, most people, including many avid golf fans, didn't recognize Payne, even when they were in the same room with him.

Charlie Bolling, a PGA Tour player from 1985 to 1988, tells a story about the time in late November 1986 when he, Payne, Larry Rinker, and Brad Faxon played a practice round at the

Grand Cypress course in Lake Buena Vista, not far from where we lived. Payne wore a nondescript outfit of casual slacks, a plain shirt, and a baseball cap. After playing twenty-seven holes, the guys stopped at the clubhouse for some refreshments before heading home. One of the Silly Season events was on television, so the fellows sat down to watch for a few minutes while they sipped their drinks.

Between Payne and the television sat a "bigmouth," according to Charlie, who recalls, "The Mouth knew every detail about every Tour player the cameras covered that day." Slightly irritated by the vociferous opinions of the local "expert," Payne decided to have some fun with the guy. He peppered him with all sorts of questions about the various PGA Tour players on the screen, acting as though he was clueless about any of them. After Payne queried him about half a dozen players and received misinformation about most of them, he couldn't resist.

"What about that Payne Stewart guy?" he asked, baiting him.

"Oh, that guy!" The expert rolled his eyes as he spoke. He then ran his mouth off wildly about Payne's cockiness, his clothes, his fancy shoes, his panache, and a litany of other disparaging comments. Payne listened attentively, nodding his head from time to time. Meanwhile, Charlie, Larry, and Brad were nearly ready to explode as they tried to hold in their laughter.

Finally, Payne stood up, walked over to the bigmouth's table, and said, "Hi, I'm Payne Stewart."

The guy was mortified. He looked as though he wanted to slither out of the bar in embarrassment. But Payne wasn't about to let that happen. Charlie recounts, "In true Payne Stewart form, he asked the guy to join us! And we all continued yucking it up about Payne's gold-tipped shoes."

Although Payne was often unrecognizable off the course, his fashion flair, trim physique, and boyish good looks increasingly caught the attention of advertisers who wanted him to sign endorsement deals to represent their companies. In 1986, Payne and I decided that we wanted to part company with the sports agency that had been representing us. Payne went to Robert Fraley for advice and asked if Robert would consider representing him. Payne respected Robert immensely, as did I. Robert agreed to take on the responsibility of managing Payne's career and helped us resolve our relationship with our former management company. Actually, Robert agreed more as a favor to Payne than out of a desire to procure us as clients.

Up to now, our relationship with Robert and Dixie had been one of friendship only. Robert's company didn't represent professional golfers at that time. Robert didn't even play golf, let alone pursue the sport's stars. Most of his clients were football and baseball stars, as well as NFL head coaches Joe Gibbs, Bill Parcells, and Dan Reeves.

Payne was the first golfer that Leader Enterprises represented and the only one for quite a while. Eventually, Paul Azinger and Lee Janzen also signed with Leader, although Lee later moved on to another agency. Robert's agency handled large contracts involving huge sums of money, yet Robert and Payne's relationship remained based simply on mutual respect and trust. Their word was all that was necessary with one another; their handshake was stronger than any contract. Robert always said, "If ever you aren't happy with this relationship, just let us know and there will be no hard feelings. Your friendship is more important to us than your business."

One of the professional athletes we met through Robert Fraley was Orel Hershiser and his wife, Jamie. We stopped by Robert and Dixie's one evening when they were hosting the

Hershisers for dinner. At the time, Orel was one of the hottest pitchers in the majors, and he and Payne connected immediately. Besides being able to hurl a baseball more than ninety miles an hour, Orel was also an avid golfer. Over the years, Orel and Payne would play together in many celebrity golf tournaments, including the AT&T at Pebble Beach, and they always were in the thick of the competition.

Payne and I loved spending time with the Fraleys and the Hershisers. Like our friends the Azingers, the Fraleys and Hershisers talked freely about their faith in the Lord, and their lives backed up their words. They never preached at Payne or me, but their example helped rekindle our own faith.

In mid-March 1987, Payne led the Hertz Bay Hill Classic almost from the start. Bay Hill Golf Club and Lodge is best known for its founder, Arnold Palmer. The Bay Hill Classic is a popular tournament with many of the PGA Tour players who live in Orlando, because everyone wants to win in his hometown.

Each day as he played his round, when he came to the twelfth tee, Payne took a slight detour off the course. He hurried over to our back porch, where our sixteen-month-old daughter, Chelsea, and I were watching and waiting for him. Chelsea pressed her face right up to the wrought iron fence as Payne pressed his face up to the bars and stretched to kiss her. On the final days of the tournament, with Payne in the lead, the television cameras followed his every move, including his hasty detour to kiss our daughter. The picture of Payne and Chelsea kissing through the fence has become an indelible part of golf history.

Payne was about to make some history of his own on the course. For four days, he had played flawless golf. He gave notice that he had come to play on Thursday when he shot a 69. He followed up with a 67 on Friday and a 63 on Saturday. The gallery could sense that the tournament belonged to Payne.

South African David Frost was also having an incredible tournament, shooting 10-under par the last two days. But his charge wasn't enough to catch Payne, who finished with a remarkable 65, besting David by three strokes. It was our first win since 1983, earning us a $108,000 paycheck.

The sports headline in the Monday edition of the Orlando newspaper read: AVIS WINS HERTZ. Payne didn't let the subtle jab spoil his victory. He was extremely excited about winning in our hometown, on our home course. A

154

few months later, Payne even consented to pose with a live chimpanzee dressed in knickers and draped around his neck for a *Golf Digest* cover story by Dwayne Netland titled "How Payne Stewart Got the Monkey off His Back." Payne knew that the press wasn't going to let his win go by without some comment, but he didn't let it dull our celebration a bit.

Nevertheless, I was still surprised when, two days after the tournament, Payne said, "Love, I think we should donate our winnings to some organization that helps people deal with cancer. I've always wanted to make a contribution to help the families of cancer patients in honor of my father. Just think how good it would be if we could help other families who are going through what we went through."

"Well, that would be nice," I replied, thinking Payne simply wanted to make a sizable donation. "How much would you like to give?"

"All of it," Payne replied.

I wasn't sure that I'd heard him correctly. "How much?"

"All of it. I'd like to donate the entire $108,000."

I was quiet for a few moments before saying, "Payne, do you really think it's necessary that we donate all the money?"

"Yeah, this is something I've always dreamed of doing," Payne replied. I could tell he was serious and not just kidding me.

"Well, if that's what you want to do . . ."

I wondered if it was wise to donate the entire amount of his winnings; how would we go about such a gesture? How would it be perceived by others in the golf community?

"Yeah, I want to do it," said Payne. "Winning and giving. That's what it's all about. I want to give it all."

Payne talked with Robert Fraley, and together they set about the task of finding just the right local organization that could handle such a proposal. We settled on the Florida Hospital Golden Circle of Friends Home in Altamonte Springs, a home where families of cancer patients in the Orlando hospitals can stay while their family members receive treatment. Payne donated the entire Hertz Bay Hill Classic winnings in memory of his father and in honor of his mother.

Beyond that, Payne's generosity gave a big boost to the ongoing Celebrity Pro-Am Golf Tournament benefiting the Florida Hospital Foundation, which over the years has drawn a hearty response from the local golf community, as well as from Bob Hope, Shirley Jones, Tommy Lasorda, Frank Viola, Julius Erving, and dozens of other celebrities.

Payne made more headlines a few weeks later at the Masters, not necessarily for his play—he never enjoyed the Augusta course, and he rarely played well there—but for his eye-catching outfits. Payne appreciated many of the traditionalists associated with the tournament, but he also enjoyed tweaking the more ostentatious of the group. In 1987, he really shook them up when he wore pink knickers, a white dress shirt with a pink bow tie, and pink kneesocks with polka dots. "It looked pretty sharp!" Payne said proudly when someone asked him about his garb. Too bad his game wasn't quite as sharp as his dress; he turned in another middle-of-the-pack performance.

After the Masters, we returned to Springfield for a visit. One day, Payne and Chelsea drove by the cemetery where Bill Stewart was buried. Payne pulled in, and he and Chelsea sat down in the grass by the gravesite. "Well, Dad, we won Bay Hill," Payne said aloud, while Chelsea eyed him in wonder. "We got 'em now," Payne said in the direction of his father's grave memorial.

As he and Chelsea sat there, Payne began telling our daughter about the grandfather she had never met and would never get to know. "I tried to explain to her just how special he was," Payne later said, "and how I missed him, and that I was sorry she was never going to know him. And then I had this big cry right there."

Payne hadn't shed a tear at his father's funeral, but now he couldn't contain his emotions any longer. As eighteen-month-old Chelsea watched the tears flowing freely down her father's face, she looked at him as though to say, "Daddy, what's wrong? Why are you crying?"

Payne's nickname for Chelsea was "Goose," as in, "You silly goose." In an attempt to answer our daughter's unspoken questions, Payne pulled Chelsea close to him and said, "Daddy's crying, Goose, because I loved my father." Payne knew that although Chelsea didn't comprehend all that he meant at the time, she would one day.

10

A Turning
Point

Payne enjoyed being different, doing things
that nobody else in golf had done before,
and he relished the attention that accompanied
his departures from the norm. When the opportunity came for him to strike a unique promo-
tional deal with the National Football League
and its subsidiary, NFL Properties, Payne
grabbed it enthusiastically, especially when
NFL Properties offered to pay a huge annual
endorsement fee to have Payne wear their
clothing and endorse their product lines.
Besides creating a new line of golf clothes for
pro shops, Payne's deal with the NFL was a
landmark agreement in that it was the first time
an active major player in one sport had become

an official spokesperson promoting another sport.

The deal was quite a coup because it involved the collaboration of a half-dozen separate companies. Robert Fraley of Leader Enterprises and Frank Vuono of NFL Properties put together a lucrative, three-year contract under which the clothing manufacturer Antigua made Payne's knickers and shirts; Cloverdale made his caps; his rainwear came from Forrester's; and his kneesocks were made by Pine Hosiery Mills. Wilson Sporting Goods, whose Whale driver Payne was playing at the time, created special NFL-logo golf balls, bags, and gloves. The outfits were designed using the colors and logos of each NFL team, and while out on the Tour, Payne wore the colors of the team closest to the location of the tournament. For instance, when he played at Doral in Miami, he wore the colors and insignia of the Miami Dolphins. When playing at Oakmont, near Pittsburgh, he wore the Steelers' black and gold.

Of course, when Payne felt like being mischievous—which was most of the time—he enjoyed stirring up a bit of controversy with his clothing selections. When he played the Colonial National Invitational in Fort Worth, in front of a gallery laden with Dallas Cowboys fans, Payne wore the colors of the Washington Redskins, the Cowboys' arch rivals. "I went to school in Dallas, but I was never a Cowboys fan," he quipped. To assuage the fans, however, he relented and wore the Cowboys' colors on Sunday during the final round.

Whether it was the excitement of the new clothing deal or the motivation of winning at Bay Hill, Payne went out and had a great year in 1988, finishing in the money at twenty-five of the twenty-six tournaments he entered. Similar to 1986, however, although we were making money at every tournament, Payne was not winning. After a few stops on the Tour, I sensed that Payne was growing too comfortable with pocketing a fat check week after week. Although many people might be content with that, I knew that Payne would never be happy just making a good living by playing in the middle of the pack. He wanted to win.

In 1986, I had shocked him out of his complacency by confronting him directly as we were leaving a tournament in Ponte Vedra, Florida. As Payne eased onto the interstate and pointed the car toward Orlando, he was obviously feeling pretty good about his latest top-ten finish.

"Well, another top-ten check, Trace," Payne said. "Another good week."

I didn't see it that way at all. "Do you know

what you are?" I asked. Before Payne had a chance to say a word, I blurted, "You're complacent!"

Payne nearly ran off the road in his surprise. "Wha—? What do you mean?"

"Well, you didn't win, did you? You're just in your comfort zone. You're happy to get a good check and finish in the top ten. That isn't what your father taught you. He'd say, 'You need to be out there winning!' He wouldn't accept just another top-ten finish. All you care about is making money. Why don't you try to win?"

Payne sulked all the way back to Orlando, but when he went back to work on his game, he played with renewed passion. He later admitted, "Tracey's words hit me like a ton of bricks. I knew she was right. It sounded like my father talking to me."

I took that as quite a compliment.

In 1988, Payne was lapsing into a similar complacency, and I jarred him again with a reminder of what he already knew: Playing professional golf wasn't about making money, and it really wasn't even about winning. It was about doing his best. His job was to be the best player that Payne Stewart could possibly be. At that time in our lives, winning the tournament was the main criterion by which we gauged our progress. Winning represented the goal, and by settling for top-ten finishes, we had been setting our sights far too low.

Payne began to work harder, but in the heat of the tournaments, he continued to tense up, putting more pressure on himself. He tried desperately to make things happen on the course, forcing shots instead of allowing his natural abilities to work for him. Inevitably, he found himself worrying more about making a mistake that might cost him a tournament rather than concentrating on winning.

Harvie Ward, Payne's swing coach, and I encouraged Payne to take some radical action. Harvie introduced Payne to Dr. Richard Coop, a professor of educational psychology at the University of North Carolina and a member of the rapidly growing ranks of "sports psychologists." At first Payne resisted, but finally he agreed to meet with Dr. Coop on the condition that if he didn't experience noticeable results quickly, he would nix the plan.

At their first meeting, "Coop," as Payne took to calling the psychologist almost immediately, spoke quite bluntly with Payne. "I told him that I had heard he was prickly, cocky, arrogant, and brash," Coop recalls.

Following their first session together, Payne called me from Coop's office.

"How'd it go?" I asked.

Payne told me what Coop had told him.

"What do you think?" I asked.

"Eh, he's probably right," Payne responded.

I breathed a sigh of relief. This could be a real turning point, I thought.

"I never wanted to admit that I needed help," Payne said later. "That was part of my immaturity, not wanting to recognize a problem. I guess that's what happens in a lot of people's lives. They are too proud or too immature to admit that something is wrong."

Coop first worked with Payne at the 1988 Provident Classic in Chattanooga, Tennessee. They spent a large amount of time together, just talking and picturing the shots it might take to win. Payne played incredibly well throughout that tournament. He was at the top of the leaderboard on Sunday, when Phil Blackmar holed a chip shot on the final hole, sending the tournament into a play-off. On the first hole of the play-off, Phil pulled off a spectacular 30-foot birdie putt to win. Payne was disappointed, but he handled the loss well. More importantly, perhaps, he felt that Coop had helped him focus better and that he should continue consulting with the doctor. That began not only a successful professional relationship but a deep friendship between Payne and Dick Coop.

He met with Dick at least once a month on

a professional basis and talked to him several times each week. Coop recognized that Payne had trouble focusing on anything for very long. At that time, research on attention deficit disorder was just beginning to be publicly accepted, but Coop was certain that Payne's difficulties in concentrating stemmed from ADD. Like many people who deal with ADD, Payne could zero in on the tough shots, but the more mundane, "easy" shots were often his undoing.

Dick encouraged Payne to establish a consistent pre-shot routine, going through the same set of motions on each shot, something that Payne had never done. "He was always fiddling with his alignment, his stance, the ball position, or something, even on the tee," recalls Chuck Cook, a professional golf instructor from Austin, Texas, who was working with the PGA Tour's then all-time leading money winner, Tom Kite, as well as Ben Crenshaw, another consistent PGA Tour contender. Coop introduced Payne to Chuck Cook, and the three of them went to work developing a structured routine with which Payne could feel comfortable and, more importantly, repeat under pressure.

A "feel" player, Payne naturally resisted being locked into a routine. He liked to be more spontaneous and became easily bored with structure of any kind. Beyond that, as Chuck

Cook quickly realized, Payne had an entire repertoire of incredible shots. But his natural ability sometimes worked against him. In a jam it was all too easy for Payne to reach into his bag and attempt to pull out a shot that he knew he had the ability to make, rather than taking the safer, and often wiser, shot that would lead to a lower score.

Dr. Coop gave Payne the phrase, "Get lost in the shot-making." By that, he meant to keep Payne in his shot routine so that he could focus more intensely on each shot. Payne worked diligently with his new mentors, and his confidence grew along with his work habits.

That's not to say that 1988 was all work and no play—quite the contrary. While on the PGA Tour, Payne and fellow players Peter Jacobsen and Mark Lye loved to pursue their rock 'n' roll musical inclinations. They talked about getting together some evening to jam, and eventually they put together a pickup band, with Mark on guitar, Peter as lead singer, and Payne playing his harmonica and singing background vocals. They called themselves Jake Trout & the Flounders and gave themselves pseudonyms and alter identities: Peter was Jake Trout; Mark was Lofton Lie, and Payne was Nick Knickers. They thought up clever golf-related lyrics and parodied easily recognized pop songs.

For instance, to the tune of "Sittin' on the Dock of the Bay," the 60s classic written by Steve Cropper and recorded by Otis Redding, Peter came up with: "Hittin' on the Back of the Range," which opened with the immortal lines

I'm just hittin' on the back of the range,
Trying to be just like Curtis Strange . . .

When Bobby McFerrin topped the music charts with his mega-hit, "Don't Worry, Be Happy," the Flounders came up with

I just saw that shot you hit.
You're playing so bad you want to quit.
Don't worry, keep swinging . . .

Jake Trout & the Flounders were not going to threaten anyone at the top of the pop music charts, but they sure had a lot of fun. And golf fans loved to hear them. At Tour events around the country, shortly after the final shots of the day had been made, the loud, raucous sounds of Jake Trout & the Flounders could often be heard at one of the corporate tents along the golf course. The guys had a blast, and fans of the game enjoyed seeing Peter, Mark, and Payne in a different light. After a hot day in the sun, and probably with a few drinks under their belts, some people actually thought that Jake Trout & the Flounders should record an album.

With the help of Larry Rinker, another PGA Tour player who was part of the original musical musings of the Flounders, the guys went to Tallahassee in 1989 and recorded their first album.

A modern recording studio can be a daunting place for the uninitiated. All the high-tech equipment, microphones, soundproof cubicles—and the recording process itself—can be nerve-racking. Peter Jacobsen remembers that although Payne came to be known as an extremely competitive player who had ice-cold blood flowing in his veins as he came down the closing stretch in a golf tournament, he was extremely nervous when it came to playing his harmonica for the first time in the studio. "I picked up Payne at the airport in a rental car," Peter recalls, "and we got to the recording studio around noon. But when Payne started playing along to the track, he couldn't get his parts right. He was just too nervous. So I sent two of the production assistants to a local convenience store. When they returned, Payne and I sat in the back of the rental car and downed six cans between us. Payne put on his dark sunglasses, went back into the studio, and played as smoothly as I'd ever heard him. I mean, he made that harmonica wail!" The self-produced album that resulted from those semi-inebriated sessions sold more than twenty-five thousand copies.

◆ ◆ ◆

On April 2, 1989, I gave birth to our second child, our son, Aaron. We induced my labor so Payne could be with me before going off to play in the Masters at Augusta National. Payne was in the birthing room, just as excited as he was at the birth of Chelsea, and when the doctors handed Aaron to him, once again Payne cried for joy. Later that week, he came in twenty-fourth at the Masters. The following week, at the MCI Heritage Classic at Harbour Town Golf Links, a tournament that Payne always thoroughly enjoyed, he won by five strokes! Obviously, parenthood was good for Payne's golf game.

Now that Payne was thirty-two years old, "the best player never to have won a major" tag began showing up often next to his name in the media. Payne set his sights more on playing well in the major tournaments. In June he led during the first round of the U.S. Open before faltering and finishing thirteenth. He had a similar chance in the last round at the British Open in July but ended in eighth place. At the Buick Open in July, Payne airmailed the green with a poor wedge shot late in the tournament, bogeyed the final hole, and ended tied for second. By August he was anxious to win again.

11

A Major
Victory

P ayne has always been cocky," Bee Stewart
once told a reporter, "but he used to be
worse." Maybe so, but his cockiness, combined
with the encouragement and correction of Dr.
Coop and golf instructor Chuck Cook, helped
prepare him for the 1989 PGA Championship
in August. Convinced he could win, Payne
worked hard at his game throughout the summer. Almost as if to emphasize his newfound
mental discipline, Payne had his hair sheared
off, leaving him with a military-style haircut as
he teed it up at Kemper Lakes Golf Club just
outside Chicago.

The PGA Championship was the fourth
and final major of the year. Payne was well

aware of the added pressure that went with attempting to win a major. "You'll never be considered a great player until you win a major," he often said. "It's the standard that a professional golfer's career is judged by."

Most of the first day's attention at the PGA Championship focused on Arnold Palmer, who shot an opening round 68, a mere nine strokes over his age. Leonard Thompson, who two weeks earlier had handed Payne a loss at the Buick Open, took the early lead. Matching him shot for shot was Mike Reid, the bespectacled, slight-of-build, straight-down-the-fairway hitter whom the guys on Tour had nicknamed "Radar," both for his accuracy and his resemblance to the character Radar O'Reilly on the television series *M*A*S*H*. Reid's radar was working particularly well on Thursday as he shot a 66, tying Leonard Thompson. Several of golf's superstars, including Tom Kite and Tom Watson, were one stroke behind the leaders. Payne's name was nowhere to be found on the leaderboard at the end of the first round. Playing with Greg Norman, Payne opened the tournament with a disappointing 74, eight strokes off the pace.

He came back strong on Friday, however, shooting a 66, and he followed that round with a 69 on Saturday. Both days saw ominous thun-

171

derstorms crawl across the Chicago skyline. Several times, play had to be postponed until the storms passed by. No one wanted to take any chances. Four local golfers had been hit by lightning in the Chicago area on Wednesday, and three more locals had been struck while playing golf on Friday, including one who died as a result.

Besides causing everyone to keep an eye on the sky, the wet weather also softened the greens, allowing the players to aim for the pin with less fear of their shots rolling off the green. The results were staggering. Cumulatively, the players racked up 153 rounds under par during the tournament, setting a new PGA Championship record. Craig Stadler shot a 64 on Friday, setting a new course record at Kemper. Clearly, the competition was intense as the players started the final round, but Mike Reid was still three strokes ahead of his nearest challengers. When a reporter asked Mike if he'd have butterflies in his stomach during the final round, he answered, "There's always butterflies. Sometimes they're in there playing hockey."

On Sunday, wearing his knickers and a golf shirt sporting the Chicago Bears colors, Payne quickly endeared himself to the fans in the gallery. With the Chicago fans cheering him on, Payne was striking the ball beautifully on the front nine. Unfortunately, he couldn't find the cup when it came time to putt. I followed him over the first half of the course as he shot a 36, even par, a good score in any major, but still five strokes behind Mike Reid. When Payne three-putted the ninth green, he was clearly frustrated but no less confident. At the turn, he looked over and saw ABC-TV's fairway broadcaster, Jerry Pate. "If I can shoot 31 on the back nine," Payne told Jerry, "I could have a chance to win this thing."

As Payne headed off toward the tenth tee, I returned to the clubhouse and picked up Chelsea from the nursery. We had left Aaron with our nanny at the home where we were staying during the tournament. I took Chelsea with me to watch the remainder of the tournament on television in the clubhouse. Call it superstition or something else, but I always felt that Payne's putting improved when I watched him on TV. Chelsea and I joined Raymond Floyd's wife, Maria, in front of the television. Raymond had been selected as captain of the 1989 U.S. Ryder Cup team, and Payne had already earned enough points to secure his berth among the ten world-class players already on the roster, with two captain's picks still in question. Points toward the Ryder Cup positions are earned by top-ten finishes—which

Payne had plenty of—with point bonuses awarded for major championship wins. Additionally, the PGA champion automatically qualified for the Ryder Cup team. Maria and I recognized that if either Payne or Curtis Strange, who was right behind Mike Reid, were to win today, it would give Raymond the opportunity to consider another player for his captain's picks, a personal choice that every Ryder Cup captain hoped to have. Consequently, Maria and I were both watching the PGA Championship closely to see how it might impact our husbands' lives—and our lives too.

The ABC broadcast team sounded convinced that Mike Reid was going to be tough to beat. Indeed, as he started the back nine, Mike continued to play impeccably. He kept hitting consistently straight, middle-of-the-fairway shots, highlighted by his approach on number 10, where he hit a 4-iron to within three feet of the pin. Meanwhile, playing with Leonard Thompson, several groups ahead of the leaders, Payne had been inching his way up the leaderboard all afternoon. He birdied number 11, then chipped in for another birdie from the rough behind the fourteenth green. On the par-5 fifteenth, he hit his third shot to within a foot of the cup, tapping in for yet another birdie. He followed that shot with a 20-foot putt for a birdie on 16 as well. When Payne stroked a 12-foot birdie putt on the eighteenth green, he instinctively crouched lower, clenched his right fist, and pulled downward as the ball dropped into the cup. Jack Nicklaus described Payne's putt to the ABC television audience as "the most important putt of his career." Payne went to the clubhouse having birdied four of the last five holes to complete a sensational back nine round of 31, just as he had told Jerry Pate he'd hoped to do.

Payne was ecstatic. He had come from behind to post an incredible round of 67 in the last round of the final major tournament of the year. Since the leaders had yet to finish, he was ushered to the scorer's tent, where he signed his card and then happily milled about, eating grapes and having fun with the people who were watching the leaders coming home on television. An ABC cameraman followed Payne's every move, and Payne gave them plenty to shoot.

Not knowing whether Payne would be going back to play another "sudden death" play-off, I didn't want to "jinx" anything by going down to the scorer's tent too early. Instead, I stayed right where I was in the club-house, unwilling to move until the tournament was over. Maybe I should have.

Rather than sitting down calmly and putting on the obligatory "worried face" that the golf world has come to expect when contenders are put on camera while awaiting the conclusion of the tournament, Payne was characteristically antsy. He was talking to everyone, mugging for the television camera, and giving NFL Properties their money's worth of publicity by pointing to the NFL logo on his clothes. Payne himself later described his actions as "immature," but his antic posturing wasn't meant to be disrespectful of Mike Reid or the other players still on the course. Payne was simply happy that he had done well, that he had finally finished a tournament the way he always knew that he could.

Meanwhile, out on the course, Mike Reid was making one mistake after another in a heartrending collapse that was difficult for me to watch on television. Playing in the final group, on the seventieth hole of the tournament, Mike Reid's radar screen suddenly went blank. One of the straightest, most consistent drivers on the Tour, Mike hit his tee shot from the sixteenth into one of the lakes for which the golf course was named. At 17, he came close to hitting the water again but caught the fringe on the left side of the green. Mike then hit a poor chip shot, landing the ball at least fifteen feet from the cup. His three-stroke lead had disappeared, but the tournament was still his to win. His 15-foot putt for par missed by an inch . . . and kept going. He watched dejectedly as his putt rolled nearly three feet past the hole.

In the scorer's tent, Payne saw the putt on television and was surprised. Suddenly, he was in position for a possible play-off. But Mike's collapse wasn't complete yet. After playing so well all week, his bogey putt, which he needed to make to remain tied with Payne, spun out of the cup and off to the right.

Payne was now in the lead! He was as astonished as anyone. "When I saw him miss the first one, I assumed that he'd make the second putt," said Payne. "Then when Mike missed that second putt, my heart was definitely beating hard!"

Mike now had to make birdie on 18 to force a play-off. His drive predictably found the middle of the fairway, and he followed up with a beautiful 5-iron to within seven feet of the pin. If he sank the putt, we were going to a play-off—and I knew that Payne would be at a disadvantage. He was 0-4 in play-offs at the time. If Mike missed the putt, Payne would be the 1989 PGA Champion.

Mike's putt rolled slightly to the left, missing the cup. Payne had won his first major!

On the way back out to the green for the trophy presentation, Payne was so happy, he tossed his hat into the crowd. When the PGA of America officials presented Payne with the huge, silver Wanamaker trophy, inscribed with the names of some of golf's greatest players, he kissed it and hoisted it high in the air. He could hardly believe it—right along with all the other legends would be the name Payne Stewart.

Payne was bubbling over with excitement. "Man, this is unbelievable!" he said. "I can't describe my feelings. I'll cherish this moment for a long time." So far, so good. But then, in an attempt to empathize with, and be consoling to, Mike Reid, Payne forgot everything Dick Coop had taught him about trying to slow down and be more structured. Payne blurted the first things that came to mind. "Believe me, I know how Mike Reid feels. I've messed up a couple of tournaments in my time."

Ouch. Even the most callous, caustic members of the press corp were uncomfortable with the winner of the tournament reminding the loser that he had messed up. It got worse. When Payne told the media about his comment to ABC's Jerry Pate at the turn, he sounded more arrogant than grateful. "I told him, 'If I can shoot 31 on the back nine, I might win.' Look what happened—I shot 31 and I did win.

For me, it's a little bit of justice." Payne was implying that after his many second-place finishes and his close runs at major championships, it was about time that a break had fallen his way. But no matter how he said it, or who Payne tried to credit and compliment, his enthusiasm kept pushing his size-12, gold-tipped golf shoes into his mouth. Even God came off sounding a little beholden to Payne. "I said a prayer in the tent," Payne told the media, expecting them to understand. "'How about some good stuff for Payne Stewart one time?' He obliged me by letting me win."

Somewhere, Dick Coop was cringing.

Making Payne's unabashed exuberance even more bothersome to many people was Mike Reid's utter humility in defeat. When he sat down to meet the media, one of Mike's first comments was, "Where can you go around here to have a good cry?" A quiet, classy competitor, better known for his attendance at Bible studies on Tour than for bombast, Mike fought back his tears as he tried to explain how he had allowed the tournament to slip out of control. Before long, his eyes teared over and his voice trailed off. "I cry at supermarket grand openings," he said, trying to cover his pain with a joke. After several emotion-packed pauses, Mike managed to say,

"I'm happy for Payne . . . because . . . he's been in that position a lot."

No one had to ask what Mike meant.

Not surprisingly, the press quickly cast a pall over Payne's victory by saying that he hadn't won the PGA Championship so much as Mike Reid had lost it. It irritated Payne that the media suggested that he had "backed into winning the championship," winning it in the scorer's tent while Mike Reid was self-destructing on the course. What the media chose to play down, of course, was that Payne had played better each day of the tournament and had closed with a true championship round on Sunday. Although Mike's falling apart was not considered unusual in view of the pressure that accompanies a major championship, and Payne's unbridled tongue at times made him sound more like a whiner than a winner, Payne had shot the lowest score after seventy-two holes of intensely contested golf. Whether anyone liked the way he had won it, Payne was the PGA champion. Dr. Coop and I did tell him that he needed to be more humble when he won in the future . . . and we were sure he'd be winning a lot.

12

Ups and Downs

Winning at golf often comes down to a player's ability to "get it up and down," a golf term for getting the ball in the cup from a location off the green or in a greenside bunker. We had plenty of ups and downs in 1989, and although Payne wasn't totally satisfied with his performance—no professional golfer ever is—it was our finest year on the PGA Tour to date. Payne finished in the top ten twelve times and brought home winnings of $1.2 million, second only to Tom Kite.

The year had started out on a downswing when Payne developed a back problem. Back pain was something Payne had endured since his college years, when he had strained his back lifting some heavy furniture. By 1989, the thousands of golf swings he had taken over the years had exacerbated the problem to the point that he was having trouble making a full hip turn without excruciating pain in his lower back. The only thing that helped was rest. Consequently, after a tie for thirtieth place at the 1989 Bob Hope Chrysler Classic, Payne missed the cut the following week at the Phoenix Open. When the pain grew worse, he withdrew from the AT&T at Pebble Beach after the first round. The following week, at the Nissan Los Angeles Open, Payne had to withdraw during the second round.

Disappointing as it was at the time, that withdrawal at Los Angeles proved even more significant at the end of the season, when the PGA of America ruled that any player who had withdrawn from a round he had started, without completing it, was ineligible to win the Vardon Trophy. One of golf's highest and most sought after honors, the Vardon Trophy is awarded to the player with the lowest scoring average of the year. In 1989, Payne had the lowest average of anyone on the PGA Tour, but because of the withdrawal due to his back, he missed getting the trophy.

On the "up" side of the 1989 ledger were Payne's victories at the MCI Heritage Classic and the PGA Championship. He also earned a spot on his second U.S. Ryder Cup team.

The Ryder Cup competition dates back to 1926, when Samuel Ryder, a wealthy British seed merchant who loved golf, offered to put up a solid gold trophy for the winner of a biannual series of matches between Great Britain and America. The Americans won the trophy in 1927 and most of the matches that followed. Over the next fifty years, the U.S. team lost only four times and tied once. The British and Irish golfers simply couldn't compete with the large number of outstanding players from which the American team could be drawn.

In 1979, the competition was expanded to include all of Europe's best players. No longer was it the U.S. versus Great Britain. Now it was the U.S. against Europe! Since 1979, the Ryder Cup has become the world's premier golf tournament—at least, that's what it was to Payne.

Played on alternating continents every two years, the Ryder Cup pits America's golf "Dream Team" against Europe's best players. The top ten players with the highest amount of Ryder Cup points earned during the two preceding years are chosen for the U.S. team. Points are awarded based on top-ten finishes at Tour events. The team captain also is granted two "captain's picks," guys who are not in the top ten but who are considered fierce competitors and who might be assets to the team. The European team is chosen in similar fashion, except for one major difference: the European team members are selected solely based on the money list in the year of the Ryder Cup. In other words, only players who are playing well during the year of the competition make the team.

Whereas the focus of most golf tournaments is on personal achievement, money, and fame, the Ryder Cup is about teamwork, honor, and national pride. On Tour, each professional golfer plays for himself and his family. If he wins or loses, it usually doesn't affect anyone outside of his own circle. But during the Ryder Cup competition, for three days every two years, golf becomes a team sport with national ramifications. Individual players, almost against their wills, find themselves drawn into a team spirit unlike anything else they experience in golf.

What meant the most to Payne about Ryder Cup play was that he represented his country. That sent chills up and down his body. The awesome seriousness with which he took Ryder Cup contests could be seen in his face as he stood listening to "The Star Spangled Banner" while the United States flag was being raised. Tears filled his eyes. Payne had never served in the military but had an extremely high regard for America's armed forces. This was as close to being in uniform as he would get, and he approached his responsibilities with tremendous pride.

Nothing in a PGA Tour player's golf experience prepares him for a Ryder Cup competition. Describing the pressure experienced by newcomers to the matches, Raymond Floyd said, "If you haven't played in one before, you can't hardly get through it the first time."

When the matches are played on European soil, the American guys are often shocked at how the crowds go wild for great shots made by the home team and how they scream equally as loudly when the American players miss a putt. It can be a bit unnerving compared to the empathetic "ooohs and aaaahs" expressed by the gallery after missed shots at most other tournaments. Furthermore, the format of Ryder Cup matches differs in large part from what the PGA Tour normally plays. U.S. golfers are more accustomed to "stroke play," where the winner is the player with the lowest number of strokes. But Ryder Cup competition is a "match play" format, which means that the player or team winning the most holes wins the match.

On Friday and Saturday mornings, the competition centers on four "foursome" matches, in which two-man teams play alternate shots with the same ball. In other words, the two members of the U.S. team in each foursome alternate hitting every other shot, as do the Europeans. In the afternoons, four "four ball" matches are also played, in which a "best ball" format is used, where the best shot between the two U.S. team members is used against the best shot of the two European team members. On Sunday, the final day of the Ryder Cup, twelve "singles" matches are conducted, in which the players compete head-to-head, with one man from the U.S. team squaring off against one man from the European team. Each match is worth one point, with half a point given to each team for matches that are tied after eighteen holes.

The Europeans defeated the Americans in 1985 and again in 1987. Payne played on the losing U.S. Ryder Cup team in 1987, which was a huge embarrassment for him and the entire team. Making matters worse, Payne's hero, Jack Nicklaus, was the captain of the U.S. team, and the matches were played at his home course, at Muirfield Village, in Dublin, Ohio. That's tantamount to the Yankees being swept in the World Series at Yankee Stadium.

After the 1987 loss, Nicklaus was under-standably put out. At the team meeting, he hammered his fellow players, including Payne. "You guys just don't know how to win!" Payne recalled Jack scolding. One of the reasons that Jack's words were so indelibly impressed in Payne's mind was because the Golden Bear had taken Payne to task in front of the other team members. "Look at you, Payne Stewart," Jack had said. "You make all this money on Tour, but how many tournaments have you won?" Then turning his wrath on the entire team, Jack chided them, "You guys need to learn how to win, or you're going to continue getting beaten in this thing."

Payne took Jack's speech to heart, and he took the U.S. team's loss personally—both for himself and for Jack. He couldn't wait for another shot at the Europeans.

Payne got that chance in September 1989, when the Ryder Cup was held at the Belfry, located in Sutton Coldfield in the picturesque English Midlands. Captained by Tony Jacklin, who had guided the European team to their two previous victories, the European force was loaded with many of the same big guns, including the indomitable Seve Ballesteros, Nick Faldo, José Maria Olazábal, Ian Woosnam, Mark James, Howard Clark, and Bernhard

Langer. Of course, the U.S. team wasn't exactly comprised of slouches. It was truly an All-Star–caliber assortment of players including Fred Couples, Mark O'Meara, Paul Azinger, Curtis Strange, Tom Kite, Chip Beck, Tom Watson, Mark McCumber, Lanny Wadkins, Mark Calcavecchia, and Ken Green.

Five members of the U.S. team were playing in their first Ryder Cup competition. Raymond Floyd did an outstanding job of pulling the veterans together with the five newcomers at the "Battle of the Belfry." The Europeans may have had a better mix of seasoned players, but the U.S. had more team spirit. Part of that was due to Payne. Each morning he awakened the entire hotel floor where we were staying with the blaring sounds of Bruce Springsteen's "Born in the USA" or Queen's "We Are the Champions" vibrating the hallway. The louder he could get his boom box, the better he liked it.

"Turn it down!" the guys would yell from behind closed doors. "I'm trying to sleep!" Payne just cranked the volume higher.

Out on the links, Payne proved an able cheerleader as well. When he finished his matches, rather than heading for the clubhouse and a cool drink, he was right back out on the course, cheering on his teammates. He raced up and down the fairways, supporting the other guys every way he could, slapping them on the back and rooting heartily for every one of them.

The American guys played well, holding their own through Saturday's matches, though the Europeans took a two-point lead into Sunday's singles play. In the early final-round matches, the U.S. team fought back, as Tom Kite beat Howard Clark and Chip Beck defeated Bernhard Langer. Chip was the only unbeaten American player that year. Paul Azinger won a heated battle against Seve Ballesteros, but it wasn't enough.

As Payne stood on the eighteenth tee in his match, he was all square with his singles opponent, José Maria Olazábal. Needing to at least tie Olazábal, Payne drove his tee shot into the water, just six inches short of dry land. He tried desperately to blast the submerged ball out of the lake, but when José reached the green in two, Payne knew that he had lost his match.

Mark Calcavecchia, nearly nauseated by the pressure, drove his tee shot into the same body of water that Payne had, and the Americans were in deep trouble. Moments later, Mark's opponent, Ronan Rafferty from Ireland, ripped his drive down the middle, and that match, too, went to Europe.

The Europeans needed only a half-point

to win, but the remaining U.S. players scrambled tenaciously and wouldn't let it happen. The 1989 Ryder Cup matches ended in a 14-14 tie, the first tie in twenty years. Although a tie was better than a loss, to the Americans it still felt like a loss, and it might as well have been. According to Ryder Cup rules, when a tie occurs, the team that last won the cup retains it. The Ryder Cup trophy would remain in Europe for another two years. The Europeans celebrated jubilantly.

"It was awful," Paul Azinger said later, "having to stand there at the eighteenth green and watch Tony Jacklin and the whole European team celebrate as though they had won—which they hadn't. They had only tied. But they retained the Cup."

Even though the tie was disappointing, Payne tried to look at the results positively. Outwardly he said, "Guys, we didn't lose. They didn't beat us." And he really meant it.

Inside, Payne felt awful. He beat himself up with "if-only's" all the way back to the States. But he had contributed much to the team effort, and to gauge his success or failure by one tee shot was not fair.

We had really jelled as a team, and Raymond and Maria Floyd had done an outstanding job as our captains. We came away from that Ryder Cup experience feeling so much closer to the other PGA Tour members on our team. Payne was completely hooked on the Ryder Cup competition. He loved every minute of it. His experience at the Belfry made him even more determined to be on the next Ryder Cup team at Kiawah Island in 1991.

Payne's next tournament was at the German Masters in Stuttgart, Germany, just two weeks after the Ryder Cup. He tied for second, finishing at 11-under par.

Back home, he played at the Walt Disney Classic, where he tied for forty-seventh place. Payne always enjoyed playing at Disney, and he played there every year after he won the tournament in 1983. Ironically, he never again won at Disney. He did, however, enjoy watching the guys tee it up in the father-child tournament prior to the main event, and he looked forward to one day playing in the event with Chelsea and Aaron.

In the season-ending Nabisco Championships, played at Harbour Town Golf Links in Hilton Head, Payne showed up with his "A" game. He played well throughout the first three days and shot 29 on the front nine on Sunday. But then, leading the tournament on the final hole, Payne three-putted the eighteenth green and ended up in a play-off with Tom Kite. They remained tied after the first play-off hole, but on the second green, Payne three-putted again, handing the tournament to Tom.

Payne was extremely annoyed with himself. Not only had he given the tournament away, but he also had lost out on several meaningful year-end awards. Prior to the Nabisco Championship, Payne had been the leading money winner for the year; Tom Kite had been second on the list. With his play-off loss to Tom, the order reversed, enabling Tom to receive the Arnold Palmer Award and the PGA of America's Player of the Year Award. Add to that his ineligibility to win the Vardon Trophy, even though he had the lowest scoring average for the year. Payne felt as though he had given away every important award for 1989 with one three-putt.

Disappointed by his failure, Payne had a passion to improve, not only as a player, but as a person.

13

Change Is Good

Winning the PGA Championship in 1989 vaulted Payne to a position of new prestige among his peers. No longer was he known as "the bridesmaid" or "Avis" or "the guy who came close but couldn't finish the tournament." No longer would he bear the stigma of "the best player never to have won a major." Now other players took nervous note of his name when it showed up on the leaderboard; they knew he was coming after them.

More importantly for us in the long run, the victory boosted Payne's confidence in his ability to remain focused under pressure. He had proved to himself that he could get the job done, and his complacency was gone forever.

From now on Payne wanted to be number one. He had come close in 1989, finishing second on the money list.

As we began the 1990 season, we had every reason to believe that the changes Payne had made were going to continue to pay big dividends. One thing that had changed in 1989 was Payne's putting consistency. Always on the lookout for anything that might help Payne with his game, I had noticed that most of the players who were consistently near the top of the money list played a different brand of putter. Payne was putting with a Bulls Eye, but many other top players used Ping. Working with Chuck Cook on a regular basis now, Payne widened his putting stance, lowered his hands on the grip, and leveled out the blade of the putter as he set up. Payne's father had taught him to place only the toe, the front tip of the blade, on the green as he addressed the ball, and Payne had not changed that part of his putting stroke since high school. With the new putter, he lowered the blade so that it rested on the heel, with the toe now in the air, and the changes seemed to help. His putting improved, and he played like a champion almost every week.

In April 1990, at the MCI Heritage Classic, Payne accomplished another feat. He beat 1987 Masters winner Larry Mize in a play-off, by sinking a 30-foot putt on the second hole of sudden death. It was the first time he had won a play-off in six attempts. Three weeks later Payne fired a final round 67, fending off Lanny Wadkins to win the rain-shortened GTE Byron Nelson Classic at the Las Colinas Sports Club in Irving, Texas. Payne always looked forward to playing well in the Dallas–Fort Worth area, and he was especially thrilled to have won the tournament associated with Byron Nelson's name. When Payne won, he told reporters, "Besides Bay Hill, this probably is the most emotional win I've had."

The following week, at the Memorial Tournament at Muirfield Village, Payne trailed Greg Norman by one stroke after fifty-four holes, when the fourth round was canceled on account of rain. Payne had been playing extremely well, hitting seventeen greens in regulation the previous day. His confidence soaring, he accepted the cancellation as an occupational hazard, but he expressed his disappointment to the press. "Two years ago, I might have felt, 'Hey, second place, great! Another $108,000.' Now, I think, 'No, that stinks. I didn't get a chance to win.'"

Payne's competitive drive continued off the course as well. Chuck Cook told me about a time shortly after the Byron Nelson win when

Payne had gone to Austin to work with him for a few days.

Arriving shortly before noon, Payne wanted to get something to eat before they started working. Chuck recommended one of his favorite local restaurants, The Texas Chili Parlor.

"What are you going to have?" Payne asked as they looked over the menu.

"Well, I'm going to have the Triple-X Frito Pie," Chuck said, "but you don't want that. It's real hot, probably too hot for you. You should get the Single-X." That's all Chuck had to say!

"Oh, if you can eat it, I can eat it," Payne declared and ordered the Triple-X.

The Triple didn't burn going down, but before long, Payne was chugging large glasses of water and iced tea. He got such a bad case of indigestion that he could hardly even practice! He and Chuck went out and played at Barton Creek, one of the finest golf courses in Austin, and Payne shot a 67 anyway!

That night, Payne said, "I gotta have me some more Mexican food."

Chuck and Payne did it all that evening, including fajitas, onions, salsa, and what Chuck called a "healthy dose" of hot jalapeño peppers. The next morning, Chuck awoke to the sound of Payne screaming. Chuck ran to Payne's bedroom and found him spread-eagle on the bed. "It hurts!" he screamed, between gales of laughter. "It hurts, Chuck . . . I mean it hur-r-rts!" That's as close as Payne ever got to admitting that he'd lost the battle of the Texas Chili Parlor.

One of the best aspects of Payne's success at winning golf tournaments and his increasing popularity on the PGA Tour was the greater impact his name had when it came to raising money for charity. Besides supporting the charities that tugged at our hearts, Payne accepted dozens of invitations to play in tournaments for his friends' favorite charities. And he was always ready to do something unusual if it might help charities that were helping people who others had passed by. For instance, one of our friends suffered from a blinding disease known as retinitis pigmentosa. To draw attention to the need for research, Payne agreed to play a nine-hole round of golf while completely blindfolded. Making matters even more interesting, he was to play the match against Pat Browne, the Blind Golfers Association champion!

Payne wore the blindfold from the time he

left the clubhouse until the round was completed. It wasn't even fair being able to see going from shot to shot. He wanted to perceive the course the way a sightless person would encounter it—in total blackness. Our friend Jon Brendle, who serves as a PGA Tour rules official, went along with Payne to help him line up his shots and direct him around the golf course. They placed Payne's ball on the first tee at Lake Buena Vista Golf Course in Orlando, and Payne took his normal, graceful swing. He connected with the ball, but just barely, knocking it about fifty feet to the left, into a ditch. "Oooooh, this is going to be tough!" Payne said with a laugh as Pat Browne's tee shot landed in the middle of the fairway.

Over the nine holes, Payne played fairly well for not being able to see his clubs, ball, or the golf course. He hit a few shots out of bounds, and he four-putted one green, missing three times from within three feet. He also nearly got hit by an errant shot from one of the other fellows playing along with them. "Fore!" several guys yelled. Not being able to see, Payne was standing next to a bunker, oblivious to the ball racing in his direction. He didn't realize that the warning was meant for him. Fortunately, the ball missed him by about two feet. But it highlighted another potential danger a blind person must deal with.

Payne had a lot of fun that day, and he drew attention to a problem that often gets lost amid the plethora of other worthy causes that clamor for attention. Pat Browne, the Blind Golfer's champ, shot a 41, while Payne zoomed to a 60 wearing the blindfold. "It was a humbling experience," Payne said of his day of darkness. "I hope what I did will make more people aware of this disease that can strike any one of us."

Payne continued to play well in 1990. In the six tournaments he played between the Masters and the U.S. Open, he won twice, finished second twice, had a seventh-place finish, and missed the cut once. He was on a roll!

Payne really wanted to win the British Open. He often called it his favorite major because it was the original, although he also revered the U.S. Open for obvious patriotic reasons. In 1990, the British Open was scheduled for St. Andrews, the birthplace of golf. Payne had grown to love St. Andrews, and he really enjoyed playing golf in the tough conditions usually associated with the Open. Inspired by the historic significance of the course and the tournament, Payne played extremely well at St. Andrews, finishing second, behind Nick Faldo.

Next, as the defending champion, Payne got fired up for the PGA Championship at

Shoal Creek in Birmingham, Alabama. He played quite well for three rounds and began the final day just two shots behind the leader, Australian Wayne Grady. Playing in the final group, along with Wayne, Payne shot a disappointing 79 and faded to a tie for eighth place.

Wayne later told me, "I knew it was going to be a great day for me when Payne showed up on the first tee wearing the colors of the Green Bay Packers, green and yellow" because the official national colors of Australia are also green and yellow. Wayne won the tournament by three strokes and credited Payne for inspiring him with the Aussie colors!

Payne's final round fade was the least of his problems at Shoal Creek, however. Prior to the tournament, it became publicly known that Shoal Creek, one of the more prestigious country clubs in Alabama, had no African American members. When the news hit the press, it became a major embarrassment for the PGA of America. The Southern Christian Leadership Conference threatened to picket the tournament. Advertisers threatened to pull their commercials from the tournament broadcast on ABC television, and ABC in turn threatened to forego payment to the PGA if the matter wasn't resolved quickly. At one point, the feasibility of moving the PGA Championship from Shoal Creek to another location was considered.

With controversy swirling around the golf course and tournament, reporters buzzed in every direction, looking for a new angle on the story. Naturally, they were quite interested in the opinion of the defending tournament champion—Payne Stewart.

When Payne was asked his opinion, he was honest enough to give it. He hadn't yet learned to be discreet with his answers. Many people, when asked for their opinions by the media, tend to give the expected, or "politically correct," answer, whether or not they believe it. But not Payne. He was too honest for that. If you asked him what he thought about something, he'd tell you!

When a reporter asked how he and the other players felt about the controversy, Payne responded, "Actually, you people in the media are the ones making a big deal out of this and blowing it out of proportion." Payne continued, "Most of the players that I've talked to in the locker room have not been affected by it. In fact, a lot of them are just telling jokes about it."

It was a simple, truthful comment, but it carried the explosive power of an atomic bomb. The media blew Payne's comments in every direction. The headlines the next day read something like: "PAYNE STEWART THINKS RACISM AT SHOAL CREEK IS A JOKE."

Payne? A racist? That was absurd, and it wasn't what he had said. Since his earliest days on the Asian Tour, Payne, of all people, had always considered himself a "world" player. He loved meeting and befriending people of every race and experiencing various cultures. To brand Payne or any of the other guys in the locker room as racists because they made jokes about an awkward situation was laughable in itself. The controversy died down when the Shoal Creek leadership agreed to invite Louis Willie, to join their club.

All in all, Payne had a great year in 1990, with nine top-ten finishes, including two victories. He finished third on the PGA Tour money list in 1990, winning $976,281. Representing the U.S., he also won the individual competition at the World Cup tournament, held at the Grand Cypress Resort in Orlando. Payne was partnered with Jodie Mudd and finished 17-under par for the event. Unfortunately, Jodie was over par for the week, and they didn't win the team competition.

Because Payne had won the individual title, he went to the media center for interviews. Meanwhile, Dick Coop, Chuck Cook, Mike Hicks, and my father, who was visiting from

Australia, decided to play a round of golf at one of Grand Cypress's other courses. After his interviews, Payne and I jumped on a golf cart and, with Payne still in his plus fours, we drove out to find them. The head pro at Grand Cypress, Paul Celano, hopped on another cart and came with us. For the rest of the day, we played a "sevensome," unheard of at any course, let alone at Grand Cypress! That Payne had just won the World Cup individual competition was less important to him than playing a round of golf with my dad and our friends.

One day, early in February 1991, Payne picked up Chelsea and let her ride on his shoulders as we were walking along. The next day he began to experience a severe pain in his neck. At first he thought that perhaps he had simply pulled a muscle and that the pain would go away. It didn't. Instead, it grew worse with each passing day. Over the next week or so, Payne tried to ignore the throbbing in his neck, but before long it became nearly intolerable. On February 20, he was practicing at Bay Hill when the pain in his neck area became so intense he couldn't take it anymore. After playing only five holes, he had to stop. Three days later, he tried to play again, but after only four holes, the neck pain intensified, this time causing Payne's left arm to fall limp. Worried, he tried to swing, but his arm collapsed again. Alarmingly, he had lost all strength in his left arm. We knew we had to get expert attention—and quickly.

We called Robert Fraley. When Orel Hershiser had experienced trouble with his pitching arm a few years earlier, Robert had recommended that he see Dr. Frank Jobe, a well-known orthopedic specialist in California. One of the most highly esteemed sports doctors in the world, Dr. Jobe had successfully treated Orel, and Orel's career had hardly missed a beat. Robert was hopeful that Dr. Jobe could do something similar for Payne.

Dr. Jobe's office was at Centinela Hospital in Los Angeles. We were familiar with Centinela because the hospital also operated the fitness trailer on the PGA Tour. Robert and Dixie Fraley flew with us to California, where we met with Dr. Jobe and Dr. Robert Watkins, another specialist. After a lengthy exam, the doctors discovered a bone chip that had broken off and lodged between the vertebrae in his neck, causing the loss of strength in his arm. Dr. Watkins gave us two choices: Payne could have an operation, or we could try to dissolve the chip through medication, which would require that Payne wear a neck brace and probably not play for eight to ten weeks. We decided that we did not want to risk an operation if we could avoid it. Besides, the recuperation might take even longer than trying to deal with the problem through medication and rest. Payne chose the medication and gradual rehabilitation.

For several weeks, he wore a neck brace twenty-four hours a day and did virtually no lifting or exercise of any kind. During the lay-off, Payne spent most of his time around the house. There really wasn't much else he could do. He could barely lift a two-pound weight with his left hand, and swinging a golf club was out of the question. Instead, he was relegated to watching golf on television. Even turning around was a big undertaking for him. Then, one step at a time, he started a rehab program to regain the strength in his arm. Physical therapy visits became the main events of Payne's week.

The rest time also gave Payne a chance to think and to evaluate those things that were important to him. "I was thinking about how fortunate I am to get to do the things I do," Payne said one day when I came in. I could tell he was wondering what life might be like if he couldn't play golf again. I tried to encourage him that, no matter what, we'd be fine.

"Don't worry about it," I'd say lightly. "If

you can't play golf anymore, it will be OK. I enjoy having you around the house more often, anyhow!" I really wasn't worried. I knew that if Payne couldn't play golf, he'd be good at whatever he decided to do.

The low point came several weeks into our new regimen when Payne had to watch the Bay Hill Classic from our back porch and patio just off the twelfth tee. As one member of the PGA Tour after another approached the tee, Payne forced himself to stay still while he followed them with his eyes, not daring to turn his head too rapidly to follow the line of their tee shots.

During this time, Payne also did some television commentary work to pass the time and to stay in touch with the Tour. As difficult as it was to see the Tour go by without him, it also fired him with mental determination to get back out there himself.

Although Payne didn't know it at the time, Dr. Watkins had confided privately to Robert Fraley that he doubted whether Payne would ever be able to play golf again—at least not at the level he was accustomed to playing— regardless of the method used to solve the disk problem. But Dr. Watkins didn't know Payne.

On March 24, Dr. Watkins came to our home at Bay Hill to examine Payne. He was pleasantly surprised with Payne's progress, but he told him to rest for another week before hitting any golf balls and then to start easy, swinging the club, hitting only a few balls per practice and gradually working the arm, shoulder, and neck muscles to regain his strength. I kept a written log, charting Payne's progress.

On March 29, Payne hit some golf balls for the first time since the injury. Payne hit seventy balls that first day. On the next day, he hit sixty balls, and the next, he hit forty balls and then putted and chipped. Payne set a goal for himself to be ready for the Masters in early April.

We went up to Augusta, and Chuck Cook came in to work with Payne before the tournament. "Your swing is perfect," Chuck reassured him. "You're swinging just as well as I've ever seen you." Unfortunately, Payne's natural swing could not make up for the radical loss of strength in his left arm. As much as he wanted to play, he had to face the fact that he wasn't ready. Payne withdrew from the 1991 Masters and continued with his rehab and strengthening exercises.

On Wednesday, April 17, the week following the Masters, Payne underwent a strength test at a hospital in Savannah, Georgia, to check his left arm. The doctors reported their findings to Dr. Watkins, and he gave Payne the green light to play that week in the Heritage Classic at Hilton Head, where he was the defending champion. Despite not competing for several months, Payne shot 68-68-70-69, and tied for fourth place. He was back.

With little more than a month to fine-tune his game, Payne set his sights on the U.S. Open in June. He'd be ready.

14

A Career
Milestone

T he Sunday night before the beginning of
the 1991 U.S. Open, Payne and I sat outside gazing at the stars and the Northern Lights
in the Minnesota sky. We had rented a home
near the tournament site and had just gotten settled in for the week. The children were asleep,
and Payne and I finally had time to relax, sit out
on the porch, and just talk for a while. Payne
was troubled and frustrated because of his slow
start in 1991 due to his neck injury. He'd had
only one top-ten finish, at the MCI Heritage
Classic, his first week back on Tour. He fretted
that his point total might not be high enough to
earn a spot on the 1991 Ryder Cup team.

"Payne, don't be so hard on yourself," I

said. "You've already played on two Ryder Cup teams. That's two more than most guys ever get to play on. If you don't make it this year, you have nothing to be ashamed of."

"I know it, I know," Payne replied in a low voice as he pulled me closer.

"You put so much pressure on yourself to do well," I continued. "Then you get there, and you end up not performing the way you want to, and you just make yourself miserable. I love you and the kids love you, no matter what happens. You don't have anything to prove to us."

Our conversation seemed to liberate Payne in a way; it provided him with a fresh sense of freedom. He knew that of all the people in the world, I wasn't going to stand by and watch him get complacent; so when I emphasized that he needed to lighten up a bit, he felt comfortable doing it. He recognized that he could still compete tenaciously, but that we had a good life whether he won or lost. He began to relax more and stopped being so critical of himself.

Of course, he still wanted to win passionately, and so did I. Payne's new attitude actually enhanced the possibility of winning. Our friend Dick Coop, the sports psychologist with whom Payne had been working for several years, reinforced my comments. He told Payne, "You have everything going for you. Your mental preparation has been great. You have been sticking to your preshot routine; your attitude is great. You have every right to feel confident as you go into this tournament." Now it was up to Payne.

The 1991 United States Open Championship was played at Hazeltine National Golf Club in Chaska, Minnesota, a Robert Trent Jones–designed course that had been mocked as a cow pasture when the Open had been played there in 1970. Since then, Jones and his son had been called upon to improve the course. By 1991, with $1 million spent in redesign work, Hazeltine was as challenging a place to play a U.S. Open as anywhere in the country. It was everything a major championship venue should be: a long course boasting generous fairways, with severe rough and greens that were hard and fast. Jack Nicklaus called it "one of the most difficult golf courses I've ever played on."

Payne's back was bothering him again, hurting so badly that he skipped his usual practice round on Wednesday, the final day before the tournament got underway. That night, he slept downstairs on Aaron's bed because the mattress in the master bedroom was too soft to support his lower back. The soreness was still there when he got ready to play on Thursday.

First-round play was suspended on Thursday morning when a violent thunderstorm tore through the land of lakes, drenching the ground and turning Hazeltine's already high and difficult rough into something similar to green mesh wire. When the weather cleared, the players and spectators returned to the course. Shortly before 1:00 P.M., however, another violent storm rumbled across the flat, Midwestern prairie. As the rain pelted down, play was suspended again, and the players ran for shelter in the vans that had been positioned around the course as a precaution. Meanwhile, forty thousand spectators sought refuge in any dry area they could find. Unfortunately, the most obvious shelters—the large Minnesota willow trees lining the fairways—were some of the most dangerous.

Huge bolts of lightning streaked from the sky. Suddenly, lightning struck a willow near the eleventh tee, where a group of spectators was huddled, trying to stay dry. Instantly, six people fell to the ground. Medical personnel at the golf course risked their own lives, running through the storm to offer whatever help they could to the victims. Five of those who were injured recovered, but a twenty-seven-year-old man, whose father was a marshal at the tournament, did not.

Payne had been scheduled to tee off at 1:30, but because of the weather delays and the tragedy, he did not begin his round until 4:00 in the afternoon. While we waited through the delay, Payne was as antsy as I'd ever seen him. Dr. Coop was with us at Hazeltine, and he did his best to keep Payne calm and focused.

It was 9:00 P.M. by the time Payne finished his first round. As darkness finally descended upon the long, gruesome day, his name was at the top of the leaderboard at 67, along with Nolan Henke.

Scott Simpson, who had won the U.S. Open in 1987 and had contended strongly in the past four Opens, was in contention again, shooting a 70 on Thursday, as did Davis Love III, Fred Couples, and Jim Gallagher Jr. On Friday the sun came out, and the playing conditions improved greatly. Thursday's rain had softened the always treacherous U.S. Open greens, so the players were fearlessly shooting at the pin while the opportunity was there. Payne shot a 70 on Friday, and it looked as though several players might catch him, including Corey Pavin, who shot a 67. At the end of thirty-six holes, however, Payne still led the tournament.

Like Payne, Scott Simpson always seemed to ratchet his game up a few notches for the U.S. Open. A warm, friendly family man and a dedicated Christian with an easygoing personality, Scott was nonetheless a fighter, a formidable foe at any tournament, but especially, it seemed, at the U.S. Open. On Saturday, Scott tied Payne for the lead with a birdie on the third hole. With more thunderstorms threatening and a twenty-five-mile-an-hour wind swirling around them, Scott and Payne jockeyed back and forth, taking turns at the top of the leaderboard. They ended the day tied for the lead.

By the fourth and final round, the 1991 U.S. Open had turned into a two-man match between Scott and Payne. Payne's deep purple shirt and white knickers, the colors of the Minnesota Vikings, endeared him to the sold-out Sunday gallery at Hazeltine, but Scott Simpson seemed to be in the driver's seat during most of the final round. At the tenth hole, he took a two-stroke lead over Payne and kept it all the way to the sixteenth, a troublesome hole bordered by Lake Hazeltine. Number 16 had been Scott's nemesis all week, and Sunday proved no different. He teed off with a 1-iron but pulled the shot and landed in the four-inch-high rough. Payne put his 2-iron off the tee right in the middle of the fairway. Simpson bogeyed the hole for the third time in four days, and Payne made par to cut the lead to one. They both parred 17, and it was down to the last hole . . . again.

Payne's tee shot on 18 landed in the fairway, but Scott's tee shot went left on him, landing a few inches off the fairway, in the rough. It took Scott two more shots to reach the green. Meanwhile, Payne hit a 5-iron shot that skipped across the green onto the fringe. He had a chance to win, but his long putt from the fringe refused to break, leaving him with a 5-footer for par. Scott had a 20-footer that would have given him the win, but his putt, too, rolled on by the hole.

When Payne made his putt, we were off to another play-off.

Rather than a sudden-death play-off, as at the PGA Championship, or a four-hole play-off, as at the British Open, when the U.S. Open is tied at the end of seventy-two holes, the players involved must return the following day for an eighteen-hole play-off. In one sense, the eighteen-hole play-off is the most fair, but it is also the most inconvenient. Everyone's schedule is disrupted, from television coverage, to players, to spectators. Payne and I had kissed Aaron goodbye and sent him home to Orlando with our nanny, Teresa Selby, on Monday morning. Chelsea stayed with us. The three of us were scheduled to depart for Ireland on Monday so that Payne could play in the Irish Open that week, but we hastily and happily changed our plans. The Irish wouldn't mind if we came in a day late, especially if we were carrying a U.S. Open title along with us.

At Hazeltine, more than twenty-five thousand spectators showed up on Monday morning for the showdown between Scott Simpson and Payne. At most tournaments, with a full field of players to watch, the spectators fan out across the golf course to follow their favorites. But at the Monday play-off, all twenty-five thousand followed the two competitors all day long, lining every fairway and encircling every green.

By Monday, the greens at Hazeltine had dried thoroughly and were fast and hard, just the way the USGA likes them. The course had grown tougher with each passing day, and with the wind still whipping, it was an even more difficult test. Payne chose a red, white, and blue outfit for the occasion. He loved to display his patriotism anytime, but especially at the United States Open Championship.

Back and forth, the momentum shifted all day long. First, Payne seized control, then Scott fought back. Then Scott moved ahead, and

Payne had to play catch-up again. One of the defining shots of the day came on the par-3 eighth hole. Payne's tee shot didn't quite clear the water, but the ball hit a partially submerged rock near the edge of the lake and bounced clear of the hazard into the rough alongside the green. Payne still had an extremely awkward and difficult chip, but at least he didn't receive a penalty stroke for losing his ball in the drink.

As they started the back nine, Scott moved ahead of Payne. Payne came right back, but when he three-putted the fifteenth, many in the crowd assumed that Simpson could not possibly be beaten.

But the difficult number 16 still lay ahead.

As they had done the day before, both players used irons off the sixteenth tee, hoping for better control of the ball, rather than taking a chance of getting caught in the high rough along the fairway. Scott's 7-iron second shot landed short of the green. Payne's shot seemed to be blocked by a towering white ash tree. Payne considered his options, then lofted an incredible 8-iron shot right over the tree, landing on the green about twenty feet from the cup. "It was just a perfect shot," Payne recalled later, "and at just the right time." The greens were hard and fast, and Payne hadn't made a birdie since the third hole, but his 20-foot putt on 16 found the center of the cup. Scott missed a 3-footer for par, and they were tied again. After eighty-eight holes of golf, with only two holes left to be played, the championship could still go either way.

On 17, Payne hit another incredible 5-iron shot right at the pin, landing about twenty feet from the hole. Scott wasn't as fortunate. He hit a poor tee shot on 17 and his ball caught the side of a steep bank and caromed into a pond. The errant shot cost Scott a penalty stroke. He then had to pitch across the water onto the green. Scott hit an incredible third shot, then sank a 12-foot putt for bogey. What a recovery! Payne managed to two-putt for a par and walked to the eighteenth tee with a one-stroke lead.

Payne's tee shot on 18 drifted to the right, skipping into a fairway bunker. Scott's tee shot hit the exact same fairway bunker as Payne's, but instead of staying in the sand, the ball squirted out the other side of the bunker and into the rough with a downhill lie. Payne's position suddenly looked pretty good, compared to Scott's. As Payne stepped into the fairway bunker and prepared to hit his second shot, he was distracted by someone on a tournament staff radio instructing, "Get the next hole ready for a sudden-death play-off if they're still tied after 18."

Payne backed away from his ball momentarily and said to himself, There's not going to be another hole after this one.

With that, Payne hit a fabulous 6-iron shot out of the sand, landing on the green and rolling off to the edge. Scott hit a 7-iron out of the rough, but the ball took a big bounce and ran across the green, leaving him a long chip to attempt to tie. By now, the Hazeltine greens were slick as an ice-skating rink, and Scott's chip ran nearly ten feet past the hole. His putt missed and he tapped in for a bogey.

Now it was all up to Payne. He could two-putt from five feet to win. He only needed one. Payne drained the 5-footer and won the United States Open Championship! He was the first player to lead a U.S. Open wire to wire, from the opening day to the winning putt, since Jack Nicklaus had done it in 1980. Payne liked being in Jack's company for any reason, but he especially enjoyed hearing his name linked with Jack's for such an awesome achievement.

Payne and his caddy, Mike Hicks, hugged and high-fived on the green. Payne picked his ball out of the hole and tossed it into the crowd, a valuable souvenir for whoever caught it. Chelsea and I had been standing alongside the green, and Payne's ball had barely rolled into the cup before she started running toward her daddy. Chelsea leaped into his arms and wrapped herself around his neck. It was hard to believe that less than three months earlier, Payne could hardly pick up one of Chelsea's dolls, let alone have our daughter hugging his neck. I was right behind her with an emotional victory kiss for Payne.

We embraced momentarily on the green, then Payne stepped over to shake hands with Scott Simpson, congratulating him on an outstanding performance. Scott smiled kindly and congratulated Payne. Despite the loss, Scott maintained his sense of humor. When someone asked him what Payne had said to him on the green at the conclusion of the play-off, Scott replied with a sly grin, "'Thanks,' I think."

Always a gentleman, Scott Simpson was especially kind in his comments after the round. "I'm real pleased for Payne," Scott said. "I admire him for his golf game, and I admire him as a person. I know that he's committed to his family, which I appreciate, and also he always has a great attitude out there playin'."

Payne was also complimentary toward Scott. "To be the champion is what I worked for, and what Scott worked for. It's just too bad that both of us couldn't be the champion."

We hardly had time to celebrate at Hazeltine because we were soon airborne on a private jet back to Orlando where we were scheduled to leave for Ireland the following evening aboard a commercial airliner. We decided to save our celebration until we reached Ireland. Payne led the Irish Open after two rounds, but our "celebrating with the Irish" every night eventually wore him down. He finished tied for sixteenth, but we didn't mind; we were still high from celebrating our major victory. Two national opens in a row might have done us in!

Payne always enjoyed sharing his success with his friends. He invited Dr. Coop, Chuck Cook, and Mike Hicks to accompany him on a golf trip to Scotland prior to playing in the British Open at Birkdale. The trip characterized Payne's personality in many ways. For one thing, he made no lodging reservations. They just drove until they found a bed-and-breakfast each night as they made their way from one famous, historic Scottish golf course to the next. Coop was amazed at Payne's sense of direction and the way he could get around the Scottish countryside without asking for directions.

After playing golf during the day, the guys went out for dinner each evening. Invariably,

Payne was the life of the party, always wanting to include everyone. Coop and Chuck recalled one of the first nights of the trip, when they encountered a group of about thirty American college students in a restaurant in Glasgow. By night's end, Payne and the students were like old friends.

"Where can we find a good pub at this hour?" Payne asked. Someone gave him directions, and the guys headed out the door—with the whole crowd of students following Payne down the street. From that night on, the guys called Payne "the Pied Piper."

One night, after they had played the historic Troon golf course, Coop and Mike turned in early, but Chuck and Payne were still awake. They went out and found a Scottish karaoke bar and stayed until the place closed. Payne was buying drinks for everyone, and they were singing up a storm. When they got back to where they were staying, about 2:30 A.M., they realized they had been locked out.

Chuck looked up and saw that Payne and Dick's hotel room window was open. "Don't worry, Payne. I can get us in."

Wearing leather shoes, Chuck climbed up the side of the building by holding on to a drain spout.

"Throw your shoes down," Payne called,

"before you kill yourself!" Chuck removed the slippery shoes and tossed them to Payne, nearly pitching them through the windows in the hotel's sunroom below. Barefoot, he inched along the slate roof of the hotel until he got to the open window. Chuck grabbed onto the gutter and swung through the window, scaring Coop half to death. From that night on, Payne nicknamed Chuck "Spider Man." Coop earned the dubious distinction of "Grandpa" for his early bedtimes, and Mike Hicks was tagged as "Homing Pigeon" because he'd often leave while the guys were partying, go away for a while, but always come back.

In addition to the U.S. Open, Payne also won the Heineken Dutch Open in Holland, his first European win. He shot an astounding 62 on Saturday and finished the tournament nine strokes ahead of Bernhard Langer, the nearest contender. In 1991 alone, Payne played in the Irish Open, the Monte Carlo, the British Open, the Dutch Open, the European Open, and the BMW International in Munich.

Payne especially enjoyed the panoramic Mont Agel course, which sits three thousand feet above sea level, looking down on Monte Carlo and the French Riviera. Payne played in the pro-am with Prince Ranier and then shot rounds of 69-68-67-66 to tie for fourteenth place. When we weren't at the golf course, Payne and his caddy, Mike Hicks, and I were guests at the Monte Carlo Beach Club. We had a fabulous time swimming and relaxing.

While in Monte Carlo, we were invited to various functions at the royal palace, and one night the discussion turned to music. When Princess Stephanie learned that Payne played the harmonica for Jake Trout & the Flounders, I knew we were in trouble! He tried to tell the royal family that he was strictly a novice, but they would not relent until he retrieved his harmonica and played for them. Whether our hosts truly enjoyed Payne's playing was debatable, but they certainly made him feel as though they did!

The "War by the Shore" was the rather dubious name tacked onto the 1991 Ryder Cup matches, held in September at Kiawah Island, South Carolina, on the Ocean Course designed by Pete Dye. Played shortly after "Desert Storm," in the aftermath of televised images depicting smart bombs, Scud missiles, and pinpoint accuracy attacks during the Persian Gulf War, the U.S. Ryder Cup team could hardly be blamed for their heightened sense of national pride coming into the matches. The Americans made it known right from the start that they intended to send the Europeans back across the Atlantic with less baggage—namely the Ryder Cup trophy. The Europeans had held the Cup for six years, their longest dominance since the rivalry began in 1927. Following the bitter disappointment of the 1989 tie, which had allowed the Europeans to retain the Cup, the United States team felt enormous pressure to bring the trophy home.

For Payne, the war of words began even before the selection of the players. As the reigning U.S. Open champion, he was asked whether he thought the 1991 Senior U.S. Open champion, Jack Nicklaus, should be on the Ryder Cup team. Knowing that Jack had not been feeling his best and had been suffering from back problems, and knowing how strenuous and stressful the Ryder Cup matches can be, Payne said that he didn't think that Jack could play thirty-six holes in one day.

Boom! Another explosion rocked the golf world, as reports hit the press declaring in essence that "Payne Stewart says that Jack Nicklaus shouldn't be selected to play on the Ryder Cup team." Again, that was not what Payne had said, nor what he'd intended.

Nonetheless, Payne was excoriated by the media and by loyal Jack Nicklaus fans (of whom Payne was one of the greatest). Letters to the editor in papers and magazines castigated him with searing comments such as, "Payne Stewart needs to get a life!" and "When Payne Stewart has won as often as Jack has . . ." and on and on.

Payne immediately called Jack and explained what had happened. Jack understood all too well, having had his own comments taken out of context or misquoted more than a few times. He said, "Don't worry about it, Payne. I understand totally."

Nevertheless, we started receiving "hate mail" long before the first shot was ever hit at the "War by the Shore."

The 1991 team was captained by two-time PGA Championship winner Dave Stockton Sr., and he had several reasons to be confident. Many of the U.S. players who made the team had played previously on one or more Ryder Cup teams and knew what to expect. Plus, we were playing "at home," although Pete Dye's new "links style" course at Kiawah, with no grass collars around the greens to slow down errant approach shots, may have been an advantage to the Europeans, who were more accustomed to such courses in their homelands. Since it was a new course, most of the Americans had not played much at Kiawah.

Payne had played a practice round on the course the previous week.

The U.S. players included Fred Couples, Paul Azinger, Hale Irwin, Lanny Wadkins, Corey Pavin, Mark O'Meara, Wayne Levi, Mark Calcavecchia, Steve Pate, and Payne. Dave Stockton surprised a lot of second-guessers when he chose as his captain's picks the 1989 U.S. Ryder Cup captain, Raymond Floyd, and Chip Beck. Raymond's reputation for being a fierce competitor was well-known across the Atlantic. That selection in itself signaled that the U.S. planned on taking no prisoners.

The Europeans sported their usual team of power players, led again by Seve Ballesteros and José Maria Olazábal of Spain, Nick Faldo and Mark James from England, Sam Torrance from Scotland, Bernhard Langer of Germany, and Ian Woosnam of Wales. Adding clout to their team, the Europeans also boasted some strong newcomers, including David Feherty of Northern Ireland and Colin Montgomerie of Scotland.

The 1991 matches proved as exciting and tension-packed as anyone could possibly have anticipated. Fred Couples, Raymond Floyd, and Paul Azinger played amazing golf throughout their matches, Freddie making one incredible shot after another. Payne played well too. In foursomes, he and Mark Calcavecchia defeated two of Europe's hottest players—Nick Faldo and Ian Woosnam. On Saturday, he and Mark beat Mark James and Steven Richardson in foursomes, and then in the afternoon, Payne and Fred Couples fought Seve and José, Europe's toughest pair, to a tie. On the last day, Payne lost 2 & 1 to David Feherty in singles.

Sunday's final matches began with the score tied at eight; by the end of the day, after three days of intense competition, it all came down to one putt—a 6-footer—by one man— Bernhard Langer—on the final hole. The pressure was immense as Bernhard, a veteran golfer with nerves of steel, labored over reading his putt. Meanwhile, the thousands of spectators gathered around Kiawah's eighteenth green and millions more who were watching on television knew that if Bernhard made this putt the Europeans would take the cup back to Europe again because of a tie. If he missed, the Americans would reclaim the Cup.

Bernhard put a good stroke on the ball; and for a second that seemed like an hour, the ball floated across the green toward the hole . . . and missed by an inch! The United States was the winner, 14½ to 13½.

The crowd went wild, rushing the green and chanting, "USA! USA!" For a few minutes, it looked like a European soccer match celebration.

Following the closing award ceremonies, with the U.S. team sharply dressed in blue blazers, white golf shirts, and dress slacks, the guys posed for a beautiful team photograph on the beach close to the water. Too close for Payne, Corey Pavin, and Mark O'Meara, who led the players in picking up captain Dave Stockton and tossing him into the ocean, Rolex and all, as a way of celebrating the tremendous victory. It was one dunking that Dave didn't mind.

In November, Payne won the first of three consecutive "Skins Games," a tournament played each year in Palm Springs, California, during Thanksgiving weekend. Four competitors vie for large sums of money, with 20 percent of their winnings going to a charity of their choice. Each hole is worth an increasing amount of money. The winner of the hole is said to have won a "skin." The beneficiary of Payne's charity earnings was the RP Foundation, which seeks a cure for the eye disease retinitis pigmentosa.

After the celebrations of Payne's U.S. Open and other victories died down, Payne seemed to get caught up in trying to "be" the U.S. Open champion. We got so busy doing all the things associated with being the champion that we forgot to take time to enjoy it. That was a mistake Payne never wanted to make again.

15

Colors of Payne

Payne turned down very few opportunities during his reign as U.S. Open champion, often playing at charitable events or for appearance fees—money that an event sponsor pays for a professional athlete to participate.

Payne felt compelled to work harder at improving his game, which sounds noble, but—as the saying goes—if it ain't broke, don't fix it. Payne's swing certainly did not need correcting, but he experimented with all sorts of adjustments, none of which worked any better than what he'd always done. In the process, he allowed all the pressures of winning the U.S. Open, and the commitments that followed, to affect his game adversely.

He focused intensely on the majors, but most other tournaments failed to hold his attention for long. He wanted to win the U.S. Open again in 1992, but it was somewhat of a relief when his reign as 1991 champion came to a close.

Chuck Cook tells a story about the day he and Payne went to Pebble Beach for the U.S. Open Media Day. That evening, after the many interviews were concluded, Chuck and Payne were sitting in the bar at The Lodge at Pebble Beach when a rather boisterous fellow approached them and said to Payne, "That guy over there says you are Payne Stewart, but I don't believe it."

"Well, if I go get the U.S. Open trophy, will you keep filling it up with whatever I want to drink?" Payne asked with a twinkle in his eye.

"You bet I will!" the guy said.

Payne retrieved the trophy and then summoned a waiter. "Bring us a bottle of Cristal champagne," he said.

"Cristal is expensive anywhere, but at The Lodge at Pebble Beach, it is really expensive!" recalls Chuck. "That guy might be the only person who was sorry he met Payne Stewart because he's a lot poorer now!"

Despite the effects of the champagne, the

memory of that night is indelibly impressed in Chuck's heart and mind. "We drank until the wee hours of the night out of that old U.S. Open cup," he recounts, "and then Payne said, 'Let's go over by the eighteenth green.' We walked out of the lodge and sat down on a retaining wall about twenty-five feet above the waves crashing on the rocks of Monterey Bay. We propped the trophy in the sand—it could have fallen over and been gone forever—and sat there for several hours talking about life." It was a special time for both men.

In late July of 1992, Robert and Dixie Fraley and Payne and I went to the Olympics in Barcelona, Spain. I remember we leased a house just outside of town. When we arrived at the house, it was extremely hot and the house had no air-conditioning. Both Payne and Robert liked having the finer things in life, and they just were not interested in roughing it. The next morning, Payne and Robert went out to play golf with Michael Jordan, Charles Barkley, and Chuck Daly, while Dixie and I went to a department store in search of some fans. Our guys played golf every day with several members of the Dream Team, and Dixie and I met them at the golf club for lunch. Our good friend Todd

Woodbridge was representing Australia in the tennis competition, so we all went to watch Todd and his tennis partner, John Fitzgerald, play their matches. We hollered and cheered and totally embarrassed them. We had a great time attending all sorts of Olympic events. Dixie and I then flew back to Orlando, and Payne and Robert went on to Munich for the BMW Tournament. Every year, Payne and Robert picked a tournament to play together. They loved being with each other. Robert was the brother Payne never had.

In October, while Payne was playing in the Texas Open in San Antonio, a young Australian girl approached him and asked if she could have her photo taken with him. Of course he agreed. She was in the U.S. with several other young Australian golfers, and they were traveling around playing matches in different cities. At the time, Payne didn't know her, but several years later he would meet her again. Her name was Renay, and she and Stuart Appleby met on that trip to the United States. They later married and we all became friends. She always joked with me that she had a crush on Payne when she was younger.

The following month, in November, Payne and Robert traveled to Japan for the VISA Taiheiyo Club Masters Tournament.

Payne had somehow talked Robert into caddying for him. During one of the rounds, Robert gave Payne an incorrect yardage. Payne questioned him, but Robert repeated his answer. Payne hit the club for that yardage and completely flew the green with his approach shot. A photographer happened to take a picture of the two of them during their yardage discussion. Payne appeared to be questioning Robert, who had a totally puzzled look on his face. Payne obtained copies of the photo and had it enlarged with a plaque underneath that read, "Are you sure about that yardage?" and gave it to Robert. That picture has graced the wall at Leader Enterprises in Orlando ever since.

Payne had a decent year in 1992, with five top-ten finishes and a slightly better stroke average (70.30) than he'd had the previous year. He won the Skins Game and also the Hassan II Trophy in Morocco. He earned $334,738 on the PGA Tour and ended the season ranked forty-fourth on the Tour money list; but because he didn't post a victory on the Tour, to Payne the year was less than a success. He embarked on a vigorous self-improvement program, eating less red meat, working out more, and trying to break his addiction to chewing tobacco. He was determined to do better the next year, and he did.

Payne started out the year with a successful tour of the West Coast. In the six events he played, he had three top-ten finishes. At the 1993 Players Championship in late March, Payne was in contention, but his putting was off. "I nearly threw my putter in the lake," he later said. "I'm glad I didn't though. That doesn't accomplish anything except for that small moment of satisfaction when it's in the air." As I watched him on television, I noticed that he was slowing down his putting stroke rather than maintaining a constant speed as he stroked through the ball. When I saw him on Friday evening, the first thing I said to him was, "You're decelerating on the putter. I could see it on TV."

Payne teased, "Hmmph! No 'Hi, honey, how are you doing?' Just 'You're decelerating on the putter.'" He took the comment seriously, though, and shot a 66 on Saturday. Unfortunately, he bogeyed the final two holes on Sunday and finished tied for eleventh.

In New Orleans, on a cool, wet, and extremely windy first weekend in April, Payne played well again at the Freeport-McMoRan Classic. He led after the first two rounds, but then on Saturday he dropped seven shots in eight holes. Payne didn't give up, though, and came charging back on Sunday. At the seventeenth green, having pulled to within one shot of the lead, Payne stroked a beautiful 18-foot birdie putt that seemed suspended in midair, rolling right over the edge of the hole but refusing to drop. On 18, he came close again, this time with a 25-footer that was headed right for the center of the cup but stopped two inches short. As the ball ran out of gas, Payne dropped his putter and covered his eyes with his hands. He finished tied for second with Russ Cochran, one stroke behind the winner, Mike Standly.

Payne chose the Freeport-McMoRan tournament to unveil another "signature" part of his persona, known especially well by fellow PGA Tour players, our close friends, and our children. Several weeks earlier Payne had some dental work done by Dr. Kurt H'Doubler, who had grown up with Payne in Springfield. Knowing what a jokester Payne was, Kurt made him a realistic-looking set of false teeth that were as awful and ugly as they could be and still looked genuine. Kurt gave the teeth to Payne at the tournament in New Orleans.

"These are great!" Payne exclaimed. "There are a few people I want to pull something on," he said with a laugh. Payne went to great pains in planning his practical jokes. Going to a novelty shop and purchasing some premade, ugly false teeth would have been far too easy. But having ones that a dentist custom-made from scratch, that was a different story. Apparently, Kurt did a great job—or an awful job, depending on how you look at it—because Payne had a lot of fun with those horrendously ugly teeth.

He experimented with the teeth in New Orleans, popping them in and out and smiling grotesquely at anyone who noticed him. The teeth were so realistic, many people thought Payne had been in an accident. Mike Hicks recalls Payne posing with two women at the tournament. The women had never met Payne before and were excited to be photographed with him, but when he smiled, exposing the horrible teeth, they did a double take. They didn't say anything to Payne, but the expression on their faces told the story. Worse yet, Payne didn't do anything to correct their mistaken impression. Somewhere in Louisiana, two women probably still believe that Payne Stewart had the worst teeth they had ever seen!

One of the first pro players to be duped by Payne's unusual dentures was our friend Paul Azinger. At the 1993 Masters, Payne popped the teeth into his mouth when he saw Zinger coming in his direction. "Hey, Paul, what's goin' on?" Payne mumbled.

Paul noticed the problem immediately. "Man, Payne! What happened to you?" he asked with genuine concern. "What's with your teeth?"

"I was with my mom last week," Payne said, sounding as though he had a mouthful of bubble gum, "and we were walking down the street in New Orleans, when some guy tried to attack my mom and steal her purse. I got into a scuffle with him, and he hit me. Caught me right in the teeth."

"Oh, man!" Paul winced. "That looks horrible. Are you OK?"

"Yeah, I'm all right, I guess."

"Is your mom all right?" Paul asked.

"Yeah, she's fine."

Just then, Payne reared back and made a high-pitched whirring sound, as though reeling in a fish. "Got you right in the boat, boy!" he chortled. "You swallowed it all, hook, line, and sinker. I just reeled you right in the boat!" Payne popped the teeth out and roared with laughter.

Zinger went wild! "Oh, you dog! I owe you big time, buddy," he warned Payne light-heartedly. A few weeks later, at the Memorial Tournament, Paul got even—on the golf course.

♦ ♦ ♦

Payne continued to play well after his ninth-place finish at the Masters. He had two more top-ten finishes in May at Houston and Dallas. I had made plans to take Chelsea and Aaron to Australia with me after Chelsea finished school at the end of May. It had been eighteen months since we had last visited my family. Payne was so busy with tournaments that it was too difficult for him to make the trip even though he loved going to Australia.

Several times each year, Payne and I took short vacations together without the children. We really enjoyed this time alone, and it helped us recharge our batteries for the hectic pace of our lives. We had become interested in scuba diving and had taken a four-day crash course with a PADI diving instructor in Orlando. I felt we had found a sport in which we were equals. Payne was an exceptional athlete, and even though I considered myself an athlete, too, we were not comparable. He was so much better at everything. It was frustrating at times, but I admired his talent.

The week before the children and I left for Australia, Payne and I went to Cozumel, Mexico. We arranged to meet our good friends Barry and Becky Snyder. We had a wonderful time and went on our first night dive while we were there. It was incredible. So many more sea creatures come out at night to feed. We saw the biggest crabs we'd ever seen. Payne and I loved every minute!

At the 1993 Memorial, at Jack Nicklaus's Muirfield Village, Payne was leading the tournament at 14-under par as he teed up on Sunday. He was partnered with Paul Azinger, who was starting the day at 11-under. Zinger was having a great year, despite a nagging pain in his shoulder. Paul and Payne wished each other luck, and then Paul said, "Look, if I go bad today, I don't want you to worry about me. You mind your own business and play your own game."

Paul didn't stumble, but Payne nearly did. When he was trying to lay up on the fifth hole, he hit it in the water. Shortly after that, on the ninth hole, he landed in the water again. Despite these setbacks, he was playing so well overall that, as they approached the eighteenth tee, he still led Corey Pavin, who had already finished his round and was in the clubhouse, and Paul by one stroke.

Payne teed off first at 18, and his 1-iron shot flew straight up the right side of the fair-

241

way in perfect position to approach the green. Unfortunately, however, the ball came to rest in a divot. Paul's 1-iron tee shot landed on the left side of the fairway—and stopped dead, plugged in the soft ground, 212 yards away from the hole. His next shot, a 5-iron, drifted left into the greenside bunker. Payne dug his second shot out of the fairway divot in the same direction as Paul's and landed in the same bunker.

Muirfield Village was one of Payne's favorite courses. He especially liked the way the bunkers were sanded because the ball almost always stayed on top. Even a powerfully hit shot into the sand at Muirfield typically didn't dive too deeply below the surface. Consequently, bunker shots were usually extremely playable.

Not this time however. When Payne finally spotted his ball in the sand, it looked like the top of an egg, just barely visible above the surface. Paul's shot was tough, but Payne's was horrendously difficult. He sized up the situation, stepped into the bunker, wiggled his shoes down into the sand—and blasted. The ball exploded out of the sand, popped up over the edge of the deep bunker, and rolled to within six feet of the hole. It was an incredible shot!

As the crowd roared, Payne climbed out of the bunker and walked up to the green, already eyeing the line of his putt. Even with a good bunker shot, Paul would have trouble getting inside Payne on this hole. But Paul Azinger is one of the best bunker players on the Tour. It wasn't over yet.

Paul stepped into the bunker and started fidgeting, checking every possible factor before he planted his feet solidly in the sand. He seemed to take forever to get ready, and when he finally swung the club, it was with tremendous force, firing under the sand beneath the ball, causing the ball to pop nearly straight up in the air and out of the bunker. The ball cleared the high edge of the bunker by a hair and hit the ground about ten feet from the pin. Up on the green, Payne watched in amazement as the ball rolled past him toward the hole. Rolling steadily on, it curled just enough and then dropped in the cup. Still in the bunker, Paul ripped off his visor, dropped to his knees in the sand, and let out a shout!

Payne was stunned. Suddenly, his 6-footer looked as though it were a mile away. A moment ago, he had been thinking that he needed to make the putt to win the tournament. Now he had to sink his putt to force a play-off. Payne stood over his ball, his heart pounding, his mind grinding. He hit it a little too hard, and the ball rolled past the hole by two feet. Clearly stunned, Payne didn't concentrate on his next attempt and missed it, too, dropping in a matter of seconds from first place to third in the tournament. The difference between finishing second or third didn't matter. Payne wanted to win.

Paul quickly approached Payne on the green and said, "Payne, I'm really sorry." It was an unusual statement for the winner of a championship, but understandable in light of his friendship with Payne.

"It's OK, bud," Payne replied sullenly. "That's part of it. That's the game."

In the clubhouse, Jon Brendle, our friend and a PGA rules official, tried to console Payne, but his best efforts were futile as well. Payne wanted to call me in Australia to be the first with the bad news. "Why don't you just wait a while?" Mike Hicks suggested, knowing how down Payne was.

"No, I might as well get it over with," Payne replied. When he called, I could tell there was no use in reviewing what had happened. All I could do was try to encourage him. The U.S. Open was coming up in two weeks, and I suggested that he start thinking about winning another major.

My pep talk must have worked because before Payne left the clubhouse locker room, he took time to mash some bananas inside Paul

Azinger's shoes. Paul didn't have to ask who had done it!

Payne played fabulously at the 1993 U.S. Open, held at Baltusrol Golf Club in Springfield, New Jersey. His steady, solid, superb shot-making had him in position to win. On the final day, Payne was paired with twenty-eight-year-old Lee Janzen, a soft-spoken but tough competitor. Lee sank a long birdie putt on 14, then chipped in at 16. Lee's four sub-70 rounds, including three birdies on the last five holes, represented U.S. Open championship golf at its best.

Lee remembers Payne approaching him on the green to congratulate him. Then, almost like a big brother, Payne put his arm around Lee's shoulder and said, "Your life is going to change. Make sure you take time to enjoy this."

As gracious as Payne was on the eighteenth green, when Lee went to put his shoes on after the U.S. Open, he, too, found them full of mashed bananas. Payne was disappointed to lose, but he was not devastated. "My day will come," he said.

In July, the week before the British Open at Royal St. George's, Payne finished second in the Bell's Scottish Open behind Jesper Parnevik. It was Payne's first encounter with the tall Swede, and he soon learned that they had much in common. Besides a quick sense of humor—Jesper's father is one of the more popular comedians in Sweden—Jesper had a penchant for flashy clothing. He quickly became known for wearing his hat with the bill upturned, cyclist style. Jesper recalls, "When I played my first season on the PGA Tour, Payne was one of the guys who made me feel most welcome."

Payne continued to play well throughout the remainder of the 1993 season and easily made his fourth consecutive Ryder Cup team. The usual cast of great players was on hand at the Belfry in England for what was rapidly becoming a grudge match on both sides of the Atlantic. Newcomers on the U.S. team that year included Jim Gallagher Jr., Davis Love III, and Lee Janzen.

In the first day foursomes match, Payne and Paul Azinger were beaten by Ian Woosnam and Bernhard Langer 7 & 5. Paul and Payne had looked forward to playing together, but it turned out to be a disaster of a match. Tom Watson, the American team captain, sat Payne down and didn't play him that afternoon. Rather than getting angry or embarrassed for being benched, Payne spent the afternoon on the practice tee, preparing to play the following day. To Payne, the Ryder Cup was not about individual achievement. If he could help the team better by sitting out a match and letting someone who was hot take it to the Europeans, he was comfortable with that. In the meantime, he'd make sure he was ready when his next opportunity to play came.

Payne was ready the next morning. Tom Watson paired Payne with Raymond Floyd, a veteran of seven previous Ryder Cup teams. Perhaps Tom knew that Raymond would be a help to Payne on the course. Raymond had partnered with Fred Couples at the 1991 Ryder Cup matches, and they had been a formidable duo. Whatever it was, it worked. Payne played incredible golf during the remainder of the matches. He and Raymond beat Peter Baker and Barry Lane 3 & 2 in the morning foursomes, and then they defeated José Maria Olazábal and Joakim Haeggman 2 & 1 in a grueling four-ball birdie fest in the afternoon. Payne then went on to beat Mark James 3 & 2 in their singles match on Sunday. Both Payne and Raymond led the U.S. team in points won, with three each. But all that mattered was bringing home the Cup, which the U.S. team did, winning the matches 15-13.

Payne also played a pivotal role in one of the more bizarre Ryder Cup controversies in recent memory. It started out innocuously enough as a private conversation between Payne and Paul Azinger during the summer of 1993, six months after the inauguration of Bill Clinton as president and three full months before the first tee shots were struck in Ryder Cup play. In late spring of that year, before the Ryder Cup team had been finalized, Paul had jokingly told Payne that Clinton's election had been a great motivation for him. Payne had looked at Paul with a bewildered expression on his face because he knew that Paul was no fan of the new president.

"Yeah, my goal is to play well enough to make the Ryder Cup team so if they ask me to visit the White House, I can say no."

Payne had laughed at Paul's joke, but he also knew that Paul's dad had fought in the Vietnam War, a war that Bill Clinton had avoided. Payne and Paul talked about the potential awkwardness that such a Ryder Cup meeting might present. Both Payne and I—and Paul and Toni—had enjoyed our previous trips to the White House, a tradition for Ryder Cup teams. But for two conservative, patriotic guys like Payne and Paul, meeting President Bush was more comfortable than meeting President Clinton.

At the U.S. Open in June, when a reporter asked about the pending White House visit, Paul was extremely diplomatic. "If Tom Watson [the team captain] wants us to go to the White House, I'll go," Paul answered. Later that week, the same reporter asked Payne about visiting the White House. Payne jokingly replied, "Well, I know Azinger doesn't want to go. His dad fought in the Vietnam War, and he doesn't want to shake hands with a draft dodger." The reporter knew that Payne was jagging him, especially since he already had Paul's statement on the record.

Nevertheless, the story hit the press, making waves from Florida to Washington. The next day, Paul and Payne were on the putting green at Baltusrol. "What were you thinking about, man?" Paul asked.

"Well, you said it, didn't you?" Payne replied.

"Sure, I said it to *you*," Paul cracked back, "but I wasn't saying it to the whole world!" Payne apologized for the embarrassment he had caused Paul, and the two of them did go to Washington to meet the president. Both Paul and Payne shook President Clinton's hand, and if the president knew about the public flap over the visit, he didn't let on. His only comment to Paul was, "I need to take a bunker lesson from you."

✦ ✦ ✦

In October, Payne and I traveled back to the United Kingdom to play in the Dunhill Cup at St. Andrews in Scotland. Payne, Fred Couples, and John Daly teamed to win the Dunhill Cup for the U.S. The weather was extremely cold, and the guys had to play with several layers of clothing and wear beanies and gloves between shots. Nevertheless, it was a fun week.

In November, Payne won the Hassan II Trophy tournament in Morocco for the second year in a row. The tournament was unusual in that the pro-am included women pros as well as men. Also, one of the "hazards" was the constant threat that a player's golf ball might be snatched from the green or fairway by the wild monkeys that inhabited the surrounding trees. The prize money wasn't particularly large, but as a special honor to the champion, King Hassan II presented Payne with a gorgeous, ornate, jewel-embedded sword. Payne hand-carried the sword in a leather case through international customs. "I don't want to let that sword leave my sight," he said. "I wasn't going to flash it around or anything, but I didn't want to check it in as luggage either!"

Next, Payne, the children, and I flew to California for Greg Norman's Shark Shoot-out and the Skins Game. We planned to spend

Thanksgiving in Palm Springs with Paul and Toni Azinger and their daughters, Sarah-Jean and Josie. From there, we were scheduled to fly by private jet to Los Angeles and then on a commercial carrier to Sun City in Bophuthatswana.

Payne had a way of making special memories with people. For instance, just before he was to play in the 1993 Skins Game tournament at Bighorn Golf Club in Palm Desert, we received a request from the Make-A-Wish Foundation, the organization that works to grant special requests for terminally ill patients. They told Payne about Joel Broering, a seventeen-year-old boy from St. Henry, Ohio, who had been diagnosed with leukemia in 1991. Joel was an avid golf fan, and Payne was one of his heroes. Joel had asked to meet Payne, and the Make-A-Wish Foundation wanted to arrange a meeting if Joel's treatment schedule and Payne's tournament schedule would allow.

To Payne, it was more than possible; it was imperative. Joel was flown to the Skins Game in Palm Desert, and Payne literally lifted him out of the car and into a golf cart. He took Joel along for a practice round and carried him when Joel wanted to get closer to the action. After the practice round, Payne took Joel into the clubhouse to meet the other players: Arnold Palmer, Fred Couples, and Paul Azinger.

251

We had arranged with Payne's clothing suppliers to provide Joel with two sets of knickers, kneesocks, golf shirts, and tam-o'-shanter caps, similar to those Payne was wearing in the two-day tournament. Throughout the Skins Game, Payne called Joel "The Star," emphasizing that Joel was the real star on the course that weekend. When Payne won the tournament—his third Skins victory in as many years, an accomplishment that no other golfer had ever achieved—he presented the trophy to Joel as a gift.

"It was the highlight of my life," Joel later said.

Following the Skins Game, we were going to Sun City, and the Azingers were going to Los Angeles so Paul could have a biopsy on his shoulder. Payne invited Paul and his family to join us aboard the private plane we were taking back to L. A. During the short flight, Paul pulled out the film plates from his recent MRI. "Hey, check out my bone-scan pictures," Paul said as he handed the images to Payne. Payne held the scans up to the window of the small plane so he could see them better. He noticed the dark spot on Paul's right shoulder. "What's this?" he asked as he pointed at the ominous image.

The normally upbeat, quick-witted

Zinger, known for his sardonic sense of humor, was unusually somber. "I don't really know yet," he replied quietly. "That's the problem right there." He pointed to the darkest spot.

Mike Hicks stretched over the seat, peering at the bone scans. "Wow!" he blurted. "You've gotta be kidding! That looks bad!" The color seemed to drain from Paul's face. I could tell that Payne was deeply concerned as well. Although he didn't want to say anything negative to Paul, the bone scans looked all too familiar. Payne's father had died of bone cancer.

The sun was dipping below the horizon as the Azingers deplaned, and Mike, Payne, and I headed for our flight to London. Paul was scheduled to see Dr. Jobe the next day, and Payne made him promise to let us know how the tests came out. It was several days before we heard the results of Paul's biopsy, and when word finally came, it wasn't from Paul or Toni—it was a call from Robert Fraley.

"Payne, I have some bad news for you," Robert said softly. "Paul has cancer."

Payne was stunned. He couldn't believe that his thirty-three-year-old friend had cancer. All the memories of his father's bout with the disease came rushing back. He remembered how quickly the cancer had consumed his father's body. Surely that wouldn't happen to

253

Paul. He immediately called Paul in California and spoke to him. He was relieved to hear his voice and to hear how confident Paul sounded about everything. Payne cared deeply for Paul, and he was worried about his friend.

Eleven days after Payne had given Joel Broering the Skins Game trophy, he telephoned the teenager and tried to brighten his spirits. "I can tell he is fading fast," Payne said following their phone call. Joel's spirit was strong, but his health was deteriorating rapidly. Two days after Payne's conversation with the courageous young man, Joel died.

Joel's death deeply saddened Payne and emphatically drove home the seriousness of Paul's condition as well.

As Christmas approached, Payne's mother asked him if we were going back to Missouri for Christmas. Because 1993 had been a very physically and mentally draining year, we really just wanted to stay home and have Christmas in Orlando and rest before the Tour started again in January. During an evening out with Robert and Dixie, we discovered that they, too, had been asked the same question by their families. So we came up with an idea.

On December 24, Payne and I woke early,

dressed the children, packed the presents for our family members, and met Robert and Dixie at the Executive Airport. We all boarded a private jet for a Christmas memory of a lifetime. The plane headed north to Payne's hometown of Springfield, Missouri, to surprise his mother for Christmas Eve breakfast. Payne's sisters, Susan and Lora, were in on our secret so they were waiting for us when we arrived.

We pulled up to Bee's house around 8:30 A.M. Bee answered the door and to her surprise, there stood her son and grandchildren! That was the best Christmas gift a mother could get. Payne went to the kitchen and started frying bacon, and we had a great hearty breakfast that lasted all morning.

We left Springfield around noon and headed the plane south to Winchester, Tennessee, Robert's hometown. His parents knew we were coming and had prepared a huge pot of Brunswick stew as well as other goodies. We ate outside in the garage they had converted into a dining hall for the festivities.

Around 4:00 P.M. we boarded the plane again, heading south to Auburn, Alabama, Dixie's hometown. We drove around Auburn looking at Christmas lights to give ourselves time to digest all the food we'd eaten! Then we joined Dixie's family for Christmas Eve dinner.

Robert joked that we could continue on and fly to Australia to see my parents, but it was already Christmas Day over there.

Chelsea and Aaron had a wonderful day. They received gifts at every stop. We boarded the plane in the dark and headed home. The children watched out the windows during the flight, looking for Santa's sleigh. We arrived in Orlando just after 11:00 P.M. and had the children tucked into bed just after midnight. Payne and I looked at each other and agreed that it would be hard to have a more wonderful day.

We would need such memories in the new year—it was going to be a tough one.

16

The Testy
Years

In the early 1990s, Payne and I began thinking about building another house. As we
traveled around the world, it was great fun to
note the features of beautiful homes we had
seen and to discuss what we wanted to build
into our dream home. Payne wanted a big
kitchen and a large den where he could informally entertain his friends. I wanted a large
master bedroom and a tennis court. We both
loved the Old World Mediterranean look. The
more we thought about the house, scribbled
our ideas, and sketched them on paper, the
larger the house grew. By the time we broke
ground, our dream home had ballooned to

about fifteen thousand square feet of floor space.

We decided to have a gated entry with a fence around the entire property and a wrap-around driveway. We planned for Mediterranean-style columns throughout the house, a fitness room, large bedrooms for the children as well as two guest rooms, a formal dining room, and majestic foyer. While I was more concerned about the layout and the interior features, Payne was determined to wire the house with enough high-tech electronic gadgets to make James Bond envious.

With all of Payne's knickers, golf shirts, and shoes to consider, the rough designs I drew out for the house included several large walk-in closets. Ours may have been one of the few houses in the country designed with the man's closet space in mind. We even included a separate closet for Payne's shoes.

We found an ideal five-acre piece of property on Pocket Lake, part of the Butler chain of lakes in Orlando. Payne was especially impressed with the parcel of land because it included an enclosed boat dock. Construction of new boat docks is permitted, but you now can't build one with walls. Payne had always been an avid fisherman—mostly catch and release. He had purchased a sleek new boat and was excited about spending time relaxing out on the water. Not surprisingly, when we finally began construction, the boathouse remodeling was the first thing to be completed.

We named our new home *Villa Serena*, "serene home." That's what it was intended to be, a sanctuary where we could come away from our hectic schedules and enjoy being a family. Much to our dismay, the house might have been more appropriately named "The House of Pain" by the time we were able to move in. The building process was a nightmare, with one delay after another, each one increasing the original price we had anticipated.

By early 1994, the building process was well underway—well, it was underway, anyhow. It was a far cry from going well. The frustration of constant price increases and construction delays began to wear on Payne. At one point, he told Kenny Williams, a building contractor and friend of ours, "I feel like I'm a fire hydrant spewing out one-hundred-dollar bills."

I visited the construction site almost every day, and with my background working with blueprints, I was able to oversee the building process without burdening Payne with a lot of the details. Still, the interminable delays and price increases took a toll on Payne's ability to concentrate on his golf game.

Even greater than the stress from the house was Payne's distress over Paul Azinger's cancer. He called Paul frequently for updates on his treatment and tried to be a source of encouragement to him. Payne was greatly relieved when Paul informed him that the cancer was localized in his shoulder and had not spread to his lymph nodes or other parts of his body.

"It's a type of cancer known as lymphoma," Paul explained, "and the doctors say it is the most curable type of cancer I could have. The statistical cure rate is about 90 percent."

Payne was thrilled when he called Paul and Toni at their hotel room after Paul's first chemotherapy treatment. "This is a cakewalk, Payne," Paul said. "Chemo is a piece of cake. I'm going to smoke this thing, buddy. The doctor says this cancer is beatable and I'm going to beat it. Chemo was easy. It was a snap."

Although Paul later changed his tune, suffering horrendous sickness as a result of his treatments, Payne was nonetheless amazed at his attitude. Paul was known as a sincere Christian and an intense competitor, and throughout his treatments his faith in the Lord kept getting stronger. Payne couldn't help noticing Paul's spiritual commitment, and it inspired him to renew his own.

A few years later, Payne explained how

Paul's cancer had caused him to renew his passion for God. "I think Paul getting cancer started me going in a more spiritual direction," he said. "I started talking to Paul about it, and I saw that he had this unbelievable faith. I picked his brain a little and asked him questions. When I saw how he handled the cancer and all the faith he had, I became more spiritual. I definitely believe that Paul's faith and good doctors brought him through that situation."

During 1994, however, Payne's concern for Paul weighed heavily on his heart and mind and undoubtedly affected his concentration on the golf course. Payne's game suffered most of all, though, because of an extremely unwise decision we made.

Although he had not won a tournament on the PGA Tour during 1993, Payne finished sixth on the money list, earning a whopping $982,875. His stroke average was 69.82, and he had twelve top-ten finishes in the twenty-six tournaments he entered. He finished second five times and third three times, so clearly he was playing incredibly well. That in itself attracted a lot of attention from equipment companies, who offered Payne large sums of money to endorse their products. He was looking for anything that would get him into the top spot more often.

Payne's previous contract to play Wilson golf products had expired. Equipment representatives contacted us constantly, trying to lure Payne away from the clubs and ball he had played so successfully. We rejected most of the deals out of hand, but then we received an offer that was too tempting to ignore.

One of the top golf equipment companies offered us a sizable contract for Payne to play their products. At the time, he was playing so well that he felt he could play almost any club and ball with equal effectiveness and success. The drawback to the contract, however, was that it required Payne to play a different style of club and a different make of ball. One such change would have been difficult enough; two significant changes at the same time could be disastrous.

Payne talked to Robert Fraley; Robert talked to Chuck Cook; Chuck talked to Dick Coop and Mike Hicks. The overwhelming consensus was that this deal might be more than we bargained for. On the other hand, we reasoned that Payne was playing incredibly well, and the new contract would virtually pay for the new house, plus more. Maybe we could do it. . . .

We signed the contract. The new clubs that Payne was required to play were investment-cast clubs, or "cavity backed" clubs as they are more popularly known. They are wonderful clubs for the serious amateur competitor, with a large "sweet spot" to help compensate for shots that are not struck dead center. To this point in his career, Payne had played a solid, forged-blade type of club, a more accurate club head, ideal for a "feel" player like Payne, who depended on instant feedback from the club and ball to help him place his shots correctly.

The new ball was a two-piece ball, which added even more backspin to his shots. The end result was that he had no control over how far the ball would fly each time he hit it. Between the increased spin and the club's compensation, all of Payne's shots began to feel the same to him. "What's wrong here?" Payne asked again and again as he tried to get an accurate feel for the clubs and ball. When he couldn't alter the effects of the club impacting the ball, he began to tinker with the one thing his father had warned him never to touch—his swing.

Chuck Cook quickly realized the devastating effects these changes might have on Payne's game. As Payne was preparing to play in the 1994 Tucson Open, he and Chuck met to practice at the PGA West Orange Grove course in Palm Springs. When Payne pulled out his new clubs, Chuck was shocked to see that the equipment company had sent Payne a set of clubs that were exactly the same as the clubs they were selling to amateurs. The irons had an offset shaft with square grooves on the club face, the kind of clubs a beginning golfer might play, not the third-leading money winner on the PGA Tour.

"Oh, it's OK, Chuck," Payne tried to reassure his coach. "I can hit 'em."

Chuck wasn't so sure. Payne had always hit extremely long iron shots, and Chuck just couldn't see that happening with the new clubs and the two-piece ball. The engineering simply did not allow for it. "OK, let me walk off some distances," Chuck said. He took some stakes and walked out 100 yards, placed a stake in the ground, and then another every 10 yards, out to about 240 yards. "Now, go ahead and hit, and let me know when you feel that you've hit a good one, and we'll see how far the ball flies with each club," Chuck instructed.

Payne started with his pitching wedge, but the ball was practically backing up in the air, it was spinning so much. On his best shots, Payne was hitting the wedge only one hundred yards, a fine distance for a beginner on a junior high golf team. Every club distance was similarly short: he hit his 8-iron 143 yards. His 2-iron, which Payne often used off the tee when danger loomed, flew a mere 183 yards on his best shot. He normally hit a 6-iron 183 yards, not a 2-iron!

Chuck charted each good shot and then walked in shaking his head. When he showed Payne the reduced distances, Payne said, "Chuck, that can't be right. Your distances must be off."

Chuck looked at him skeptically, but he knew that Payne had to see it for himself. "OK, you walk with me, and let's check these yardages." Together the guys remarked the yardage stakes. Chuck's distances were correct. Payne's shots were much shorter than the clubs and balls he was accustomed to playing. To be sure, they went through the same routine, hitting balls and charting the distances. The results were the same.

Payne went to Tucson and had a tough time playing the new ball and clubs. He continued to work on his game, but the results weren't much better at his next two tournaments. Then finally, at the Bob Hope Classic in Palm Springs, he finished fifth, after a final round of 63.

"Hey, maybe I'm gonna be OK with these clubs and ball," he said to Chuck.

"We'll see," Chuck replied, fully aware that for Payne, the clubs he used most in Palm Springs were a driver and a wedge. Since he was still playing the Whale driver, he was certain of a fair number of good tee shots. Chuck's worst fears were soon realized. Payne kept trying to get the ball to go farther with his irons, and it was just not happening. "That's when he began compensating, and he messed up his swing by doing that," Chuck recalls.

"He got to the place where he was swinging with his body so far in front of the ball, trying to diminish the loft, that he got to swinging real steep, trying to make the ball go farther. And it just wasn't working for him. As a 'feel' player, Payne was totally lost. A more analytical type of player might have been able to figure some way to make up for the differences, but Payne didn't process information that way. He had to feel the shot. When he couldn't accurately feel the ball coming off the club, he was in big trouble."

Payne's game went progressively downhill in 1994. Not only was he not winning, he wasn't coming close! With each passing tournament, Payne grew more frustrated with his new clubs. After a while, he didn't even want to be on the golf course. It wasn't fun for him if he wasn't contending seriously.

He became so disgusted that he avoided practicing. Instead, he preferred to go out on his boat and sulk. He spent long hours out on the lake, ostensibly fishing, but frequently he did more drinking than fishing. Payne knew that he couldn't drown his golf course demons with alcohol, but for a while, he seemed intent on trying.

His frustration with his golf game showed up in other areas of his life. Ordinarily, when Payne walked into a room, his countenance lit up the place. Now he was frequently downcast, moody, and sullen. Often he was short with people he loved; so much so that our good friend Lamar Haynes, one of Payne's college roommates, referred to this period in our lives as "the testy years." Even his relationship with Mike Hicks, his caddy since 1988, grew strained. "I think we need to take a break from each other for a while," Payne told Mike.

"Yeah, I agree. We're not winning anything anyhow." Mike went back to his home in North Carolina, where he and his family started a business embroidering sports logos onto clothing.

Payne's 1994 season was his worst since he had earned the right to compete on the Tour in 1982. He had only two top-ten finishes in twenty-three tournaments, no wins, and he plummeted to number 123 on the PGA money list.

Payne became so discouraged that he was ready to quit the game. One night he said, "I'm gonna quit. We don't need the money, and I don't need the aggravation."

His words didn't surprise me. I knew how disappointed he had become, and to me the high-priced contract wasn't worth it. What good is money without happiness? I knew Payne would do well at whatever he wanted to do, whether on the golf course or off.

Nevertheless, I was not about to let him walk away from the game he loved without a fight. I put on my own "game face" and said, "Oh, yeah? You've played golf since you were four years old. You've always wanted to play golf for a living. What else are you going to do?"

My words brought Payne back to reality. He knew in his heart that golf was what he was good at. That's what he did for a living, and he did it better than about 99 percent of the men in the world. He calmed down and determined that he would learn how to win with the new ball and clubs.

As the year continued, however, something more was happening inside Payne, something imperceptible at first, but nonetheless real—something that had been stirring in his spirit for a long time.

17

Working Out the Kinks

B y mid-May 1994, we felt confident that our friend Paul Azinger was well on his way to recovery. Payne had kept in close contact with Paul, going over to visit him in Bradenton and talking regularly by phone. Paul lost all his hair due to the chemotherapy treatments, but he handled his baldness with his usual sense of humor. Payne said, "I knew Paul was going to be fine when I heard him say, 'Hey, bald is in. Just look at all those NBA basketball stars; they all have bald heads. As a matter of fact, as soon as I lost my hair, I went out to our basketball hoop in the backyard. Within seconds, I was dunking shots.'" Obviously, Paul was recovering well. Although it would be some time before life returned to normal for our friends, Payne worried much less over Paul's condition as the year progressed. By 1995, Paul was back on the PGA Tour. His faith in God and his physical recovery were a tremendous inspiration to us.

In January 1995, we finally moved into Villa Serena, two and a half years after we first broke ground on the property. Payne was getting ready to leave Orlando for the West Coast swing, and we were scheduled to move in while he was out of town. Payne had grown so irritated with the slow construction progress and so tired of answering questions about when we'd be in that before we actually had our certificate of occupancy, we threw a couple of sleeping bags on the floor and slept in our new bedroom the night before he left, simply so he could say, "I slept in the house last night. It's almost done."

Although Payne loved our new home, construction problems continued to plague us even after we moved in, which distracted Payne from his golf. Kenny Williams, our contractor friend who lived nearby, became an invaluable aide to Payne and me. We hired him to do the punch-sheet repairs on the house, and Kenny not only fixed whatever was wrong, he improved it! From then on, Kenny took responsibility for keeping the house in shape.

Everything from air-conditioning to landscaping became his domain. Payne trusted Kenny's judgment, skill, and integrity, which freed Payne to concentrate on playing golf rather than worrying about plumbing leaks and a long list of picayune problems that needed to be fixed at our home. He and Kenny became good friends, and Kenny became a regular part of our "family." Slowly but surely, the pressure lifted off Payne's shoulders.

Every media person who covered golf knew that Payne Stewart was "eminently quotable," that whenever they needed a PGA Tour player's opinion on almost any subject they could almost always wrangle a quote out of Payne. When he played poorly, Payne sometimes wasn't as cooperative or as patient with the press, but he always spoke his mind, and the media were right there to pick up on every word he said. Consequently, he was often portrayed in the press as cocky, arrogant, surly, churlish, or rude. Interestingly, people who knew him well, including the players who competed against him, whether they liked Payne or not, did not see Payne in that light.

"He could be a real jackass at times," one PGA Tour player said, "and say some things that may not have been appropriate at the moment, but he never purposely said or did anything to hurt anyone."

At Robert Fraley's and my insistence, Payne agreed to attend a media relations class in Dallas. The class was good for Payne in several ways. Just to admit that he might benefit from such training was a major step forward, but he also learned how to provide the media with the sound bites they needed without sticking his foot in his mouth . . . or at least not quite so often.

After attending the media training seminar, Payne was somewhat more cautious about teasing the other players, and he thought through his comments more carefully for the media. He still gave his opinions, often with the point of a needle, but he was more judicious in the way he worded what he wanted to say.

Payne began the 1995 season well, finishing fourth at the Phoenix Open and fifth at the Pebble Beach AT&T. Although he was still struggling with the new clubs and ball, he was getting better at compensating for the changes they made in his game. His equipment sponsor helped by designing him a new set of clubs.

Payne never blamed his poor 1994 performance on the new clubs and ball. Instead, he took the responsibility onto his own shoulders.

"It's not the equipment; it's my attitude that needs improving," he said. "I've been my own worst enemy. When I missed a cut, all I wanted to do was go home, sit in my boat, and feel sorry for myself, instead of practicing and working on my game."

In March, Payne narrowly missed winning the Players Championship—considered by many on the PGA Tour as the "fifth major" because of the difficult configuration of the course, with extremely hard greens, narrow fairways, and deep rough. He tied for third with Corey Pavin and Gene Sauers, only one stroke behind Bernhard Langer and two behind the champion, Lee Janzen. Lee later said, "Payne seemed to take on a role almost like a big brother to me as we played together in the final group on Sunday. After Baltusrol in '93, we had played together on the Ryder Cup team and had gotten to be pretty good friends. So at the Players, even though we were trying to beat each other, his attitude seemed to be, 'If I don't win this thing, then you better!' I felt that Payne was genuinely happy for me."

By the time he got to the Shell Houston Open in May, Payne was back on his game; if not his "A" game, at least a strong A-minus. Our friend Scott Hoch, who along with his wife, Sally, had first encouraged us to move to

Orlando eleven years earlier, was nursing a five-stroke lead over John Cook and Charlie Rymer at the end of the third round. Payne was seven shots back. After nine holes on Sunday, Scott stretched his lead to six shots ahead of the pack at The Woodlands. His game had been nearly flawless that weekend, until he became protective and started missing opportunities to maintain or increase his lead.

Playing patiently and consistently, three groups in front of Scott, Payne chipped away at the leaders all afternoon. When he finished his round with a birdie on 18, Payne was still two shots off the lead. Scott bogeyed the sixteenth hole; on 17 he hit his tee shot into the fairway. He then pushed his second shot, a 7-iron from 148 yards out, landing in the water to the right of the green. When Scott took a double-bogey, Payne suddenly had a one-shot lead! On 18, Scott approached the green looking at a 40-foot putt for birdie. Scott waved to Payne, who was waiting patiently next to the green, and Payne called back gingerly, "Knock it in."

Scott did. We were going to a play-off, Payne's first in a long time.

If Scott's long putt on 18 shook Payne, he didn't show it. He went about his business, hitting a great tee shot as they replayed number 18 as a play-off hole. His approach found the green, leaving him a 15-foot putt for birdie.

Meanwhile, Scott hooked his drive into the left rough. Next, his approach shot flew the green, landing in the back side of the bunker on a downhill slope—an awful lie. The angle from which he attempted to hit the ball was so awkward that while he was trying to get into position, Scott lost his balance. In front of the large gallery watching around the green and the Sunday afternoon television audience, he toppled over backward onto the ground. The entire gallery laughed along with him. Scott picked himself up, brushed off, and tried to get into position again. This time, he quickly blasted the ball out of the sand, sending it twenty feet past the hole.

Lying two, Payne could breathe easier. He hit his 15-foot putt a little more firmly than he wanted and left himself with a 4-footer coming back. Scott left his putt for par just right of the hole and tapped in for bogey. Payne later said, "When I looked at my putt for par, I said to myself, 'OK, this is the time to be a champion again, so put a good stroke on it.'" He bore down on the 4-footer and dropped it right in the heart of the cup. After a four-year dry spell on the PGA Tour, Payne had won again!

Fully aware that his victory had come at the expense of a friend, Payne went to Scott and tried to offer kind words. Scott was understandably distraught. He had started the day with a five-stroke lead, stretched it to seven strokes, and ended the day in second place. He wasn't much in the mood for words of any kind, declining the usual postchampionship interview. Nevertheless, a slew of reporters peppered him with questions as he made his way to the clubhouse parking lot. Scott attempted to make light of the loss, saying, "You can print it now. That's why 'Hoch' rhymes with 'choke.'"

When Payne heard about Scott's statement, he felt awful for him. Payne knew all too well how the word "choke" seared into a player's heart. "I hate that word," Payne said sadly. "I'm sorry to hear Scott use it. It's a nasty, hard word. . . . But Scott's a great player. He'll bounce back."

The victory did more for Payne than simply add another piece of silver to our trophy case. It inspired him to believe he could win another major—and the U.S. Open was coming up.

Payne arrived later than planned at Shinnecock Hills, where the 1995 Open was held. Originally, he had been slated to work with Chuck Cook on Monday, as he had done the previous week when he finished in the top ten at the Kemper Open near Washington, D.C. By arriving late, Payne missed his session with

Chuck, who was already committed to working with Tom Kite and Corey Pavin on Tuesday and Wednesday. Payne was miffed, and he told Chuck that he was going to go it alone from then on. He had felt for some time that, no matter what he and Chuck came up with, as long as he was playing the clubs and balls he had committed to playing, nothing they did would be a lasting change. He was not yet halfway through the contract he had signed with the new equipment company. They had paid us well, and Payne desired to honor the commitment he had made.

Payne and Chuck parted amicably, and Corey Pavin won the U.S. Open that week. Payne was genuinely happy for Corey, but it was like a smack in the face. He couldn't help but wonder whether he might have been the one to bring home the trophy had he kept his appointment with Chuck.

Payne played well at both the U.S. Open and the British Open in 1995, but he fell short of achieving one of his main goals—earning enough points to make the Ryder Cup team. Because of the disappointing season he'd had in 1994, his two-year accumulation of points was too low unless he could win a number of tournaments or a major. Because he was playing so well, however, Payne thought that Lanny Wadkins, the 1995 Ryder Cup captain, might choose him as one of his captain's picks. Just prior to the selection deadline, Payne was paired with Lanny during the first two rounds of the Buick Open at Warwick Hills in Grand Blanc, Michigan. Payne shot two outstanding rounds of 65 to lead the tournament after two rounds, eventually finishing tied for eighth. When Curtis Strange missed the cut at the Buick Open, Payne thought that it might increase his own chances of being picked. Instead, Lanny chose Fred Couples and Curtis to round out the team.

Despite a nagging back problem that had troubled him for more than a year, Fred had been playing well. Lanny's choice of Curtis Strange, however, proved controversial from the start. Curtis had not won a tournament on the PGA Tour since the 1989 U.S. Open, and when he faltered during the matches, many people questioned his position on the team even more. But Lanny stood by his choice. Payne could only sit at home and watch the U.S. team go down to an ignominious defeat. "I thought I had a pretty good shot," he said, "but apparently Lanny didn't think so. I was playing well enough to be on the team. I didn't make it, they didn't win, and life goes on."

✦ ✦ ✦

To help Payne get through Ryder Cup week, we drove over to Tampa, Florida, and caught a plane to the Cayman Islands. We went scuba diving with the stingrays and hung out on the beach for four days. Because Payne was so deeply disappointed by not being on the Ryder Cup team, it caused him to sit back and reflect on what was really important in his life. We spent hours just talking. He told me then that the most important thing to him was our relationship and his relationship with his children. He wanted us to spend more time together as a family. He wanted to be there with his children while they were growing up. He didn't want to blink and miss it. He had decided that he didn't want golf to be his driving force in life anymore. Golf would have to take a backseat; his family was much more important.

Dick Coop had suspected from his earliest days of working with Payne that he had some sort of disorder that made it difficult for him to focus for long on anything. He needed a raft of stimuli around him all the time. Lana Cook, Chuck's wife, said that when she first visited in our home she was amazed at the amount of activity—Payne's loud music blaring, the big-screen television on in the great room, the small

TV blasting in the kitchen, phones ringing, voices coming out of intercoms, various people trying to have a conversation, others scurrying in all directions. "It was overwhelming," Lana said.

Payne needed that sort of controlled chaos around him, and he thrived on it. In 1995, Dick Coop formally diagnosed Payne with attention deficit disorder. The doctors prescribed Ritalin, hoping to improve Payne's ability to focus. Payne tried it for a while, but we really couldn't discern any measurable difference between the days he took the drug and the days he didn't. Payne stopped taking the drug, but simply being aware of the problem helped him to exert a greater effort to concentrate.

Always looking for something new and challenging, Payne decided he wanted to develop his own line of clothing when our contract with NFL Properties expired near the end of 1995. Payne had been wearing the NFL team colors for six years and had enjoyed a good relationship with NFL Properties. Known for his flashy haberdashery, Payne and a group of designers worked together to create a line of golf clothing that would include his trademark knickers, kneesocks, shirts, and hats. The clothing they designed all bore Payne's name, plus an easily recognizable logo image of Payne wearing knickers, standing with his legs crossed, leaning on a golf club.

Beyond the golf clothing, Payne was excited about developing an entire line of men's casual wear, including sport jackets, jeans, shorts, slacks, and dress shirts. "Ralph Lauren, watch out!" Payne quipped.

Payne ranked twelfth on the PGA Tour's money list in 1995, earning $866,219, with six top-ten finishes. He closed out the year by playing in the Hong Kong Open and then invited Lee Janzen to play with him in the Diner's Club Matches in Palm Springs. In the first round, they drew Paul Azinger and Phil Mickelson as opponents.

Talk about needling! The jibes were flying back and forth among the guys, playfully poking fun at one another, making sarcastic predictions and verbally shredding each other—all in fun, of course.

"Just take the last four holes out of your yardage book," Lee told Payne. "We won't need those holes, because we'll have those guys dusted by then."

Payne felt compelled to use Lee's comment to needle Paul and Phil. "Ohhhhh! You guys can take the last four holes out of your yardage books, 'cause we'll have you guys dusted by then!" Payne should have kept that information to himself. If there are two guys not to give any incentives to, they would be Paul and Phil.

Payne played incredibly, shooting eight under. On the final four holes, however, Phil and Paul came storming back. On 15, with Payne and Lee two up, Payne had an 8-footer, straight in, uphill. Phil was in a bunker about sixty feet away. It looked almost certain that Payne and Lee were going to cruise the rest of the way home to victory. But then Phil Mickelson, who was known for making seemingly impossible shots, did it again. He holed his bunker shot!

When Payne missed his putt, Paul and Phil poured it on. Phil birdied the last four holes, winning each one—the same holes that Lee and Payne had suggested they tear out of their yardage books. It was a loss that the guys were not going to live down anytime soon. Paul and Phil would make certain of that!

18

Awakening
the Giant

In early 1996, we began to sense a need for a stronger religious emphasis in our home. We wanted our children to have at least as strong of a spiritual foundation as we had enjoyed in our own upbringings. Payne and I both had gone to church intermittently since childhood, and our faith was important to us. After we married, we visited a wide variety of churches, although we never aligned ourselves with any particular congregation. With Payne's career, it was difficult to be deeply involved in a local church because we were gone for at least half the Sundays each year—or hoped to be!

Both of our children were now school-aged. Aaron was in first grade and Chelsea in fourth. Chelsea had been attending a private school in downtown Orlando, which was usually a thirty-minute drive from Lake Buena Vista. But as anyone who has ever driven Interstate 4 knows, a single accident can turn that stretch of roadway into a two-hour nightmare traffic jam. Payne and I hoped to find a good school closer to home.

Corey Pavin's wife, Shannon, spoke highly of the school their children attended. It turned out that The First Academy, an ancillary ministry of First Baptist Church, was located on the west side of downtown Orlando, closer to our home. We knew that the Pavins were sincere Christians who held many of the same values that Payne and I did, so we felt strongly that we should look into the school. When we visited The First Academy, we were quite impressed. We became confident that our children would receive a top-notch education in a spiritually based environment, couched in love and discipline.

When we enrolled Aaron and Chelsea, we were thrilled with the way they responded to their new school. They loved their teachers and new friends and felt abundant love in return. Payne and I dropped by the campus regularly, driving the children to and from school and taking them to various activities. Soon much of our lives off the golf course began to center on our children's school. The faculty and families of The First Academy treated Payne like any other parent, not as a golf superstar. They accepted us for who we were as people, not simply based on what Payne did professionally. Before long, our circle of friends included a number of The First Academy parents.

Because of our desire for a stronger spiritual foundation in our home, and our children's involvement at the Christian school, we found ourselves drawn back to church more frequently, although we still could attend only sporadically. With the children in Christian school, however, every day was like Sunday. When they brought home Bible verses to learn for their classes, we made copies each week for both cars and reviewed them with the children to and from school each day. We learned some of the Scriptures right along with Aaron and Chelsea.

The school's curriculum emphasized the important interaction between faith and reason in every academic area. As Chuck Cook often said, "Aaron and Chelsea brought the Christian life home every day from school." The resulting spiritual stirrings within Payne caused him to strive to be a better person.

In recent years, much has been written

about the spiritual transformation that took place in Payne; but it wasn't like the apostle Paul's experience on the road to Damascus, where he suddenly saw the light. With Payne, it was more like awakening a giant faith within him. His faith in the Lord had been there since childhood and had shaped his life for years, but now it was beginning to be expressed in practical ways. Payne and I wanted to live the Christian life, not just talk about it.

Just as Payne had expressed to me on the beach in the Cayman Islands, we made a point of scheduling more time together as a family. We went skiing in Aspen, Colorado, for a week in February. We traveled to the Florida Keys for four days in early June. During our trip to the Keys, we went deep-sea fishing. We were fortunate enough to come upon a school of Mahi Mahi. It was amazing. We couldn't get the fish in the boat fast enough. Payne hooked a bull straight off, so he was busy trying to get it into the boat. Aaron was catching fish as big as he was. I was worried that he was going to be pulled overboard by these huge fish, but he hung in there. Both Chelsea and I were reeling in fish left and right. By the time we were finished, we had caught our maximum of seventy fish. The captain prepared a couple of fish for us to take home, and he sold the rest to restaurants in the area. We had so much fun on that trip.

Two weeks later, we went to Nantucket for our annual vacation with three other couples from Payne's days at SMU—Todd and Melanie Awe, Barry and Becky Snyder, and Billy and Cathy Lacy. We have maintained such a close friendship over the years that even though we didn't see each other often, whenever we were together as a group, it seemed like we had never been apart.

Throughout 1996 and 1997, Payne played well, even with equipment he did not particularly like. He had seven top-ten finishes each year and earned more than $500,000 on the PGA Tour both years as well. In 1996, he tied for third at the Honda Classic and finished second at the Walt Disney World–Oldsmobile Classic, losing by one stroke to the hot new phenomenon on the PGA Tour, Tiger Woods, who had just turned pro. Payne was one of Tiger's strongest supporters when he first came out on the Tour. Payne wasn't jealous of the huge endorsement fees Tiger received or of the vast amount of hoopla surrounding his every move. He knew that Tiger was going to be great for the game of golf, and he and Tiger became friends. Nevertheless, after coming so close to beating Tiger at the Walt Disney World Classic, Payne told Chuck Cook, "I'd like to have another shot at him one day!"

Payne had noticed a soreness in his right elbow during the Walt Disney tournament, but he was told that the pain was caused by tendinitis. He had received a couple of cortisone shots and thought the pain would subside with time. He went on to play at the Sarazen World Open in Georgia and finished third. He had a couple of weeks off, then prepared to play in the Wendy's 3-Tour Challenge in Las Vegas. The PGA Tour Team won the event, and we then traveled on to Springfield, Missouri, for Thanksgiving. Payne played golf sporadically over the next four weeks but continued to be bothered by the pain in his elbow. Robert Fraley was concerned that Payne's condition had not improved. He made an appointment for Payne with a doctor he knew in New York City. Dr. Stephen J. O'Brien had met Robert through his association with the New York Giants football team. Steve was the Giants' team physician.

We flew to New York on December 26. Payne was unaware that he had crossed paths with Dr. O'Brien over three years earlier. During the 1993 U.S. Open at Baltusrol in New

Jersey, Steve had coerced his eight-year-old son, Conor, into going to the tournament with him. Conor was a fantastic young athlete, but he had recently had brain surgery and had been told that it was unlikely that he would ever play contact sports again. Steve was hoping to get his son interested in golf by watching the best professionals compete at the U.S. Open. When they arrived in the parking lot, they saw one of the top U.S. players arriving to play. Conor approached him and asked for his autograph, but the player turned him down. He returned to Steve with tears in his eyes. Suddenly, another golfer walked up behind him and said, "Hey, buddy! How are you doing? Why don't you hang out with me?" It was Payne. He proceeded to sign an autograph for Conor and continued to acknowledge him while he practiced that day. Conor was so thrilled that he followed Payne all day long. He is now fourteen, loves golf, and shoots in the mid-80s. Payne had no idea that the small boy that he was kind to that day at Baltusrol had a father from whom Payne would seek help three years later.

At the appointment in New York, Dr. O'Brien looked at Payne's X-rays in what they call "Round the Clock" views and discovered that Payne had a loose chip inside his elbow. On December 31, Payne underwent an arthroscopy of his right elbow. Interestingly, they found two loose chips in his elbow. One was stuck in the ulnohumeral articulation and was difficult to reach. Knowing that opening Payne's elbow to get at this loose chip would be hard, Steve persisted in using a trochar to jack open the joint, as one would in raising a car to fix a tire. He was able to then successfully remove the other loose chip. Inspired by this success, this procedure became a technique that Dr. O'Brien has recommended to the orthopedic community.

Because of the elbow surgery, Payne didn't start the 1997 season until mid-February at the Tucson Open. When he returned to the Tour, Payne was surprised to learn of the locker-room buzz over a twenty-five-year-old player named Casey Martin. Casey was born with a rare circulatory disorder, Klippel-Trenauney-Webber Syndrome, making it nearly impossible for him to walk eighteen holes of golf without severe pain. Doctors agreed that Casey's condition was degenerative, that it would only get worse, and that walking the golf course—even if he could do it—was more than should be expected of him.

Later, when Casey Martin and the PGA Tour became embroiled in a lawsuit over his right to use a golf cart while playing, Payne was supportive of Casey. A quiet, personable young man, who had played his college golf with Tiger Woods at Stanford, Casey just wanted to play on the Tour, and was trying to earn the right to do so. The PGA Tour's position was that walking the course was an important part of the game; that a player who could ride would have an advantage. It was reasonable to assume that if they allowed Casey to ride, players with back injuries or other maladies also might expect to be able to ride a cart.

When a judge's ruling allowed Casey to join the PGA Tour, Payne welcomed him personally and publicly. "He still has to make the shots," Payne said, "no matter how he gets to them, whether walking or in a cart. Let the guy play." What bothered Payne the most in the Casey Martin case was that the PGA Tour players were not given a chance to vote on the matter. The Tour spent huge amounts of money fighting a losing cause to keep Casey out of the cart; but except for members of the PGA Tour Policy Board, the players were not formally consulted. That didn't seem right to Payne. Nevertheless, in the midst of a maelstrom of publicity swirling around him, Casey maintained a consistent Christian testimony, never losing his temper or speaking harshly against those who opposed him. Payne was tremendously impressed with Casey's poise, and even more so with the peace that Casey displayed under pressure. It was the sort of peace that was becoming more apparent in Payne's life.

One of the questions Payne and I were asked frequently was, "Who are your best friends on the Tour?" That was always a tough one to answer because although we have many wonderful friends on the PGA Tour, it's difficult to maintain close relationships with more than a handful of couples. Every week, we competed against one another; and no matter how strong the friendship, that competitive edge needs to be there in order to win.

That's probably another reason we established many of our friendships with people who knew us apart from the golf course. Some of Payne's best friends were the guys he knew from his SMU days—Barry Snyder, Todd Awe, Lamar Haynes, and Billy Lacy—who all remained close to Payne throughout his life. Payne needed some guys around him with whom he could just be himself, have fun, and not worry about where anyone stood on the PGA Tour statistic sheets. One guy with whom Payne forged such a friendship was Chris Millsaps.

Chris's daughter, Megan, is in the same grade as Chelsea at The First Academy. Each year, the fifth graders go on a campout at Wekiva Springs State Park, an overnight, fun-packed trip for the entire fifth grade, accompanied by some of the teachers and parents of the students. Payne and Chris were "counselors" in a couple of the boys' cabins. That was like letting thieves guard the bank! Those two were the biggest "kids" of all! They hit it off immediately because they were the jokesters at the camp. The subject of golf never even came up; they were just mischievous dads, having fun with the kids.

Before going to camp, Payne stopped by a toy store and loaded up on gags, including a bagful of rubber snakes, spiders, and other ominous-looking bugs. That night, after everyone was supposed to be gathered around a bonfire, Chris and Payne distributed their rubber snakes and bugs in all the wrong places, including the campers' bedding, the rest room facilities, anywhere they thought they could scare someone. They even put a rubber snake in the gas cap of a vehicle owned by one of the moms, knowing she wouldn't find it for several days. One teacher got even by sneaking into Chris's cabin and swiping some of his underwear. The teacher ran Chris's underwear up the camp flagpole for all to see.

Another man whom Payne got to know at the campout was J. B. Collingsworth, one of the ministers at First Baptist Church. J.B. and his wife, "Shugie," didn't fit the usual clergy stereotypes. They enjoyed being considered "just regular people," and their kind, gentle, loving spirits were contagious. Putting J.B. and Payne together at Wekiva, though, was dangerous! J.B. was as much a prankster as Payne and Chris. It was J.B. who got caught that night when the guys rattled the girls' cabins, attempting to scare them.

Payne loved cutting up with the kids at Wekiva. He'd do anything to cause trouble and have fun with them, and the kids tried to get him right back. One boy was giving Payne trouble all night long; so when the youngster wasn't looking, Payne slipped some packets of jelly in the boy's back pocket. Payne was wrestling around with the boy, and they were having a good time. Later, when the boy sat down, he heard a squishing sound. His entire backside was sticky with jelly.

Payne threw himself into helping in the kitchen, preparing the meals, cleaning up, the whole deal. Some of the parents were surprised to see him having so much fun, but Payne was just doing what he loved to do: pitching in, helping out, and serving others. He didn't do it to be noticed; he did it because that's who he was.

Payne's real passion in life was not golf—it was being a father. Payne loved doing anything with Aaron and Chelsea, whether it was driving them to school or helping to coach their sports teams. Beyond that, he just loved kids! On the golf course, he was known as a fashion plate, the consummate professional. Off the golf course, he was a jeans-and-T-shirt sort of guy, a dad who was just as comfortable in shorts and sneakers as he was in his knickers and gold-tipped golf shoes.

Not long after the overnight camping trip, a need arose at The First Academy for a volunteer coach for the fifth-grade girls' basketball team. "Hey, why don't we do it?" Chris suggested to Payne. "Our girls are playing, and we'll probably want to be there every game anyhow."

"Great!" Payne answered. "I know I can't be there for all the practices, but if we can do it together, I'd love to." Payne and Chris became the coaches of the team. Three other dads also attended the practices and games, so before long they, too, were coaches.

Chelsea's team had only nine players and five adult coaches! They looked like an NBA coaching staff. Payne and Chris were by far the

most vocal, yelling instructions and encouragement constantly during the practices and
games.

Five of the nine girls on the team could
barely dribble the ball, but Payne didn't mind.
He enjoyed teaching them the basics of the
game. One little girl couldn't even stand still
and dribble, let alone run, dribble the ball, and
shoot. Payne took a special interest in her,
working with her on the fundamentals of the
game. "Nice shot!" Payne encouraged if she
came anywhere close to hitting the rim. "Way
to go!" In the last game of the season, she
finally scored her first basket. To Payne, that
was tantamount to winning the Ryder Cup! He
was whooping and hollering loud enough to be
heard all over the gymnasium.

After the opening jump ball, Payne was
oblivious to everything but the game. During
one game, the girls were playing terribly, making bad passes, missing easy lay ups, and Payne
was going wild as a result. He was leaning forward, yelling directions from the bench, almost
down on his knees, bellowing at the girls.
Suddenly, the noise in the stands subsided, and
the only voice that could be heard in the gym
was Payne's, yelling, "You girls are clueless!
You just don't even have a clue!" Payne never
noticed that the entire gymnasium had fallen

silent, and every parent and child in the room could hear him. I grimaced at Payne and said, "Payne, you can't say that!" He looked back at me with a bewildered expression and replied, "But they are!"

I just shook my head, and he went on with his instructions for the next play. All the girls on the team thought it was funny that Mr. Stewart had called them clueless.

Chris and some of his other buddies got together occasionally to play cards, go to a ball game, or do some other activity just as a night out with the guys. All of the men were Christians, and most of them attended First Baptist Church in Orlando, although the "men's fellowship" was not a group connected to the church in any way; nor were their activities necessarily overtly "Christian." Men's Fellowship was just a name they had tacked on to their night out with the boys. Every so often, when Chris mentioned something about having a "men's fellowship," Payne's curiosity was piqued. "Well, when am I going to be invited to one of these men's fellowship meetings?" he wanted to know.

"I don't know," Chris teased him. "This group isn't for just anybody. You have to be invited; you can't just drop in. We have to get financial statements on you and do a background check. It's a whole process, and to tell you the truth, you may not be able to get in."

"Whooooooh, what do you mean I can't get in?" Payne roared. "You better let me know the next time you have one of those men's fellowships, and I better get an invitation!"

"We'll see," Chris answered with a twinkle in his eye.

The group met several more times without Payne, and whenever he heard about it, he got right after Chris. "Hey, I'm beginnin' to get a little insulted here. How come I never get invited to these men's fellowships? I feel like I need to be a part of this."

"All right, Payne," Chris said. "Next time we have a men's fellowship, I'll be sure to let you know."

True to his word, the next time the group met, Chris took Payne along. They met in the sparsely decorated apartment of one of the single fellows, Alan Avriett, a dentist. The other guys always called Alan by his first name, but as soon as Payne met him, he tagged Alan as "Doc" and the name stuck. As the guys set up the metal card table with folding metal chairs, Payne gawked all around at the bare walls. "Hey, Doc, how long have you lived here?" Payne wanted to know.

"Oh, about three years," Alan replied.

"Doc," Payne said as he rubbed his chin, still looking around the room, "nice art."

For a moment there was dead silence in the room. Except for Chris, the other guys didn't know Payne well and were unaware of his sense of humor. They weren't sure whether he was insulting their friend or not. Then somebody started to snicker, and all five guys convulsed in laughter. Payne was accepted immediately.

Payne grew to love his "men's fellowship" guys—Jim Maloof, Brian Bowen, Mike Lowder, Scott Taylor, Alan, and Chris. They treated him as one of them—just regular, every-day guys getting together without any of the hoopla or pretense sometimes associated with the church or the golf world. It wasn't a Bible study group; nobody preached or taught a lesson. They weren't a Promise Keepers–type of accountability group, helping one another to toe the line. They didn't even plan to sit around and talk about spiritual issues, although as could be expected in such a group, the conversations sometimes took on a spiritual tone. They were simply a group of guys who exerted positive peer pressure on one another as adult men.

Nor did they meet on a regularly scheduled basis; they'd call or run into each other somewhere, and one of the guys might say, "It's about time for another men's fellowship, don't you think?" They'd plan some group activity and simply enjoy being with each other, whether going to a ball game or sitting around a card table playing penny-ante poker.

Before long, Payne became the point man, organizing many of the men's fellowship get-togethers. "Hey, it's time for a men's fellowship, isn't it? I need one," he'd say. "Let's get together next Monday night at my place to watch the Magic game and play a little cards."

The men's fellowship group was a good balance for Payne, one he enjoyed and needed. Despite the influence of his new, spiritually oriented friends, Payne could still be impatient with himself at times when he didn't play up to his expectations on the golf course, knowing that he was close but not quite where he wanted to be in his game. Beyond that, sometimes he unintentionally offended people by something he said or did.

For instance, he had a standing rule that he refused to sign golf balls other than the brand he was contracted to play. To do otherwise, Payne felt, was to promote another company's product. Consequently, when someone asked him to sign a ball from a different manufacturer, Payne often said, "Sorry, bud, I don't sign golf balls." He'd autograph hats, pictures, cards, T-shirts, and just about anything else within reason, but he would not sign a brand of balls he didn't play. People who weren't aware of Payne's contractual obligations didn't understand and sometimes took offense.

Payne didn't mind signing almost anything for genuine collectors, people who had a love for the game of golf. But Payne had little patience with the autograph mongers who collect autographs simply to sell them at greatly inflated prices. Moreover, he hated the idea of someone else profiting by using his name illegitimately. Knowing how much Payne loved children, a standard ploy of collectibles vendors was to pay a child a few dollars to approach Payne with a batch of items to sign. A twenty-five-cent photo could skyrocket in price when Payne's signature was added to it. When he thought he was being used, Payne did his best to reduce the marketability of the products. For instance, he once was approached by a boy asking him to sign a picture. In his peripheral vision, Payne caught sight of a known vendor, waiting for the child's return.

"What's your name, son?"

"Benjamin," the little boy said innocently.

"Great; here ya go, Benjamin," Payne said, as he signed in large letters: TO BEN-

JAMIN, BE A GOOD BOY, YOUR FRIEND, PAYNE STEWART. By personalizing the picture to the child, Payne immediately eliminated the resale value for the vendor, while giving the boy a special present.

On the other hand, Payne often went out of his way to autograph something that was special for someone. Sixty-seven-year-old Don Bobillo has served as caddy master at the Phoenix Open for twenty-eight years. Don watched with interest as "Mr. Stewart," as Don always referred to Payne, was approached by a six-year-old boy and his mother, asking for an autograph.

Don recalls, "Mr. Stewart took off the tam-o'-shanter hat he was wearing. He signed it and gave it to the little boy.

"The next day, I saw the mother," said Don, "and she told me, 'My boy slept with that hat on last night.'"

Don is a bona fide collector of autographed golf balls, with more than two thousand balls in his collection, eight hundred of which are signed by tournament winners, including Ben Hogan, Jack Nicklaus, and Tiger Woods. Yet when Don asked Payne to sign a ball, he refused. "Sorry, Don. I don't sign golf balls," Payne told him.

"OK, good luck today," Don answered.

On Sunday, when Payne finished the tournament, he sought out Don and signed one of his own personal golf balls, imprinted with the initials PS. He handed the ball to Don, and then took off his golf glove, signed that, and handed it to Don as well.

19

Lights, Camera, Action

Payne's patriotism and his identification with the men and women of the American armed forces got an enormous boost in June 1997, when he was asked to host a segment of the television program *Inside the PGA Tour,* to be filmed aboard the aircraft carrier USS *George Washington.* Payne was excited about the opportunity to see an aircraft carrier in action. The *George Washington* spent much of its time away from U.S. shores, plying the dangerous waters of the Middle East; but at the time of Payne's visit, the ship was about one hundred miles off the coast of Cape Hatteras, North Carolina.

Commander Ward Carroll hosted the television crew and Payne during the trip. As director of the Carrier Air Wing One Golf Association (CAWOGA), a bona fide, USGA-sanctioned body, Commander Carroll was as excited to meet Payne as Payne was about being on board the ship.

"I walked Payne through the standard VIP itinerary," the commander recalled of his first encounter with Payne, "observing flight operations between the catapults, standing on the landing signal officer's platform, chatting with the captain on the bridge, and schmoozing with the air crew in the ready rooms. When we had finished, Payne's only question was, 'Where does the crew eat?'"

Payne wanted to meet the "everyday men," the guys who serviced the jets, the cooks, and the young sailors aboard ship who did the grunt work. Commander Carroll took Payne to the "mess deck," where, he remembered with a laugh, "Payne began exchanging golf stories with the guys. Before long, Payne had attracted a huge crowd, hanging on his every word. Several hours later, we finally managed to persuade Payne to break himself away from the crowd of enlisted men who had gathered around him on the mess deck."

Payne had always been a staunch supporter of the American military, but having experienced a taste of life on the aircraft carrier, he was even more impressed and inspired. The filming went well, concluding with Payne, with Commander Carroll as his caddy, hitting golf balls off the flight deck. Payne stayed overnight aboard ship, and he and the commander connected as golfers and as patriots, but also as fathers and friends. Before Payne departed the following day, Admiral Mike Mullen, the battlegroup commander and an avid golfer, asked Payne, "Have you ever flown in a military jet?"

"No," replied Payne, "but I sure would like to!" The admiral, Commander Carroll, and Payne talked of a possible return trip sometime during the next year.

Months later, with Iraqi leader Saddam Hussein once again stirring up trouble in the region, the *George Washington* was deployed to the northern part of the Arabian Gulf. Tensions were high, and it seemed that war was inevitable. The crew was on almost constant alert, working long days and nights, planning strikes against targets in Iraq. According to Commander Carroll, "the plan changed daily, and frustration levels were high" among crew members aboard the ship.

After three months at sea, late one night, as he sat exhausted after another day of managing more than 250 pilots' flight schedules, Commander Carroll noticed an E-mail from

Payne Stewart Enterprises on his computer screen. The message, recalls Commander Carroll, was short:

Dear Ward,
   Drop 18 bombs on Saddam and CAWOGA will have a new golf course. Fly safe. We'll see you guys when you get home.
        Payne

In Payne's eyes, Ward Carroll and the men and women aboard the USS *George Washington* were serving our country, protecting our freedoms, and helping keep the world safe, but to Commander Carroll, Payne's message was equally part of the effort. "Words can't describe what that simple sentiment did," said Commander Carroll, "not just for me, but for the entire air wing, as the E-mail was circulated from squadron to squadron. Payne Stewart cared; therefore, we assumed America cared. We zipped up our G-suits and went back to work."

Not surprisingly, after his experience aboard the carrier, Payne's goal of making the 1997 Ryder Cup team was even more important to him. It was an uphill battle, but he felt he was capable of achieving it. He reconnected with his former swing coach, Chuck Cook, and began training again with him. "I need your help," he told Chuck. "I just can't do it by myself."

He also hired Mike Hicks back full time as his caddy. Payne's confidence soared with Mike on the bag and "in his ear." Payne encouraged Mike to talk to him throughout the round, to remind him of the shot routine he had established, and to keep him informed on distances and potential hazards on the course. Mike talked to Payne all right—so much so that other caddies thought Mike was overstepping his bounds—but that was the relationship Payne and Mike had, and that's what Payne wanted from his caddy. "Mike knows what drives me," Payne said. "That's what you need in a caddy, someone who understands your moods, your game, and your tendencies, both good and bad. Mike does."

Payne was striking the ball well, making good shots, and playing patiently, but his best finish was a tie for second at the Honda Classic. He wasn't winning any tournaments.

Worse even than not winning, Payne's Ryder Cup point total was low again, which meant that he would have to win a couple of tournaments or rely on being a captain's pick. Prior to the British Open, Payne went to Valderrama in Spain to play a practice round on the course where the 1997 Ryder Cup matches were scheduled to be played in September. He was excited about the possibility of making the team. His dreams of helping to recapture the Cup for America were dashed, however, when captain Tom Kite announced his two picks: Fred Couples and Lee Janzen.

Payne was sorely disappointed, but instead of dwelling on it, we packed our bags and flew to Lyford Cay in Nassau. Our friends, Joe and Jane Lewis, had invited us and several other couples down to stay with them on their yacht during the Ryder Cup matches. Joe and Jane were originally from England, so we all had fun teasing each other about the rivalry. We watched the Europeans defeat the U.S. team. Millions of viewers around the world saw European captain Seve Ballesteros cheering on his team as the Europeans retained the Ryder Cup by a one-point margin, 14½–13½. Payne vowed that he would never again allow himself to be in the position where he had to rely on a captain's pick to make the U.S. team. Every Ryder Cup team on which he had played had been on the basis of earning enough points to automatically qualify. He was determined that he would do the same to earn a spot on the 1999 team.

In December 1997, the children and I met Payne in Los Angeles and we flew to Australia. Payne had arranged to play in the Schweppes Coolum Classic with our good friend Todd Woodbridge as his pro-am partner. Todd and Payne played great and won the pro-am competition by four strokes. Todd said that he was more proud of the trophy that he won with Payne than any of the fourteen Grand Slam tennis trophies he had displayed in his trophy case. We stayed in Australia with my family over Christmas and then returned to Orlando on January 3.

Before the beginning of the 1998 golf season, Aaron, Chelsea, Payne, and I sat down as a family to lay out our schedule for the year. Everyone's input was welcome because we were deciding our priorities as a family. I had a list of the tournaments in which Payne had played well over the previous years, and we laid that on the table along with our calendar of family events. One of the highlights of Aaron and Chelsea's year was a monthlong stint at Kamp Kanakuk, a Christian-oriented sports camp directed by Joe White. The camp is located in Branson, Missouri, in the heart of the picturesque Ozark Mountains, about forty miles from Payne's hometown of Springfield. We had heard of the camp through friends, and when Payne and I visited Kamp Kanakuk, we were quite impressed. The program was fun but challenging, spiritually uplifting but not over-bearing. We usually let Aaron and Chelsea attend camp during the month of July while Payne and I traveled to the British Open.

Together we planned out our schedule for 1998, including school functions, golf tourna-ments, practice days with Chuck Cook, spring break, vacations, holidays, and, of course, sum-mer camp. We talked about which tournaments we especially enjoyed going to as a family and which tournaments Payne might travel to alone, mostly those on the West Coast. Our bottom line as a family at the beginning of 1998 was that we wanted Payne home more often, and he was happy to oblige. Payne loved being home with the family, doing ordinary things with Chelsea and Aaron, making them pancakes for breakfast when their friends stayed overnight, driving them to various games and school activ-ities—playing taxicab driver, as Payne put it. The children, of course, couldn't see enough of their father.

Aaron, our nine-year-old, is as straightforward as Payne. In comparing Aaron to himself, Payne often said, "The apple didn't fall very far from the tree!" When we were discussing how Payne might be able to play fewer tournaments in 1998, Aaron cut right to the chase. "Just play better, Dad, and you won't have to play so much."

Payne cracked up at Aaron's blunt honesty and his simple solution. "Oooooo . . . kaaay, I can do that," Payne said as he leaned back and laughed. Sometimes the obvious answer is the best, although not always the easiest!

Payne was quick to admit that his priorities had changed. "My family comes first and foremost, and golf is second. It didn't used to be like that, but now it is." In order to have more time at home, he purposely chose to play a lighter schedule in 1998. Ironically, just as Aaron had suggested, Payne indeed played better. He entered twenty-one tournaments, had six top-ten finishes, and earned $1,193,996 on the PGA Tour. The lighter schedule also allowed time for some of Payne's "extracurricular" activities.

One day, Van Ardan of Leader Enterprises called our home and asked, "How'd you like to be on *Home Improvement?*"

"On what?" Payne asked.

"On television, on the ABC series *Home Improvement,*" Van repeated.

"What do I have to do?"

"Just be yourself," Van replied.

"I can do that," said Payne.

Van arranged to have a script sent over, and when Chelsea saw it, she said, "Dad! You've gotta do it. Jonathan Taylor Thomas is on that show!"

Van and the show's producers worked out the details so Payne could appear on the program during the PGA's West Coast swing early in the year. During the Buick Invitational in February, Payne spent several hours on the ABC set. He had a blast cutting up with Tim Allen and Richard Karn.

When Jonathan Taylor Thomas first saw Payne, he asked, "Can I get your autograph?"

Recalling Chelsea's excitement, Payne said, "Let's see if we can work a little trade here. I've got two kids back home who want your autograph pretty bad."

"And I've got a couple of buddies who are golf nuts who would love this!" Jonathan offered. They worked a deal in which Payne autographed some caps, and Jonathan signed some pictures for Aaron and Chelsea.

Payne thoroughly enjoyed his guest spot on the show and welcomed future appearances. "Hey, I'd do it again if they asked me," he said. "Think of it. I'm working on my acting career, my rock-and-roll career . . . you know, after twenty years in golf, maybe I'll go on to something else. . . ."

As for Payne's "rock-and-roll career," he was still active with Jake Trout & the Flounders, along with Peter Jacobsen and Mark Lye. Over the winter, the band had recorded another album of golf parodies, turning such classic rock songs as "Love the One You're With" into "Love the One You Whiff." The guys talked several of their musician friends into appearing on the album with them, including guest artists Glenn Frey of the Eagles, Stephen Stills, Graham Nash, Alice Cooper, and Darius Rucker of Hootie and the Blowfish. The album included introductory comments by actor Bill Murray, Arnold Palmer, Greg Norman, and John Daly. The Flounders even signed a recording contract with EMI-Capitol—the same company that distributed the Beatles, the Beach Boys, and a host of new artists. Jake Trout & the Flounders performed "live" before an enthusiastic crowd of more than one thousand golf fans at the 1998 AT&T Pebble Beach National Pro-Am. Joining the guys on the stage, located just off the famed Pebble Beach Golf Links' eighteenth green, were Glen Campbell, Glenn Frey, and Alice Cooper. It was quite a change from the days when Bing Crosby crooned at Pebble Beach.

Coinciding with the release of their CD, Jake Trout & the Flounders did a music video that aired on VH-1. In the video, Payne, Mark, and Peter are seen riding around in a golf cart as they perform "I Love to Play," a parody of Randy Newman's early 1980s hit, "I Love L. A." "Guest artists" appearing on the video included Arnold Palmer, Jack Lemmon, former president Gerald Ford, Leslie Neilson, and Marcus Allen. Chelsea, Aaron, and I thought the video was hilarious, and Payne had a good time filming it.

Although Mark Lye was enthusiastic about the band's potential, and Peter was actually a decent singer, Payne never took it too seriously. "This is fun, guys, but I'm a golfer," he'd say. Of course, the kids and I never let Payne's role in Jake Trout & the Flounders go to his head. Once when the group appeared on the Golf Channel, Payne was really getting into the moment and got a bit too close to his microphone. We could actually hear him singing background vocals. That was not good. When he got home, I told him, "Payne, please don't sing so loudly. Let Peter sing. Let Mark sing if he wants, but you—please, don't sing."

I wasn't the only one who saw the band's

limitations. Another time when the group played, Mike Mills, of the band R.E.M., and country music star Vince Gill played guitar on stage with them. Vince and Payne had become good friends through their mutual interests in music and golf. A scratch golfer himself, Vince hosts an annual charity tournament in Nashville.

After their performance on stage together, Payne asked Vince, "So what do you think?"

"Well, Payne, it's kinda like you playing in a pro-am," Vince deadpanned. "Having you guys up here on stage with us is our pro-am."

With his low-key sense of humor, Vince loved to needle Payne whenever he could. Once, at a charity dinner and auction in Orlando, Payne attended wearing a bright yellow sport jacket. It was a free shot for Vince. From the stage, Vince called attention to Payne's presence in the audience, and Payne stood briefly, waved to the crowd, and sat down. "I'm glad to see that the Bay Hill pro shop finally sold that yellow jacket," Vince quipped.

In March we went to Deer Valley, Utah, for a family ski vacation. The children were at the perfect age for all of us to ski together. Payne enjoyed snow skiing, but he was always aware of the danger of falling and injuring himself, so he was quite happy to ski on the green and blue slopes with the rest of us. Personally, I think he enjoyed the snowball fights with Chelsea, Aaron, and me more than the skiing.

Payne didn't play in the Masters in 1998. It was the second year in succession that he had not been invited to Augusta because he had not won a tournament that year on the Tour. Although Augusta National wasn't Payne's favorite course, he was nonetheless disappointed to miss the first major of the year. "If you think of yourself as a world-class player, you have to play all four majors," he often said.

In early June of that year, we flew to the island of Aruba for a family vacation. Payne was committed to play Nick Price in a Shell's Wonderful World of Golf match there five days later. We spent our time swimming and relaxing on the beach. One day we went deep-sea fishing, with a film crew tagging along to record our every move. Unfortunately, it was quite windy and rough that day out on the ocean. Chelsea had just climbed to the top platform, where Payne and I were sitting, to tell us that she wasn't feeling very well. Aaron was following her up the ladder when suddenly, Chelsea began throwing up. With the wind blowing directly into Aaron's face, he got a faceful. Well, he immediately started to throw up while he was still holding on to the ladder, with the film crew below him. People were ducking everywhere. It was total chaos! We turned the boat around and headed in. We told the film crew that they should name the segment, "Fishing with the Spewarts."

Back at home, Payne approached the 1998 U.S. Open with nervous excitement. The Olympic Club in San Francisco had hosted three previous U.S. Opens, including the 1955 Open in which Payne's dad had played. It was a top-notch golf course, and Payne regarded it as a stiff challenge. He had missed the cut at the 1987 Open at Olympic and had finished near the bottom of the field in the 1993 Tour Championship played there. It was not going to be an easy week.

Chelsea and Aaron were getting ready to go to Kamp Kanakuk, so I stayed home with them, and Payne took his mom along with him to San Francisco. "Just believe in yourself," I told Payne as I dropped him off at the airport. "I'll be watching you on television."

20

I'll
Be Back

On Tuesday afternoon, Payne and Mike Hicks mapped out a game plan for the Olympic Club course. "Par is a good score," Payne said as he surveyed the layout, configured in typical U.S. Open fashion with rock-hard greens, narrow fairways, and high rough. "Par is always a good score at a U.S. Open. There's nothing wrong with making par on any hole out there."

"The key to winning the U.S. Open," said Mike, "is staying away from the double-bogey. You're going to get a few birdies, you're bound to make some bogeys, but stay away from losing two at a time."

Playing together with Hale Irwin and

Curtis Strange, Payne took immediate control of the tournament, opening with a birdie on the first hole and grabbing the lead. He played well all day and birdied the sixteenth hole. On number 17, a 468-yard hole that normally played as a par 5, but which had been modified by the USGA officials to a par 4 for the Open, Payne sank a sensational 45-foot putt for another birdie. He finished the day with his third straight birdie by nailing a 12-foot putt on the eighteenth green. That gave him an incredible 4-under-par round of 66, which shot his name to the top of the leaderboard.

Friday's round turned out to be a nightmare that many PGA Tour players and a few USGA officials will never forget. Many of the problems stemmed from the hole location on the eighteenth green. At first glance, number 18 at Olympic looks almost too easy to be a finishing hole in a major tournament. Relatively short for a par 4, the hole is an iron shot for most pros, straight off the tee, downhill to the landing area, and then a wedge back uphill to a small, treacherously sloped green. This presented a challenge for Tom Meeks, the USGA director of rules and competitions, who was the man most responsible for the selection of hole positions during the Open. A twenty-three-year veteran with the USGA, Tom was a consummate professional, a man who knew his job and did it well. His job was to make the holes difficult but fair.

At Olympic's eighteenth, however, the hole location on Friday was almost unplayable. The cup was eighteen yards from the front of the green and eight yards from the left edge, which would not be considered unusual by the difficult U.S. Open standards. But because of the green's slope and speed, any putt that was hit below the hole would not stop; it would keep rolling and, depending on the speed, could end up all the way off the green.

Payne started his round on Friday the same way he had finished the afternoon before: he birdied the first three holes, sinking two 15-foot putts and a 25-footer. What a great way to start a round! Again, he played well all day long, sticking to his game plan. "Par is a good score," Mike reminded him repeatedly. As he approached the eighteenth tee, Payne was at even par for the day, still four strokes under for the tournament, and he had a three-stroke lead. After his second shot, his ball lay ten feet to the right of the hole.

Mike and Payne looked over the green as Payne lined up his putt. Both guys realized that if he missed the putt, the ball was going to go south, but neither of them could have guessed just how far. "In hindsight, I should have told him to go for it," Mike said later. "Don't baby it. Put some paste on it. Be aggressive. Try to drain it because if you miss it by trying to dive in or ram it in to the back of the cup, it isn't going to matter. The ball will be going to the same place anyhow. Instead, I made a mistake and cautioned Payne to be careful, to try to play the break."

That's exactly what Payne did. He put a smooth stroke on the ball, aiming just above the hole, trying to lag it up and waiting for it to turn to the left and break toward the cup. It broke all right, but it was just short of the hole when it did. Instead of diving into the cup, the ball kept rolling. Payne could only stand and watch, with his arms folded across his chest, as the ball trickled a full twenty-five feet below the hole. He ended up getting a bogey on the hole, giving him a 71 for the day. He was still leading the tournament, but now by only one stroke. As Payne walked off the green, he said to Pete Richter, the USGA official walking with Payne's group, "Isn't that pin location bordering on ridiculous?"

Mike Hicks was amazed. Said Mike, "The 'old' Payne Stewart would have said some things he might have been sorry for later, but Payne didn't. He sure wasn't happy about dropping a couple of strokes, but he seemed much more mellow than I had seen him in the past. He exercised amazing restraint, not one of Payne's better-known virtues. When he went into the media tent, he hardly talked about the eighteenth hole at all."

Instead, he talked more about how much he had enjoyed being home with our family more that year. To the shock of most of the media, Payne admitted that a high ranking on the money list didn't really matter all that much to him anymore, that his driving average wasn't nearly as important to him as his driving Aaron and Chelsea to school when he was home. "I've got a beautiful wife and two lovely kids at home that I'm really enjoying spending time with," Payne told the reporters. "I'm a taxi service at home and I love it."

The mesmerized members of the media looked at one another in amazement and shook their heads. Was this the same Payne Stewart they loved to hate?

In some ways it was, and in many ways it was not.

On Saturday, as the course conditions grew tougher and the greens faster, Payne rebounded with an eagle on the first hole. He finished with a 70, even par at Olympic, stretching his lead again to four shots over Tom

323

Lehman and Bob Tway and five shots ahead of Lee Janzen. It was the largest lead any player had held in a U.S. Open in twenty-eight years.

As he had done after the first two rounds, Payne spent a long time in the media tent on Saturday night. The big question was, "Can you keep it up, Payne? How can you withstand the pressure that goes with leading the U.S. Open three days in a row?"

Payne's answer was simple. "If I go out and play Payne Stewart's game, the game I've been playing for three days, then I'll be standing here with the trophy," Payne told the media. By the time he finished answering questions, the sun was beginning to set. Payne shook his head. He had wanted to go hit some balls on the range and spend some time on the putting green before dark. But the sun was dipping quickly over the Pacific Ocean, taking with it Payne's opportunity for some extra work before the final round.

The fourth round of the U.S. Open was played, as always, on Father's Day, and Payne couldn't help but think of his dad. Bee Payne-Stewart, the name Payne's mom went by after Bill's death, told a group of reporters, "Payne adored his father." It was true, and in times such as these, Payne especially missed his father. He always envied our friend, Mark O'Meara, whose dad frequently attended tournaments, proudly wearing a shirt, hat, or logo that reminded him of one of Mark's more recent victories. Payne was glad that Mark could have those precious moments with his dad, and he wished that his own father could have lived long enough to enjoy his success. Payne often said that the victory he cherished most—even more than winning a major—was the one his father saw at Quad Cities in 1982.

As if there wasn't enough nerve-racking emotion to the day already, Payne was paired on Sunday with Tom Lehman, who had led or shared the lead at the past three successive U.S. Opens only to finish third in 1995, second in 1996, and third in 1997. The 1996 British Open winner got off to a tough start on Sunday, bogeying the first hole. Tom never truly recovered, shooting a 75 for the day.

Playing in the third to the last group, slowly making his way up the leaderboard, was the 1993 U.S. Open winner, Lee Janzen. Although six strokes behind Payne at one point on Sunday, Lee had already caught two incredible breaks, both of which were significant enough to make anyone think he had a chance to win the tournament. On the fifth hole, Lee hit his tee shot into one of Olympic's giant cypress trees, known for snagging golf balls and not giving them back. By the time Lee arrived at the tree, his ball still had not fallen out of the thick branches. Discouraged, Lee started walking back up the fairway toward the tee to hit another ball when suddenly a ball stamped LMJ, for Lee Michael Janzen, dropped to the ground. The marshals and Lee verified that it was indeed his ball.

"I still had to hit out of the rough," Lee recalls, "and then my 6-iron flew the green!" Fortunately for Lee, he caught a good lie, off the green but not in the thick stuff. If he was going to stay in contention, it was now or never. On his next shot, he hit a chip that just barely landed on the pinnacle of the green, rolled down the slight slope, and disappeared into the cup. With thirteen holes to go, Lee started climbing up the leaderboard as nearly everyone else was sliding backward.

Payne had some incredible developments of a different sort on number 12, where his tee shot landed in a divot that had been filled with sand—a "fairway bunker" as Payne referred to it. Most PGA Tour and USGA courses now make it a practice to have maintenance crews go out each evening after a round to fill the many divots with sand so that they can be reseeded to preserve the flat, smooth look of the fairway. In the old days, it was considered a breach of golf etiquette for a golfer to take out a large chunk of grass on a shot and not replace it. If replaced immediately, the roots will remain alive, and the grass from a divot can actually begin to grow again within a short time. Nowadays, many pros and their caddies don't bother replacing the divots because they know that the maintenance crews will fill them with sand. That sand, however, as Payne said, becomes almost like a mini-bunker for a professional. Furthermore, the player is not allowed to put a club, stick, or even a finger into the sand to measure the depth of the divot.

Payne said, "I'd rather see them remain unfilled. If it's a hole, you know what's going to happen. When they fill them with sand, you don't know how deep that sand is . . . you don't know if there's a quarter-inch of sand in there, or what's under the sand. If they repair it, that spot ought to be considered 'ground under repair.' . . . I feel that if you're in a sand divot, where they've come in and intentionally put sand in there to replace it, you should be able to call the official over and say, 'I'm in a divot; I should get a drop.'" As with any other "ground under repair" on a golf course, the player could then pick the ball out of the divot and drop it in another spot within a club's length and no closer to the hole.

The USGA and the PGA Tour, however,

do not see it that way. The rules say, "Play the ball where it lies," even if it is in a divot filled with sand. On the twelfth fairway, Payne and Mike debated the wisest club selection, since they weren't sure how the ball would come out of the sand. Payne finally decided on his 9-iron. His next shot landed in the bunker at the front right side of the green.

As if that weren't bad enough, USGA official Tom Meeks approached Payne and said, "You just got a bad time."

Payne could hardly believe his ears! He was playing an extremely delicate shot, in the final group, on the final day of the U.S. Open, and they were well ahead of the time allotted in which to finish to accommodate the television coverage, yet he was being warned about taking too much time on his shots. The USGA allows forty seconds for a shot when players are "on the clock" or out of position because of playing too slowly. Payne had taken one minute, twenty seconds to figure out how to hit his ball out of the sand-filled divot. Consequently, Tom was officially issuing Payne a warning. "That's one bad time," Tom said.

"What happens if I get another one?" asked Payne.

"You'll get a one-stroke penalty," replied Tom.

"Thank you very much," Payne answered, which was better than what he meant, which was really, "Thanks for nothing!"

But the warning from Tom Meeks was indeed something. It was enough to break Payne's concentration and rattle him more than the usual frayed nerves that accompany being in contention on the last day of a major. Payne hit a great shot out of the bunker, but he missed the subsequent 10-foot putt for par. After bogeying number 12, he watched his 5-iron tee shot roll off the thirteenth green into the thick, deep rough. It took Payne a chip and two putts to finish the hole. For the first time since the start of the tournament, he was now one stroke behind Lee Janzen.

"Hang in there," said Mike Hicks. "Your swing is fine. We're going to make a birdie sooner or later." Although Mike dared not even hint at it, shades of Baltusrol 1993 flitted across his mind. Payne and Lee . . . Lee and Payne . . . Lee, by two strokes.

But this was 1998, not 1993, and Payne was much more mature and at peace with himself. He came right back on number 14, reclaiming a share of the lead by sinking a 12-foot putt for birdie—his only birdie of the day, but an important one.

Lee Janzen faced his nemesis at 17, one of

the toughest holes on the course because of the USGA's transformation of it from a par 5 to a par 4. In the three previous rounds, Lee had bogeyed it once and double-bogeyed twice. On Sunday he played it almost perfectly, walking off the green with a par.

When Lee finished with a par at 18, he recorded a 68 for the day, putting him at 1-under for the tournament. He signed his score-card and then waited in the basement of the clubhouse with his wife, Beverly, as Payne and Tom Lehman came down the final stretch.

At number 16, a long par 5, Payne drove his tee shot through the fairway into the rough. When he subsequently bogeyed the hole, some people may have thought he was out of the tournament. But not Payne. And not Lee Janzen.

Payne nearly birdied 17 with a sensational chip shot but had to settle for par—not a bad score. He then needed a birdie on 18 to force a play-off.

On 18, Payne hit the fairway off the tee, the first time he had done so all week. As they walked to the ball, he looked over at Mike and with the impish smile he was known for said, "Wouldn't it be something if I holed this shot for two?" He had 105 yards to the pin, uphill, into the wind. It was definitely too risky to go with a sand wedge, as much as Payne would have liked to put some extra backspin on the ball. Instead, he used a pitching wedge and put the ball within twenty feet of the cup.

Back in Orlando, Chelsea, Aaron, and I watched nervously as Payne lined up the putt. It looked makable on TV, but out on the green, Mike and Payne realized that the putt had to be perfect—perfect speed, perfect line, breaking from about six feet above the hole. Payne knew that he couldn't leave the putt short or it would miss the break, and hitting it even the slightest bit too hard would send the ball rolling down the green. It had to be a perfectly finessed putt, and if there was anyone on the PGA Tour who could do it, Payne was that man.

Payne later said, "I just told myself, You have to make this putt so you can play tomorrow [in a play-off] and have a chance to win the tournament. Because you didn't get it done up to this point, you have to make this putt."

Payne put as perfect a stroke as possible on that putt, aiming at the spot about six feet above the hole. Watching on TV in the clubhouse, Lee and Beverly Janzen hardly dared to look. Watching at home in Orlando, Chelsea and I dared not to look. For a long moment, everyone knew . . . it was on its way to being in the hole . . . it was rolling right on line, past the

331

spot six feet above the hole . . . to within three feet. But then the ball wiggled, veered slightly, and stopped six inches away from the cup. Payne tapped in for par. Par is a good score at a U.S. Open, but sometimes it's not quite good enough.

In Orlando, Chelsea burst into tears.

In the clubhouse basement, Lee and Beverly Janzen lost it, too, but for an entirely different reason. For the second time in his career, Lee was the U.S. Open champion. And for the second time in his career, Payne finished as the runner-up.

After congratulating Lee privately and complimenting him on the green during the trophy presentation ceremonies, Payne hugged Beverly on the green and went to the media tent to face what he knew was going to be one of the toughest press conferences of his career.

As was his custom, Les Unger, the moderator of the press conference, opened the session by asking Payne to review his birdies and bogeys. "The birdies won't take long," Payne said almost playfully. "The bogeys will though." Even hardened members of the press corps could barely suppress a smile. They braced themselves, however, when Les pressed Payne about the sand-filled divot on 12 that he had referred to as a "fairway bunker." Les asked, "That tee shot, which wound up in the bunker in the middle of the fairway—did you get any feeling that maybe this wasn't meant to be?"

In years gone by, Payne might have looked back at the person asking such a question and answered, "What kind of question is that? You know how I feel about those sand-filled divots." Instead, Payne replied, "Well, I sat up here yesterday and told you all that if I go out and play good enough—played Payne Stewart's game—that I'd be standing here with the trophy. And I didn't do that. But first off, you've got to give Lee Janzen all the credit in the world."

Rather than making excuses for his errors or blaming the course, Payne went on to extol Lee's tremendous performance at the Olympic Club. "There was nobody in contention in the golf tournament that shot under par except for Lee Janzen. So he deserves to be the champion today."

For nearly an hour, Payne answered every question patiently and without a word of sour grapes. In similar circumstances in the past, Payne might have endured the grilling for fifteen minutes, or half an hour at the most, and even then his answers might have seemed perfunctory and curt to some. Everyone in the tent recognized that some sort of transformation had happened to Payne Stewart. Most of the writers wrote glowingly about the metamorphosis they had suddenly noticed in Payne. Only a few were willing to acknowledge the reason behind what they heard from, and saw in, Payne that evening.

Mike Hicks was waiting for Payne outside the clubhouse. "Are you OK?" Mike asked.

Payne smiled, and Mike could tell that he was smiling through the hurt. "Yeah, I'm OK," Payne said. "We did accomplish one thing," he continued.

"What's that?" Mike asked.

"I know that I can win again."

As soon as the reporters spotted Payne, a group surged around him again. "Don't worry about me, boys," Payne told them. "I'll be back."

21

A New Foundation

While Payne finished his interviews on Sunday evening following the 1998 U.S. Open, Justin Leonard and D. A. Weibring were waiting for him at the airport aboard a Learjet 35 that would whisk the three of them to Quincy, Illinois, where Payne and Justin were scheduled to play in a charity event hosted by D. A. on Monday. Knowing that Payne had just lost the U.S. Open by one shot after leading for nearly three-and-a-half rounds, the guys weren't looking forward to the next few awkward hours as they made the cross-country trip. "How do you console a guy like Payne," asked Justin, "who has been there at the top and knows what it feels like to win?"

To their surprise, when Payne and his mother boarded the Lear, Payne was as ebullient as ever. "Looking good!" he called to D. A. and Justin. Payne was the consummate host, digging around in the luggage, finding food and drinks for everyone on board.

In Quincy, it was late by the time they settled into their hotel rooms. Justin was unpacking his suitcase when the phone rang. It was Payne. "Throw some jeans on," Justin recalls Payne saying on the phone. "We're going out."

Justin remembers, "D. A.'s caddy had a friend who owned a bar and grill in the area, who was willing to open it up for us. At three o'clock in the morning, with the music vibrating the walls in the place, Payne was cooking cheeseburgers for everyone on the grill at a restaurant owned by somebody he had just met after he had just lost the U.S. Open! Talk about bouncing back. He wasn't about to sulk all night. The guy was incredibly resilient!"

Payne may not have been a sourpuss at D. A.'s outing, but when he saw the pairing sheets the next day for the first two rounds of the Motorola Western Open, he was less than thrilled. He couldn't believe his eyes. He was paired with Frank Nobilo and Lee Janzen! It was as though the PGA Tour was rubbing

Payne's nose in the loss to Lee by having the guys play together the next week.

Lee was shocked, as well. "It really wasn't fair to Payne," he said. "It was a no-win situation for him. I assumed it was the PGA Tour computer that had made the match because I figured that nobody would actually do that on purpose. Then we found out later that the pairing was actually done intentionally."

After a major, the field in the tournament that follows is sometimes lighter and needs some added pizzazz to create television interest. NBC had carried the U.S. Open, and CBS had the Western. For a variety of reasons, several big-draw players had chosen to sit out the tournament, and CBS put heavy pressure on the PGA Tour to pair their best two draws for the Thursday and Friday broadcasts. Following the U.S. Open that week, there were no bigger names in golf than Lee Janzen and Payne Stewart, both of whom were committed to playing in the Western.

Not only was the pairing intentional, it was done by our good friend Jon Brendle, who is also a good friend of Lee's. Jon and Martha Brendle live right next door to us in another home that we own; and between Jon and Payne, they had fed most of the large catfish that populate Pocket Lake, adjacent to our property. It got to the point where they practically viewed the fish as their own pets! Together, they certainly poured enough fish food into the lake to claim ownership of at least a few.

In fact, once when my dad was visiting in our home from Australia, Payne came home to find him proudly displaying his catch of the day, a plump, well-fed catfish. "Norm!" Payne shrieked. "You killed my pet fish!" For a fraction of a second, my father thought Payne was serious.

When Payne heard about the Western Open pairings, he was in Jon's face faster than Jon could cut bait and run. "I'm sorry, Payne," Jon apologized sincerely. "CBS had to have a top-notch pairing, and you and Lee were it."

"Oh, yeah. Well, do you know what I'm gonna do?" Payne fired back.

Jon's worst nightmares flitted across his mind. He could easily imagine Payne speaking his mind to the media or, worse yet, withdrawing from the tournament. After all, he'd had a tough week at Olympic, and a few days off would be understood by everybody—except, perhaps, CBS. "Now, Payne, let's think—"

"I'm gonna raise your rent!" Payne interjected.

Both Jon and Payne broke into laughter. Payne played in the Western Open, but it certainly wasn't one of his more enjoyable weeks on the golf course. Jon didn't hear the end of it for a long time.

"It was tough for Payne," Lee Janzen said later. "He could have won the tournament, and I could have missed the cut, and that wouldn't have given him one bit of satisfaction because I was the guy who had the U.S. Open trophy. Our conversation wasn't as easy that week as it was normally, but the way Payne's heart was, I knew he didn't hold any grudges against me. It was just an awkward situation."

We had always given generously to worthy causes within our community and to help other charities with which we were involved, but in 1998, we decided we wanted to do more. Along with our children, Chelsea and Aaron, we formed the Stewart Family Foundation to help other Christian-oriented organizations assist less-fortunate children.

Payne didn't want to simply write checks and throw money at problems. He wanted to get involved in the lives of underprivileged children in a hands-on fashion. He wanted Chelsea and Aaron to do the same, partly so they would learn the joy of helping others, and partly so they would better understand how blessed our family has been. "Our kids are fortunate," Payne said, "but we don't want them to ever think they can turn their backs on other kids just because they may not have as much."

All four of us gathered around the table and talked about the needs and how we might best get involved. Our main criterion in sorting through the many worthy causes was (and still is today): "How can we help other children?" Payne and I made the final decisions on whom we should help and how, but Chelsea and Aaron had a vote in the matter as well. They especially enjoyed helping inner-city children experience the fun of going to summer camp at Kamp Kanakuk and other camps around the country.

In April 1998, Navy Commander Ward Carroll visited Payne during the pro-am at the MCI Heritage Classic, and they finalized plans for Payne's familiarization flight aboard an F-14 Tomcat. A four-star admiral had granted approval for Payne's adventure, and the date was set for October.

Payne was as excited as a little boy in a toy store as he flew to Oceana Naval Air Station in Virginia for his two-day look into the life of a navy "Top Gun" fighter pilot. Commander Carroll and his superiors had arranged for

Payne's Lear to land at Oceana, a rare privilege usually reserved for U.S. senators and congressmen. Allowing Payne's plane to land at the air base was a huge compliment and demonstrated the high regard they had for Payne.

The navy put him through their rigorous swimming and physiology training, including basic survival training, a run through the altitude chamber, and helpful instructions such as "Here's how the ejection seat works." Payne loved it!

He also experienced hypoxia training, in which he was strapped into a pressure chamber with other pilots, oxygen masks on, and run through a simulation of an aircraft suddenly losing pressure at twenty-five thousand feet. The training shows pilots how quickly they can become disoriented when oxygen is deficient, and how easily they can become hypoxic, losing all rational thought and control of their physical and mental abilities. At a simulated twenty-five-thousand-foot altitude, the instructor commanded, "OK, drop your masks and start playing patty-cake," the childhood game in which two people pat their hands together. The trainees in the pressure chamber soon discovered that they had very little coordination. They quickly became light-headed and experienced a strange, tingling sensation, accompa-

nied by a euphoria similar to a feeling of intox-
ication.

"You've got to get your oxygen mask on quickly," said the instructor, "before you lose consciousness. In a real situation, there will not be anyone to strap this mask onto you. You must do it for yourself."

"Payne did the right thing," Commander Carroll later said. "As he felt himself beginning to get woozy, he reached for the oxygen mask and put it over his face. Once the mask is in place, and the oxygen flows back into your lungs and bloodstream, you're fine, and Payne did well."

That afternoon, following his training sessions, Payne presented a free golf clinic for the sailors at Oceana, as he did wherever he met with American military personnel around the world. Then Payne played nine holes with Admiral Mullen, Commander Carroll, Vinnie Spagnuola, the pro at the Oceana course, and Captain "Flea" Smith, the base executive offi-cer. More than two hundred people followed the fivesome, making for a rather unusual gallery, and Payne bantered with the naval crowd, just as he would the spectators at a celebrity charity event. He intentionally topped the ball on his first tee shot, and the gallery gasped as though someone had fallen overboard. Payne smiled and then ripped a drive 270 yards right down the middle of the fairway. Payne shot what Commander Carroll referred to as an "oh, by-the-way, 33" for the nine holes.

That night, Payne was the keynote speaker at a banquet on the base. His message was simple: "Thank you to the navy for opening doors of opportunity to me, and for the freedoms the sailors help to provide for all of us—freedoms, unfortunately, that most Americans take for granted."

The next day, Commander Carroll carefully strapped Payne into an F-14 Tomcat fighter jet behind the squadron's second-in-command, "Pokey" Molidor, a former Top Gun instructor. The pilot didn't pull any punches. This was no kiddy ride. Pokey put the pedal to the metal in a supersonic demo and gave Payne the ride of his life, breaking the sound barrier, flying inverted, experiencing the chest-pounding force of six-and-a-half times the normal pull of gravity, and simulating a genuine bombing pattern. When the F-14 taxied to a stop, Payne proudly displayed his empty airsickness bag—a badge of honor among the civilians who have dared to take such a flight. If Payne could have played the Ryder Cup matches just then, he'd have probably defeated the Europeans single-handedly!

Commander Carroll helped him out of the jet, and as soon as Payne's feet hit the ground, he sought out the sailor whose responsibility it was to service the jet between flights and keep it in tip-top condition. Payne gave the young sailor a high five, and the sailor smiled back as though Payne had given him a million dollars.

As Payne walked back to the hangar, television reporters and cameramen surrounded him and asked for his impressions of the flight. Payne was literally pulsating with patriotism. "Most Americans don't realize what these guys do each day to keep the rest of us safe." He pointed toward the flight line and the maintenance crews. "Just look at them working out there. It's incredible."

With the camera rolling, Payne said, "It makes me proud to be a taxpayer." Wow! It must have been a great ride!

Payne also received another surprise in November 1998, when he was honored by the Alumni Association of Southern Methodist University with the Distinguished Alumni Award. Although Payne's college buddies Barry Snyder, Lamar Haynes, Billy Lacy, and Todd Awe teased Payne about the judging criteria for such an award, Payne was always truly honored to represent his alma mater. Anytime he could do something to help SMU, he was glad to do it.

In the midst of all the other activities in 1998, Payne played some pretty good golf. Besides his second place at the U.S. Open and the Greater Vancouver Open, he tied for third at the MCI Classic in Hilton Head; tied for fourth in the L. A. Open and the Michelob Championship; and shot an incredible 65 at the Players Championship in Ponte Vedra, Florida, on his way to a tie for eighth place. In all, he had six top-ten finishes, with a 69.93 stroke average, and was nineteenth on the PGA Tour money list, earning $1,193,996. Not a bad year!

Perhaps most of all, Payne was excited because his equipment and golf ball contracts had expired. He had represented the company well, and the parting was amicable. Several companies clamored for Payne to endorse their products, but he wisely decided to move slowly. We didn't need the money, but Payne needed to win. And for the first time in five years, he was free to use whatever clubs and balls he wanted. It was time to play some golf.

22

Mr.
No-Name

"Do you like that bag?" Payne asked Mike Hicks. "How about this one?" he pointed to another golf bag. "Whoa! Check this out!" Payne pointed to a plain black, canvas, triangular-shaped golf bag. "Hey, Mike, I love this one. Look at all the little pockets. Isn't that great? Zippers everywhere. I can stow all kinds of stuff in there. What do you think?"

"Looks a little funky to me, but it's OK," said Mike. "I can carry that."

Payne and Mike were in the Edwin Watts Golf Shop not far from our home in Orlando, and Payne was looking for new equipment as he prepared to head to the West Coast to begin the 1999 PGA Tour season. With our former equipment contracts expired, Payne wanted to check out every possible alternative before he decided on what he wanted to play. We had received lucrative contract offers to endorse clubs and balls from a wide variety of manufacturers, but Payne wasn't interested. He wanted to find some clubs he was comfortable with, whether they were name brand or not, and regardless of whether the manufacturer offered us money. Most of all, Payne wanted forged blades for his irons—clubs that he felt he could win with.

Payne had taken two and a half months off between the 1998 and 1999 seasons. We didn't travel to play overseas during the winter, and while he was home, he hardly lifted a club. He concentrated instead on working out and getting his body in top shape. Part of Payne's success over the years was due to his stringent workout schedule. He had discovered early on that if he worked out regularly and stayed in shape, he could minimize his lower-back problems. But if he got lazy and allowed himself to slack off, the back problems returned with a vengeance. Moreover, Payne had to be in shape to make his long, flowing, graceful swing work for him. Otherwise, the swing was off, and so was his game.

Payne bought the plain black golf bag and

filled it with an assortment of new clubs. He liked the Titleist driver, Orlimar fairway woods, Cleveland wedges, and a Scotty Cameron putter. He completed the set later with Mizuno irons.

The Mizunos were a godsend. Before Christmas, Payne had talked by phone with Lamar Haynes, telling him about his search for a new set of irons. "Lamar," he said, "I just can't find what I'm looking for."

"Payne, they can make golf clubs any way you want. What exactly do you want?"

"Lamar, all I want is a real thin blade, with a thin top line, and no offset."

"Well, I still have those Mizunos," said Lamar.

"What Mizunos?"

"The ones you gave me ten or twelve years ago," Lamar replied.

"I don't remember giving you any Mizuno clubs," Payne said.

"Well, you sure did. I've had them ever since, and they are like brand-new."

"Send them over to me."

Lamar contacted Harry Taylor, a Tour rep and club designer for Mizuno who lived in Nashville, and explained that Payne wanted to try the clubs, but he needed a few minor changes on them. Harry agreed to have the clubs sent to Mizuno's manufacturing location, where the clubs were regripped with the style of grips Payne used. They calibrated the degree of loft on each iron to the exact specifications that Payne felt he needed to play his "feel" type of golf.

When Payne received the clubs, he was ecstatic. He called Lamar and said, "They're perfect! Why you kept these clubs all these years, I'll never know, but thank God you did!" Payne put the Mizuno irons in his new golf bag as he headed out on Tour in 1999. He didn't sign an endorsement deal with Mizuno; he was just happy to play the clubs.

Though Payne spent hundreds of dollars stocking his new bag, the only endorsement contract he signed was with Titleist. He was committed to playing a Titleist 90-compression professional golf ball. All the coaching that Chuck Cook could give him or the mental tips that Dick Coop could provide or the pep talks or motivational speeches I could give him couldn't compare to the renewed confidence that Payne felt as a result of having his favorite ball back in his bag. As Mike said, "Payne needed to be playing that Titleist. Payne Stewart could make that Titleist jump!"

Payne was an anomaly on the PGA Tour that year. Here he was one of the all-time leading money winners, a winner of two major championships, yet he was going out on the Tour without a major equipment endorsement. By contrast, many players were wearing as many as four sponsors' logos on their shirts and hats, and had other paid endorsements for using a certain brand of golf bag, clubs, and ball.

Payne told Van Ardan, whose job it was to procure such endorsements for the athletes he represented, "Look, don't worry, Van, that I don't have a club contract. Don't worry that I'm going out on the West Coast swing without a company's name on my bag. It's not an issue for me." The most important consideration for Payne was finding the right equipment, the clubs he felt he could play with and win. If that meant not representing anyone, Payne was not concerned.

He and Mike practiced in Florida for a few days, then went to Austin to work with Chuck Cook for three days before starting their year at the Bob Hope Chrysler Classic, the Phoenix Open, and the AT&T at Pebble Beach. After his hiatus, Payne felt refreshed physically, emotionally, and spiritually. He was ready to play.

When Paul Azinger saw that Payne was again playing the clubs and ball that he wanted, he told Mike Hicks, "Payne will win twice this year." Paul's words proved to be prophetic.

◆ ◆ ◆

Although the AT&T Pebble Beach National Pro-Am golf tournament is held on three gorgeous courses—Poppy Hills, Spyglass Hill, and Pebble Beach—only one set of practice tees services all three courses. To accommodate the players and their wives who are waiting in the range area during the tournament, a lunch tent is erected. The range is also the place where many caddies and equipment representatives gather during the days before the tournament begins.

On Wednesday, Payne played a practice round at Pebble Beach. The weather that week was nasty—wet and windy, as it often is on California's Monterey Peninsula in January, and Payne struggled all day with his putting. "Payne, don't worry about it," Mike said. "These greens are so wet, the ball's not going to roll where you're looking anyway." Payne knew that Mike was right, but he was frustrated nonetheless. He was hitting the ball well from the tee, and his confidence in his irons was through the roof now that he was back to playing blades. But his putting still wasn't where he wanted it to be.

After finishing his round, Payne went into the tent for lunch. Mike Hicks stayed out at the

351

range, talking with some of the other caddies and equipment representatives.

About that time, Arnie Cunningham, an equipment representative from the SeeMore Company, approached Mike to show him the company's new line of putters. "Have you seen this?" he asked.

"No," Mike replied. "What's the big deal?"

"You're going to love this putter," Arnie said. At the time, SeeMore was not a household name in the golf club industry, but Payne and Mike had known Arnie for about fourteen years, and they had developed a mutual respect. Arnie had previously represented major golf companies such as Taylor Made and Cobra and had a reputation for honesty among the players. Golf manufacturers spend millions of dollars to develop new equipment, but if the pros don't use it, the chances of success in the marketplace are slim. Consequently, at almost every tournament, professional golfers and their caddies get inundated with the latest and greatest fads and state-of-the-art technology. It is easy to become callous and not want to see any more new clubs, balls, bags, or gizmos. But every once in a while, something comes along that really works. For Payne, the SeeMore putter was one of those rare finds.

Just as Arnie began explaining how the SeeMore differed from other putters, Payne came out of the lunch tent. Arnie didn't miss a beat. He started over with his presentation, explaining to Payne the way the SeeMore putter could help keep his putts on line by assuring him of proper alignment. "It's one of those things where you just have to put your ego aside and see if you can get better at putting. What do you think?"

"I don't have a problem with that," Payne said with a laugh. At that point, he was so frustrated with his putting that he might have been willing to try a hockey stick if someone had promised it could help him. He looked at Arnie's new putter and said to Mike, "Well, put it in the bag, and we'll hit some with it when we go down to the putting green."

Later that afternoon, Payne, Mike, and Arnie went down to the putting green across from the Lodge, and Arnie worked with Payne for about two hours. It took Payne a little while to get used to the new putter because at first he seemed to be lining up "off line" compared to the putters he had used previously. The secret to the SeeMore, Arnie explained, was amazingly simple. The putter has two white lines and a red dot on the blade. The putter has no offset, so the shaft goes straight into the top of the blade. By positioning the shaft so it appears to be between the two white lines, and holding the blade so that the red dot cannot be seen while looking down the shaft, the putter blade will be perfectly lined up with the target. The more Payne used it, the more his putts started dropping. When he was done, he looked at Mike and said, "What do you think?"

"I think it's got to go in the bag," said Mike. "You're making putts from all over the practice green."

"Yeah, I think you're right," said Payne.

"I was hoping for a change," Payne said later, "anything at all that I felt would help me get the ball rolling on the greens, so I worked with it for a while, went to a meeting, and came back and worked with it for another hour. The putter had never been in competition, but I said, 'I'm going with it tomorrow.'"

Mike Hicks later acknowledged, "Few players on the PGA Tour would be willing to play a tournament using a putter without ever playing a round of golf with it. But Payne did. And he filled it up every day of the AT&T tournament."

Chuck Cook noticed the difference in Payne's putting immediately. "The new putter made Payne set up in the correct alignment every time," observed Chuck. "That had a profound impact on Payne because it stopped him from fidgeting with his putter all the time."

Payne agreed. "I have a tendency to move my hands and head if I'm not putting well, but the putter makes me set up the same way every time."

The combination of the new clubs, the new putter, and the spiritual peace that Payne had in his heart and mind gave him a light-hearted freedom in his game that Mike, and others who knew Payne well, had not seen in a long time. Using his "new" clubs and a putter with which he had never before sunk a putt in tournament competition, Payne shot 69 and trailed by three strokes after the first round. In the second round, his game was absolutely masterful. Starting the round on the back nine, he opened with an eagle on the tenth hole and followed with birdies on 11 and 12. Even in the inclement conditions, Payne was striking the ball well and putting incredibly! Before the day was over, Payne added four more birdies, and not a single bogey, shooting a sensational 64, 8-under par for the day. As he walked off the last green at Poppy Hills, he was 11-under and led the tournament by three strokes at the end of the second round.

Payne's third round at the AT&T was played at Spyglass Hill, one of his favorite courses in the world. The weather on Saturday, however, was horrible. Gusting wind and pelting rain made for miserable playing conditions. Despite the weather, Payne still had a share of the lead with Frank Lickliter as he approached the eighteenth green. From 185 yards out, he pulled out his Mizuno 5-iron. Brimming with confidence, Payne stiffed it, dropping the ball one foot from the pin! He sloshed up the fairway, tapped in for a 73 for the day, 10-under for the tournament, and held a one-stroke lead after fifty-four holes.

"That's the kind of finish we like," Payne said to Mike as he plucked his ball out of the cup.

A steady, driving rain on Saturday night turned the famed Pebble Beach Golf Links into a series of ponds along the bay. Some of the players with early tee times on Sunday started out across Pebble, but before long, the sirens blew, calling the tournament to a halt. Payne was declared the winner, since he was the leader after three completed rounds.

Almost immediately the naysaying began. "Payne won in fifty-four holes, but when is he going to win a seventy-two-hole tournament? Sure, he can lead for three days. That's great. But when is he going to finish all four days on top?"

Payne didn't discount the skeptics. Instead, he agreed with them! Holding the gorgeous crystal AT&T Pebble Beach trophy, Payne said, "I've been on the other side of the fifty-four-hole deal before, and this time, I'm on the right side of it. And I'm not going to lie to you; it feels pretty good." Payne was referring, of course, to the four times he had been close to winning in a tournament that had been called because of weather, most notably at the 1986 Vantage Championship and the 1990 Memorial Tournament, where he had been one stroke back when play was canceled.

He went on to acknowledge his desire to prove that he could still get the job done all four days of a tournament. "I really did want to prove to myself that I could win again in seventy-two holes. I wanted that opportunity." Then with a smile, he added, "But I'm going to take this and run."

Following his victory at the AT&T, Payne reiterated his priorities. "My game is exciting me," he said. "I have to go out and believe that ... but I'm not going to blink and miss my family growing up. I took two and a half months off last year, and I'm not going to play this fall. I'm going to be a father. It's very important to me. Golf is secondary to my family."

Payne also attempted to express his faith

publicly after his win at Pebble Beach. "I just want to thank the Lord for helping me out there today," he said. It wasn't an overt witness, but it was genuine. Payne went on to say, "I've got a great grip on life right now. I have a wonderful family, and I'm in touch. When I'm at home, I'm a father, and when I'm on the road, I'm a golfer. I love my life."

Payne's faith in the Lord was getting stronger, and his growing spiritual awareness made him want to win more, rather than less—but for a different reason. More than ever before, Payne recognized that along with winning came more visibility, which translated into more opportunities to present a testimony concerning his faith. He never could have imagined how much of an impact his testimony would have before the year was over.

23

W.W.J.D.

D uring Major League Baseball's off-season, between the fall of 1998 and the spring of 1999, our friend Orel Hershiser taught a Sunday school class at First Baptist Church in Orlando. Orel invited Payne and me to attend, and because we were home more frequently through the winter months, we occasionally dropped in on Orel's class. Payne and I sensed a warmth and friendliness among the people there. The class was structured informally and comprised primarily of men and women our age, so we felt extremely comfortable in attending. We were used to seeing Orel on the pitcher's mound or on the golf course, so his presence in front of the class made it all the more interesting for us.

Before he left for spring training in 1999, Orel passed out two devotional books to each member of the class. *Handbook to Prayer* and *Handbook to Renewal*, both compiled by Kenneth Boa, were simply daily Scripture readings arranged under several topics. Orel encouraged the class to read one section from the devotional each day of the month, cautioning us against trying to do too much at once. "Just read one section at a time, and try to think about what that means and how it applies in your life," instructed Orel.

Payne and I started reading the devotional sections together, but before long I noticed that he was much farther along than I was. He'd read the Scripture from the devotional every night before he went to bed.

"What day are you on?" he'd ask occasionally.

"Er, ah . . . I don't know. What day are you on?" I'd waffle. Although I might miss a day or two of my reading, Payne rarely did. He read the devotionals "religiously." He took them with him when he went on the road as well.

"I saw Payne reading the devotionals quite frequently," said Mike Hicks. "He wouldn't say much about it, and he sure never tried to stuff his faith down anyone's throat, but he did take it seriously."

Payne also began reading the Bible. Nobody tried to talk Payne into what he should believe or how he ought to live out his faith; he simply set out on his own journey with God. The Scriptures themselves were the most powerful influence on Payne's life.

Frequently, he'd get all excited about something he had discovered in the Scripture book and couldn't wait to tell me. For instance, when he ran across the apostle Paul's instructions about marriage in Ephesians 5, he thought he had hit the mother lode. He jokingly said, "Hey, it says right here that you're supposed to submit to me!"

"What?" I cried.

"It says right here, 'Wives, submit yourselves unto your own husbands, as unto the Lord.' That's Ephesians 5:22," he said with a bit of feigned cockiness. Payne thought the idea of my submitting to anybody was pretty funny.

"OK, whatever . . . ," I said. "Wait a minute! Let me see that book." I looked at the passage and noted verse 21. "It says here that we are to submit to one another!" I said. "And it says on down here that you are to give yourself up for me. . . ."

"Whoa, whoa, whoa," Payne boomed facetiously. "I haven't gotten that far yet!"

Payne never claimed to have great knowledge of the Bible. Nor did he try to tell anyone else how to live. "I'm not a 'Bible thumper,'" he said. "I can't get up there on a rock and tell you what it all means because I don't know. But I'm learning, and I like what I'm learning."

Once, for example, Payne was with Chris Millsaps at The First Academy, and someone gave him a card with a Scripture reference that said "1 Thess." Payne was touched by the card and the Scripture reference, and said, "Look at that—First Theologians . . ." Chris didn't have the heart to tell Payne that the book he was referring to was First Thessalonians!

Payne was very much a "Christian in process," not someone who felt he had arrived spiritually. He never pretended to have the answers and probably didn't know what some of the questions were. But his faith was genuine, and as he understood the Bible, the issue wasn't about how much faith he had but whether his faith in Christ was real. And everyone close to Payne knew that his faith was real.

Payne was excited to be home more often, and the time away from the course seemed to do him good. When he went back out to play, he was enthusiastic about being there. Payne had played extremely well on the West Coast swing and had a good feeling about the spring and summer tournaments. "This is the best West Coast swing I've had in a long time," he said. "I think this could be a banner year for Payne Stewart."

Our friends Frank and Kathy Viola had recently finished construction on a beautiful new home on the same lake as ours, just around the corner. Kathy called Payne one day and asked if he could do her a BIG favor. She wanted to know if Payne could arrange for Frank to play Augusta National. Payne called a dear friend of ours, Joe Ford, from Little Rock, Arkansas, and asked Joe if it would be possible to arrange it. For years, Payne had talked about wanting to take my dad up to Augusta to play, but he never seemed to get around to it. Mum and Dad were visiting with us from Australia, so Joe kindly agreed to host the men as his guests. Payne, Dad, and Frank flew to Augusta early on March 4. They played golf all day until the sun set. They even stayed overnight in one of the cottages next to the eighteenth fairway. Frank and my dad were overjoyed. They played again the next morning and flew home that afternoon. I'm so thankful they made that trip together.

The following week at the Honda Classic, Payne was in contention all week, shooting 9-under par for the tournament and finishing in second place, two strokes behind Vijay Singh. He came close to winning again at the MCI Classic in Harbour Town, shooting a solid 68 in the opening round and then shooting a 64 on Friday. Payne shot even par over the weekend and ended up joining Glen Day and Jeff Sluman in a play-off. Payne seemed to have the advantage when after their second shots to the green, Payne was closest to the hole. Unbelievably, Glen Day sank a 35-foot birdie putt. When Payne missed his 18-footer, Glen had won the tournament.

"You just have to give Glen Day credit," Payne said graciously. "Glen shot 5-under par at Harbour Town, with the wind swirling, and then he came out and birdied the first hole of the play-off." Payne was disappointed that he hadn't won, but his attitude was upbeat, and he started setting his mind on the U.S. Open coming up at Pinehurst in June.

In April, Payne signed an equipment deal with Lynx, a subsidiary of Golfsmith, one of the largest manufacturers of golf clubs in America. Payne felt especially good about the agreement because it specifically stated that he could play whatever clubs he wanted until Lynx designed a set of irons that suited him. The Golfsmith people were delighted to have Payne on board, and Payne felt confident that we could all work together to develop some great new golf products.

About that same time, Aaron came home from school one day with several bracelets bearing the initials W.W.J.D., which stands for "What Would Jesus Do?," the theme of Charles Sheldon's classic book *In His Steps*. In Sheldon's book, the question, "What would Jesus do?" became the guiding principle that people chose to live by, regardless of the consequences. In recent years, the slogan "What would Jesus do?" had become a resounding theme for many contemporary Christians as well.

As Aaron was showing Payne his bracelet, he said, "Here, Dad. Why don't you wear one?"

"OK, I will," Payne replied. "Thanks, Aaron." Payne put the bracelet around his wrist and fastened the clasp. He wore the bracelet everywhere, during golf tournaments, out for social occasions, wherever he went; he wasn't ashamed to be seen with the W.W.J.D. bracelet on his wrist.

Bobby Clampett, golf commentator for both CBS and TBS television networks, was having breakfast with Payne at the Memorial

Tournament in late May. A former PGA Tour player, whose Christian testimony on the Tour is highly regarded, Bobby noticed the W.W.J.D. bracelet Payne was wearing. "Tell me the story behind the bracelet," Bobby ventured.

Bobby recalls Payne's response. "Payne told me the whole story—how Aaron had given him the W.W.J.D. bracelet and how it was sort of a silent witness to his faith. Then Payne turned to me, and looked at me as only Payne could do, and said, 'How come you're not wearing one?' Payne had a way of saying things as a friend with a jabbing manner but always with a message behind it. I sat there, and I had absolutely no response to Payne's question. Finally, I stammered, 'I . . . I . . . don't know.' Basically what Payne was saying was, 'Hey, I'm a public person, and I'm not afraid to talk about my faith in Christ, and I'm not afraid to wear it, and to let people know that it's a big part of my life, and you should too.' I went home and I thought about that, and it kept gnawing at me. I said to myself, 'I know I'm going to do this. I have to do this.'"

Bobby put on a W.W.J.D. bracelet and has been wearing one ever since.

✦ ✦ ✦

Payne was so intensely focused on the 1999 U.S. Open that he didn't play well at Memphis. Mike Hicks recalls that their attitude that week was basically, "Let's get through this week so we can get on to Pinehurst." Payne wasn't concentrating well, and Mike could tell that although his body was in Memphis, his heart and mind were already at Pinehurst. Mike didn't talk to Payne for most of the last nine holes.

Payne missed the cut, and when Chuck and Lana Cook arrived on Saturday, they flew on to Pinehurst to prepare. After they had played a practice round at Pinehurst, Payne confronted Mike about his quietness at Memphis. "You didn't do your job last week, Mike."

"Payne, you didn't want to be there, and neither did I," Mike replied.

Payne and Chuck walked the course on Saturday and Sunday, mapping out a game plan, noting the dangerous spots on the greens and the hazards. "If you get over in that rough," Chuck cautioned, "you won't be able to get it up and down." Chuck literally wrote down the spots where he and Payne decided he should aim, plotting out each possible scenario, as much as possible, for situations Payne might encounter during the tournament. They studied the golf course as though they were two generals poring over terrain maps, planning an attack.

On Tuesday, Payne did the first of many interviews he would give that week. Tom Auclair, a sportswriter with Worldwide Media Corporation, had followed Payne's career for years. Tom had written about Payne's victory at the PGA Championship in 1989 and at Hazeltine in 1991, and Tom had written about Payne's losses to Lee Janzen at Baltusrol in 1993 and at the Olympic Club in 1998. Tom had covered Payne in good circumstances and in tough times.

Tom immediately noticed that Payne had a special bounce in his step during his practice rounds at Pinehurst. "The guy knew!" said Tom. "I'm convinced that Payne Stewart felt deep down inside that he was going to win the U.S. Open. On Tuesday, I asked him, 'Payne, I've noticed something different about you; I know that you're excited, but what is it?' It was so obvious. It was as though he knew in advance that he was going to win. When I wrote my article, I compared Payne to my two kids who went to the prom this year for the first time, and they had what I called 'nervous anticipation.' They just couldn't wait to get there. I saw something similar in Payne during the days before that tournament. He just couldn't wait to get it going. There was something special going on there. I've seen guys in major championships for years, and I'd covered Payne throughout his career. I believe that Payne Stewart went into the U.S. Open believing that he was going to win."

As a highly respected sportswriter, Tom appeared on several sports-talk shows prior to the Open. Whenever the question came up of who was going to win the U.S. Open, a dozen names of top competitors were always bandied about. Tom stuck to his guns. "It's going to be Payne Stewart," he predicted.

In the pretournament haze of talking-head television and radio interviews, newspaper and magazine columns, nearly every reasonable name was tossed out as a possible winner of the 1999 U.S. Open. Some said it was a shoo-in for Tiger Woods. It was Tiger's time. Others said David Duval was due, or that Phil Mickelson was poised to win his first major.

Only one player publicly predicted that Payne Stewart would win the 1999 U.S. Open. That player was Lee Janzen.

24

An Overcoming Heart

J. B. Collingsworth was baffled. What should he do? As a Baptist minister, he was not accustomed to speaking directly into another person's life, at least not in a predictive sense. Yet J. B. felt a strong urging to call Payne and share a verse of Scripture with him that the Lord had given him in his devotional time that Saturday morning. J. B. felt God wanted Payne to know something before he went into the final rounds of the U.S. Open.

J. B. dialed Payne's cellular phone number from the bedroom of the condo in Whistler, British Columbia, where the Collingsworths were vacationing.

"Hi! You've reached Payne Stewart's

phone. He's not with it right now, . . . but if you leave a message, I'll tell him you called." Payne's voice mail message played through, and J. B. took a deep breath as he heard the tone.

"Payne this is J. B., and I'm just calling to let you know we love you and will be praying for you . . ." That was generic enough, but then the minister took a leap in his own faith. "And Payne, I believe that I have a verse the Lord wants me to share with you as you go into the final rounds of the U.S. Open." J. B. quoted from Psalm 16:8, "'I have set the Lord continually before me; Because He is at my right hand, I will not be shaken.' Payne, I believe you are going to win this week. I believe God is going to give you the win because you have been faithful and you have really been striving to put the Lord first in your life. As this verse says, you have set the Lord continually before you, and I believe that God is going to honor that." J. B. hung up the phone, trusting that he had indeed heard from God and imparted his message.

The Collingsworth children, Mary Margaret, Rob, and Wes, along with J. B.'s wife, Shugie, were aware that J. B. had gone to the back bedroom to call Payne. When J. B. came out of the bedroom, Rob asked, "What did you tell Mr. Stewart, Dad?"

371

"I told him that I believe he's going to win and that God just gave me this verse to give to him."

"I don't usually do stuff like that," J. B. recalled later, "but I felt confident that this was a word from the Lord. I felt confident enough to tell my family that Payne was going to win before Payne had hit his first shot on Saturday."

Chris Millsaps felt similarly impressed to leave a voice mail message for Payne on Saturday morning, right before he was ready to go out to play the third round of the 1999 U.S. Open. "Payne, men's fellowship checking in," Chris said. "I don't know why this came to mind, or how you'll take this, but I feel like I need to call and tell you something. You know my son, Lance, has this verse of Scripture displayed in his bedroom. It's been sort of a theme verse for him in his high school athletics. It's the same verse they have on the softball field fence at The First Academy. And I guess I'm supposed to share it with you. It's Colossians 3:23, 'Whatever you do, work at it with all your heart, as working for the Lord, not for men.'"

Later that day, Payne called Chris back. "Hey, loved the verse. That was a real encouragement; I appreciated it. Colossians 3:23. Got it."

By Saturday evening, Payne had made believers out of a lot of skeptics as he maintained his lead in the tournament. In doing so, he established a new record, having led more rounds at U.S. Opens than any other golfer in history.

Mike Hicks spent Saturday night at home in Hillsborough, North Carolina, a short drive from Pinehurst. On Sunday morning, as he prepared to return to the golf course, he turned to his wife, Meg, and said, "If we can get four birdies today, we'll win." Everyone associated with Payne that weekend could think of only one thing: "He's going to win."

Dick Coop approached Payne as he prepared to step up to Pinehurst's first tee box on the last day of the tournament. Coop intended to offer Payne a word of encouragement, a last-minute reminder as he always did right before a round. "Just give yourself—"

Payne finished Coop's sentence. "Yeah, just give myself a chance."

Coop smiled. His student had learned well. Dr. Coop usually said, "You have the skills, you have the talent, you have the game; don't try to force it; just give your natural ability an opportunity to work for you." Few people other than Coop, Chuck Cook, and Mike Hicks ever understood what a miracle it was that

Payne could even focus his attention long enough to complete a round of golf at the professional level. That he could overcome the effects of ADD without medication was in itself a tribute to his determination. To win on the PGA Tour was an even greater credit. This time, Dick didn't need to remind Payne. He watched as Payne stepped up to the tee. He knew his friend was ready; nothing else needed to be said.

Payne had played confidently all week long, and Sunday was no exception. I could tell that he was working to maintain his concentration, though, and trying hard not to allow the pressure or anything else to distract him from getting the job done. He had hit only seven greens in regulation, but his putting had been incredible. He came to the final hole of the tournament having birdied four holes but needing to sink a 15-foot putt to win the championship. He had one-putted eleven greens, putting only twenty-three times over the first seventeen holes. Could he possibly one-putt one more time?

A 15-footer is difficult under any circumstances but even more so on the final hole of a major championship, playing for the U.S. Open title. As much as Dick Coop had reminded Payne that every shot counts exactly the same, whether on Thursday or Sunday, the pressure of putting with millions of people watching your every breath is undeniably greater than putting in the middle of the pack, out of contention.

People all around the world watched with anticipation as Payne sized up his putt. Would he make it? Could he make it? Oddsmakers eagerly reminded their patrons of a similar scenario a year earlier, when Payne had needed a 25-footer to force a play-off and had missed it.

In the house that Bev and Lee Janzen had rented for the week of the tournament, the Janzens and several of their friends were glued to their seats in front of the television. One of Lee's friends looked at him and said, "What do you think? He's not going to make this. It's too tough of a putt."

Lee looked at Bev; Bev looked back at Lee, and they both said the same thing almost simultaneously: "No, he's going to make it."

Lee later commented, "Any putt outside of three feet under those conditions is just all nerves. The chances of a pro making a 15-footer are slim, but sometimes guts just take over; and you could tell by the way Payne had played those last three holes, he was going to will himself to victory."

Payne rolled the putt across the eighteenth green, dropped it in the cup, and the party at

Pinehurst began! I fought my way through the crowd and finally reached him. We kissed and hugged each other tightly, and he said to me, "Luv'ie, I kept my head down all day long. I kept my head down!" Then I said, "I know you did. I am so proud of you!"

Payne later said, "People are telling me that it was the best Open finish of the century, one of the greatest Opens ever. But I never thought about how this would go down—especially during the Open itself. I thought about getting the job done. Once the job's done, then you reflect on it and think, Wow, those last three holes were pretty special."

Downstairs in the clubhouse, chaos reigned while I waited for Payne to sign his scorecard. When he came out of the scorer's room, we kissed again. I felt the fatigue and stress draining from his body. He looked as though he had just run a marathon—and in a way, he had. Tom Meeks came down the stairs, quickly made his way to Payne, and embraced him. Tom was genuinely happy for him. He had visited Orlando sometime after the 1998 U.S. Open, and he and Payne had played a round of golf together. "We had a good talk about what happened at Olympic," Payne said, "and we ironed out our differences."

In his post-tournament interview, Payne

compared the win to his loss the year before. "What happened last year, I really built on that. If you can learn from defeat, then I think that makes you a much better player. Last year, everybody said, 'Great try.' Well, I didn't want to hear that again. I didn't want to hear that when I got back to Orlando, and all my friends came up and said, 'Boy, you sure tried.' That motivated me."

Payne reiterated that his priorities hadn't changed just because he had won the U.S. Open. "I don't plan on changing my schedule," he said. "I plan on doing the same things that got me into position to win today, which is working out and spending a lot of time at home. . . . I'm not going to run after the elusive dollar because I've been invited to go play here, there, and everywhere. As soon as Valderrama is over, which is the seventh or eighth of November, I'm not playing again until January. I had so much fun being at home, being a father, getting up in the morning, making breakfast, taking my kids to school, going to school athletics; that's what my life is about right now." It was, after all, Father's Day.

Payne was also excited that his win at Pinehurst guaranteed him a position on the 1999 Ryder Cup team. "I've contended all year, and the Ryder Cup is what motivated me.

That's one cup that isn't sitting on this table right now. It's on the wrong side of the ocean. Hopefully, I can do something about that. I knew that the only way I could make a difference was to get on the team . . . and 300 points [today] will put me up to 917, thank you very much, and I will be on the team." The media tent shook with appreciative laugher at Payne's enthusiasm for playing in the Ryder Cup matches.

The reporters listened respectfully as Payne talked about his faith in the Lord. "I'm proud of the fact that my faith in God is so much stronger, and I'm so much more at peace with myself than I've ever been in my life," Payne said. "And that's the reason that I was able to gather myself and conduct myself. And where I was with my faith last year and where I am now is leaps and bounds. And that gave me the strength to stand up there and believe in myself and get the job done."

Payne continued to answer questions for nearly an hour, and at the close of the press conference he said, "I'm a lot more mentally prepared to deal with these situations than I have been in the past. I'm going back to the fact that my faith is strong. And the Lord's given me the ability that he wants me to use so I can stand up here and give him the praise."

It was late by the time we finally left the clubhouse. Payne looked at me and said, "Let's enjoy this one." I knew what he meant. We'd savor the taste of this victory, but we would not allow the whirlwind of attention that surrounds the U.S. Open to rule us. We returned to our rented house and quickly gathered our things. There was no time to celebrate because I had to catch a flight back to Orlando to be with our children, and Payne was going with Mike to play in a Monday charity tournament in Mike's hometown.

As they rode in Mike's van, Payne returned phone calls to people who had called offering congratulations. "The boy can putt!" he told Lamar Haynes. When they finally arrived at Mike's house, the guys stayed up celebrating and watching various sportscasts rebroadcasting the highlights of Payne's victory. They finally went to bed at 4:00 A.M. and had to be up, ready to play golf at 9:00 A.M.

Late Monday afternoon, Payne finally arrived back home in Orlando. Chelsea, Aaron, and I were waiting to surprise him at the airport, along with Robert and Dixie Fraley, Martha and Jon Brendle, the men's fellowship guys, and other friends. When he emerged from the Challenger, provided for the winner of the U.S. Open by Business Jet Solutions, the same

379

company with whom we had been flying since 1996, Payne hoisted the U.S. Open trophy high for everyone to see. "Looking good!" he called from the aircraft's steps. He greeted everyone, making sure that every person there felt special. "Fellowship!" he yelled as he saw the guys, while they all whooped in glee. He showed Aaron that he was still wearing his W.W.J.D. bracelet. Later, in talking with Aaron about the celebration on the green at Pinehurst, Aaron responded, "The celebration was cool, Dad, but you and Mike missed the high-five"—which they had.

Payne approached Lance Millsaps and said, "Colossians 3:23, right?" Lance beamed with pride, knowing how special that Scripture had now become to both him and Payne.

That week, we had a celebration at Isleworth, a private golf course community near our home, where Payne played and practiced. It was a relatively small party attended by some of our close friends. When Shugie and J. B. Collingsworth arrived at the party, they greeted Payne, offered their congratulations, and let Payne know how excited they were for him.

Later that evening, the video of the last three holes of the U.S. Open filled the television screen. As the video played back the winning putt, Payne put his hand on his chin and struggled to maintain his composure as the tears started streaming down his face.

Thinking that he was reliving the overwhelming emotions of that intense moment at Pinehurst, J. B. and Shugie walked over to him, and J. B. put his arm around Payne's shoulder. "Payne, I appreciate your heart," J. B. said.

With tears in his eyes, Payne said emotionally, "J. B., I just want everyone to know, it's Jesus that has done this for me." Then, almost as if to make sure that J. B. understood, Payne repeated, "It's Jesus that has changed my life."

The following week we celebrated my birthday. As a special vacation, Payne and I had planned a trip to the Bahamas, but he surprised me by secretly flying in my sisters, Deidre and Andrea, from Australia, to join us on our trip, along with our friends, Mike and Annalisa Gutierrez. I was absolutely flabbergasted. Payne's love and consideration spoke volumes to me: At a time when he could have basked in the adulation of being the U.S. Open winner, he instead took off for a week with his wife, family members, and friends.

Lee Janzen called to congratulate Payne after he got home from Pinehurst. Without identifying himself, Lee said, "Hello, is this the current two-time U.S. Open champion?"

"Why, yes it is. Is this a former two-time U.S. Open Champion?"

Lee and Payne talked briefly and before saying good-bye, Lee said, "I don't care what anybody says about you making that last putt. They can say it was destiny, or that you had putted well all week long, or that it was your skill, but it was none of that. Your heart was too much to overcome."

25

Giving Something Back

True to his word, Payne didn't allow winning the Open to change him. He was as down-to-earth as ever. One morning, he went over to the Edwin Watts Golf Shop near us. Naturally, most of the salespeople in the store knew Payne, so the subject of the day was the U.S. Open. They talked for a while before Payne suddenly said, "Hey, do you guys want to see the trophy?"

"Are you kidding? Of course, we'd love to see it."

Payne drove the several miles back to our home. He carefully nestled the large silver cup on the front seat of his 1984 Porsche, and with the convertible top down, he drove back to the golf store and placed the U.S. Open trophy on the counter. For the next hour or so, he greeted everyone in the store and took time to tell the story of the final three holes at Pinehurst again and again.

He found plenty of time for his friends as well. Prior to playing in the British Open in July, Payne, Mark and Alicia O'Meara, Tiger Woods, Joanna Jagoda, Mike Gutierrez, Stuart Appleby, David Duval, Lee Janzen, and Todd and Natasha Woodbridge arrived early to do some fishing and golfing in Waterville, Ireland. It was the second time the group had been invited as guests of J. P. and Noreen McManus. While Payne was there, he arranged to have a special gift made for each of the guys that he fished with on the trip. Sean, their fishing guide, framed two-by-four-foot maps of Ireland, with real fly-fishing lures used in various parts of the country displayed accordingly on the map. It was a highly unusual gift, the kind that takes time to design and produce. In fact, the guys didn't get the gifts until Christmas 1999. When Mark O'Meara opened the large box in which the gift arrived, he gazed at it and nearly cried as the memories of the guys' fishing trips wafted back over him. "It's one of the most special gifts I have ever received," he said.

Payne loved walking through the small town of Waterville, talking to the shop owners and the people in the restaurants. The people of Waterville responded warmly, adopting Payne as one of their own. Since the town was too small to have a mayor, the highest honor they could give Payne was to name him as the honorary captain of the Waterville Golf Club. They bestowed the honor at the Ryder Cup matches in September at a special ceremony at The Country Club in Brookline, Massachusetts.

On July 11, 1999, Annalisa Gutierrez and I flew from Orlando to Scotland to meet up with our husbands. Our friend Vivienne Silverton and her dad, Joe Lewis, were again hosting a number of the golf professionals from Isleworth Country Club and Lake Nona Golf Club at The Old Course Hotel in St. Andrews during the British Open at Carnoustie. This was the third time that Joe Lewis had hosted us during the British Open. Each day, the guys were transported by helicopter to and from the golf course. Joe and Jane stayed on their yacht just offshore at St. Andrews while the rest of us occupied most of the third floor of the hotel. We especially enjoyed the trips to and from the yacht at low tide. The skiff could only take us so far before we had to get out and walk the rest of the way to the shore. Most of the guys had to give their wives piggyback rides through the freezing water to the beach. It was a pretty funny sight, and it made for some great memories.

A couple of days after we arrived home from the British Open, Payne and I flew to Springfield, Missouri, to pick up the children from camp. We stayed at our eighty-acre farm just outside of Springfield for a few days, and then Payne, Chelsea, Aaron, and I flew to Jackson Hole, Wyoming, for a family vacation. Payne had won a bid on the vacation package during a charity auction for cystic fibrosis. We had a great time white-water rafting, sightseeing at Yellowstone, relaxing, and just being together as a family.

Payne got cranked up early for the Ryder Cup competition. He was so excited to be a part of the U.S. team again! After a practice round with team members Justin Leonard, Davis Love III, and Tom Lehman, Payne told the media, "I'm tired of us losing. I haven't been on a team in six years," Payne said. "You better believe I'll be flag-waving."

Tom Lehman couldn't keep from smiling. "He wears his feelings right there on his sleeve for all the world to see," Tom said. "Payne's a fantastic teammate and partner. If you have a problem being excited about what's going on when you're around him, you have a real problem!"

The European team was captained by Ryder Cup veteran Mark James. Miguel Angel Jiménez, José Maria Olazábal, Jesper Parnevik, Paul Lawrie, Sergio Garcia, Lee Westwood, Jean Van de Velde, Darren Clarke, Andrew Coltart, Padraig Harrington, Jarmo Sandelin, and the European stalwart, Colin Montgomerie, were intent on retaining the cup.

The U.S. team, led by captain Ben Crenshaw, was chock-full of talent, including Payne, Tiger Woods, Phil Mickelson, Jim Furyk, Mark O'Meara, Steve Pate, David Duval, Hal Sutton, Jeff Maggert, Tom Lehman, Davis Love III, and Justin Leonard. More than sheer ability, however, the team had an incredible sense of camaraderie. Payne suggested to Ben Crenshaw that the U.S. team play Ping-Pong at night in the team room to help relieve the stress and bond them as teammates. Ben liked the idea. "Payne was right. It was very tense up there," he said later, "so the Ping-Pong provided a nice little release." Personal egos and achievements became secondary, and the guys truly melded as a team. The attitude of the players was "I'll do whatever it takes."

It soon became apparent that it was going to take that sort of attitude, and more, to win back the Cup. The Europeans streaked ahead of the U.S. team during the Friday and Saturday match play. By Saturday night they had a commanding 10-6 lead, and European star Colin Montgomerie sent word to the press, declaring, "You know we've won, don't you?"

But Colin, like many in the raucous Ryder Cup crowd, underestimated the determination of the U.S. team. Ben Crenshaw surprised everybody, when at the conclusion of a dicey interview on Saturday with his team deeply in a hole, he said, "I'll leave you with this. I am a strong believer in fate, and I have a good feeling about this." In an impassioned plea at the emotionally charged U.S. team meeting on Saturday night, Payne told the players, "Let's not let them embarrass us again!"

When the U.S. team showed up for singles matches at The Country Club on Sunday, they were wearing matching golf shirts emblazoned with pictures of former Ryder Cup winning teams. The Americans were brimming with determination, even though they faced the largest deficit any team ever had to overcome in the Ryder Cup's seventy-two-year history. Tom Lehman got things going with an emotionally charged victory over Lee Westwood, 3 & 2. Hal Sutton, who had played in two previous Ryder Cups but had not played in a Ryder Cup match since 1987, was awesome. The leading scorer for the Americans with 3½ points, Hal sent Darren Clarke packing, 4 & 2. Much like Payne, playing for pride was plenty of motivation for Hal. He and Payne had known each other for a long time, their lockers in close proximity to each other on Tour, but the 1999 Ryder Cup brought them closer together as friends. Close in age to Payne and having come out on Tour around the same time, Hal had traveled some rocky paths in his career. By 1999, he was back on top, playing better than ever, and nobody was happier for Hal than Payne.

Phil Mickelson, Davis Love III, Tiger Woods, and David Duval all won their singles matches as the American team fought from behind. The score was now U.S. 12–Europe 10, but of the six matches still on the course, the U.S. was down in four of them. Mark O'Meara was even with Padraig Harrington, and Justin Leonard was behind in his crucial match with José Maria Olazábal. Playing just behind them, Payne was battling Europe's lion-hearted Colin Montgomerie in what would become one of the most notorious Ryder Cup matches in recent history, not simply for the great playing, but because of the rowdy Brookline crowds. The crowds repeatedly taunted Colin, jeering at him and hurling insults in his direction; the behavior was abominable by any standards.

Payne was ashamed of the conduct of a few American spectators, so he asked the Ryder Cup officials to remove several of the worst offenders from the premises, which they did. Nobody on either side of the Atlantic approached Ryder Cup play any more passionately than Payne, but it was important to him that the Americans conduct themselves with good sportsmanship, regardless of the outcome. Payne later explained, "We had numerous instances of heckling in the gallery; we had a couple of people removed. I appreciate the gallery that we had here, but it's a golf event for pride and honor. You have to understand that it's not life and death.

"On the fifth fairway, I said, 'Colin, if you have a problem, I will take care of it. This is not what it's about. Some of our fans are out of control and not appropriate.' I told him that I would have security or whatever take care of it. . . . I wasn't going to let the fans be out of control and influence one of his shots because of the heckling. I think he respected that from me."

Mark O'Meara lost his point to Padraig Harrington, but Steve Pate won his match against Miguel Angel Jiménez. The attention now centered on Justin Leonard and José Maria Olazábal on the seventeenth. Justin had willed his way back to being all square. The United States now needed only a half point to win the Cup back because Jim Furyk had closed out Sergio Garcia 4 & 3. The American players gathered around the green to watch Justin, who was lining up a monstrous 45-foot putt. Justin struck the ball solidly. The putt raced up the slope, suddenly disappearing into the hole!

The roar that went up from the crowd was deafening. Payne and Colin were standing in the middle of the seventeenth fairway. What they saw was one of the most memorable sights in sports history—although, admittedly, not the most sportsmanlike—as the American players, wives, and friends spontaneously spilled out onto the green. Supercharged with emotion upon seeing the putt drop, Justin instinctively raced to the left side of the green, an action not unlike many other emotional responses throughout the matches. In their chaotic attempt to congratulate him, the fired-up U.S. players chased after him, onto the green, with the photographers and TV camera operators hurrying right behind. The celebration contin-ued until somebody must have realized, Ooops! José still has to putt! We haven't won this thing yet.

José Maria Olazábal is one of the best putters in the world, and although he was facing a tough 40-footer himself, everyone recognized that if it could happen once, it could just as easily happen again. Understandably, José took several minutes to line up his putt. When he finally putted and missed, the victory celebration began for real! Captain Ben Crenshaw knelt down and kissed the green.

Meanwhile, standing back in the fairway, Payne realized that the U.S. had won the Ryder Cup even though his match with Colin Montgomerie was not yet over. They continued to play out the hole, although to Payne it seemed meaningless. If he had had a choice, he would have just ended their match right there on the seventeenth. We had won back the Ryder Cup, so his goal was already accomplished, and he was ready to celebrate with his teammates and the rest of the country. Payne and Colin were still even after 17 holes, and as they walked off the seventeenth green, Payne looked over toward Colin with a quizzical look as if to say, "Do we have to play the last hole?" They continued on and played the eighteenth hole.

As Colin prepared to line up his 20-foot birdie putt, Payne walked over, picked up Colin's ball, walked across to Colin, and handed it to him, conceding the putt and the match 1 up. It was an extremely gracious act on Payne's part, but it didn't really matter to anyone except Colin because the U.S. team had already won the Ryder Cup. To Payne, that's what it was all about, not his individual win-loss record. When Colin realized what Payne was doing, he smiled and started applauding before Payne got halfway across the green with his ball. It was a class act all around.

The celebration moved to The Country Club's clubhouse, where the U.S. team, almost giddy with joy, stood on the bell tower overlooking the area and sprayed spectators and each other with champagne. All of the guys, especially Payne, credited Ben Crenshaw with the team's success. Davis Love III summed it up, "It's all because of Ben Crenshaw. He fired us up and made us believe we could do it." Tiger Woods agreed. "We won it for Ben." Later that night, the celebration continued as many of the players and wives gathered in the team room at the hotel where we were staying. Before long, Payne, dressed in chili-pepper pants and a peach T-shirt, was dancing on top of the piano, leading the cheers and the songs. It was an incredible night.

As things calmed down a bit, Payne and Hal Sutton struck up a conversation. A successful horse breeder, Hal invited Payne down to his ranch in Louisiana. "You know, Hal, I don't like horses that much, but I'm going to come to your place and ride a horse," Payne promised. They laughed, told stories, and shared special memories of the Ryder Cup matches for more than an hour. Payne said, "Hal, I know one or both of us will be the captain of the Ryder Cup team one day. But if I'm ever selected as the captain, then I want you and Paul Azinger to be my assistant captains." Hal heartily agreed, knowing that other than winning the British Open, the only goal Payne had yet to reach was to be a Ryder Cup captain.

The party slowly reached ebb tide, but Payne didn't want to leave. He was enjoying it too much, even though I could see his head nodding and his eyes struggling to stay open. Finally, as he nearly drifted off to sleep in the chair, I said, "Come on, Payne. It's time to go to bed." Reluctantly, he let me help him back to our room. "Tracey," he said as he crawled into bed, "this completes my year."

On October 15, Payne was presented with the first annual Legacy Award by the First Orlando Foundation, a community service ministry affiliated with First Baptist Church. The award honors someone whose life is an example of giving back to the community. At the banquet that evening, Randall James, president of the First Orlando Foundation, announced publicly that Payne and I had committed to donate $500,000 to The First Academy to help build a sports complex at the school. Prior to the public announcement, Payne and I had hosted a barbecue at our home, where we informed some of our friends of our intentions to help with the sports facility. Many of them got excited about it, as well, and before the night was over, we had commitments of another $700,000 toward the project.

At the Legacy Awards dinner, Payne was asked to say a few words following the presentation. His voice cracked with emotion as he said, "I think that we all have something in common in that we have dreams. And the thing about dreams is that sometimes you get to live them out. I've always dreamed about playing golf for a living. And here I am living out my dream.

"It's pretty special. I've accomplished quite a bit in my career, and this year has been extremely special, but really what excites me, probably as much as winning, is being able to make a difference in people's lives. Tracey and I and our children have started this foundation [the Stewart Family Foundation], and through it, and through TFA and First Orlando Foundation, we are making a difference in people's lives.

"It's not that hard to give something back. I've been blessed with an ability; I think God chose me to play golf, and I use that podium; I use the golf course to give him the praise that he deserves and to make a difference in people's lives . . . so it's not that hard to give a little bit back."

It was the middle of October. Payne was scheduled to play in the Walt Disney World National Car Rental Classic the following week. Then Payne was going to Houston for the Tour Championship, then on to Valderrama in Spain for the American Express Championship. Payne was scheduled to play in the Grand Slam in Hawaii and then the Skins Game in Palm Springs. After that, we planned to take a couple of months off and just enjoy being together as a family. We could not have imagined the turns our lives were about to take.

26

My Soul Mate
Forever

The phone rang incessantly the week of the Walt Disney Classic. As always, our family was going to be busy that weekend. Chelsea had a volleyball game in Vero Beach on Friday night. Aaron had a football game on Saturday, and of course, Payne was scheduled to play golf, assuming he made the cut. Since he had only missed three cuts all year—one of which had been at Memphis when he had been focused on Pinehurst—it was a good bet that he'd be playing on Saturday and Sunday. On Monday, he was scheduled to play in a "Champions for Children" charity event at Bay Hill for the Arnold Palmer Hospital for Children and Women, an event that Arnold hosted and which we had supported for several years. Our friends Scott Hoch, Mark O'Meara, and Lee Janzen were also committed to play in the charity pro-am.

It had already been an eventful week. During a rain delay in the tournament on Thursday, Payne was having fun with an interview when he was asked about the derogatory comments made by British golf commentator Peter Alliss in regard to the American Ryder Cup team. Still bristling over the mayhem that had taken place on the seventeenth green, Alliss had told the *Daily Telegraph*, "Americans are totally different to us. They might as well be Chinese." Payne couldn't resist firing a volley back across the sea. Clearly jesting, Payne squinted his eyes and attempted to talk in broken English with a Chinese accent as he said, "I just want Peter Alliss to know that all of us American golfers on the Ryder Cup team, we are Chinese too. Thank you very much."

Almost immediately, Payne's comments were blown out of proportion, giving the impression that he was insensitive to Chinese racial issues. It was ironic and almost funny that the media would say that about Payne, who began his golfing career by playing two years in Southeast Asia. Nevertheless, Payne apologized rather than allowing the flap to escalate.

When I heard the news on Thursday night, I just wanted to shake him! I said, "Payne, you can't say such things!"

"Well, whatever happened to freedom of speech in this country?" he protested.

"Payne, the media doesn't have a sense of humor."

Payne missed the cut on Friday at Disney. That was unusual because he had played those courses so many times, but he really wasn't concerned; his sights were already focused on the Tour Championship, a tournament in which the top thirty money winners of 1999 would be competing a week later in Houston. Besides, the last time he had missed a cut was in Memphis, the week before the U.S. Open. Payne seemed almost happy that he had missed the cut because having Saturday and Sunday free gave him the opportunity to go to Aaron's football game, which Payne loved to do. It also allowed a little extra time to pack for his trips to Houston and Spain.

After his round on Friday, Payne was much more mellow with the media. Toward the end of an interview, he said, "I set some goals this year. I always set them very high at the start of the year, and this is the first year that I've achieved all the goals that I set."

After Payne left to play golf on Friday, I

left to meet Chelsea at school to go to her volleyball game in Vero Beach. Meanwhile, Leader Enterprises was working on a trip for Payne on Monday. Cindy Lisk had called and faxed concerning the possibility of a trip to Dallas to explore a prospective site for a golf course design project. The plans had not been finalized until late Friday afternoon. When I talked to Payne by phone on the way back from the game, he told me he had missed the cut, but he didn't mention the trip to Dallas.

It was very late by the time we got home that night, and Payne was already in bed, so we didn't discuss his travel plans. As far as I knew, Payne had kept the entire weekend open for the tournament at Disney and was still planning on playing at Bay Hill in the charity tournament on Monday.

Since he wasn't playing at Disney, Payne, Chelsea, and I went to Aaron's football game on Saturday morning. Mark and Alicia O'Meara's son, Shaun, was playing in the game prior to Aaron's. Mark, like Payne, had missed the cut at Disney that weekend, making it look suspiciously like they had done so on purpose so they could attend their boys' football games. The guys didn't mind. They were delighted to have the day off.

Aaron caught a touchdown pass during his

game, and Payne went wild. "Way to go, Aaron!" Payne shouted. "Wooooo-weeee! That's my boy!" Kenny Williams and his family were at the game that day, as well, because Kenny's daughter, Kimmy, is a cheerleader for Aaron's team. Kenny caught Aaron's touchdown on videotape.

After the game, we went to lunch and then went by the Christian bookstore because Chelsea needed some items for a school project. We stopped and bought some stone crabs for dinner that night and then dropped Aaron off at his friend Connor's house, where he was spending the night. My mum and dad were visiting with us, so we sat down and spent a lovely evening together just talking. Payne repeated to my parents what he had told the reporters at Disney. "I'm having a hard time getting excited about playing right now. I don't really have any desire to play the rest of the year because I've already done everything I set out to do this year. I've won a tournament, I've won a major, I made the Ryder Cup team and we won—I'd just as soon stay home the rest of the year. But I have obligations; I've already committed to a couple more tournaments through the Skins Game. Then I'm going to take December and January off. That worked pretty well for me last year, so that's what I'm going to do again."

I listened as Payne kept emphasizing that he wanted to stay home to be with the kids and me. It wasn't anything that I hadn't heard him say before, but it seemed to be more important to him than ever before. Mum and Dad listened intently, as well, and agreed wholeheartedly with Payne's plan. It was extremely late by the time we got to bed, so we slept in on Sunday morning.

Later that day, Payne went over to Isleworth to practice, and I enjoyed a leisurely afternoon at home. Payne picked up Aaron on the way home, and by the time we had dinner, it was time to start packing for his two-week trip. Payne needed ten outfits for the tournaments, plus his casual clothes. I was planning to meet him in Houston on Sunday, so I didn't need to pack until later.

It wasn't until late Saturday evening that Payne first mentioned that he was going to Dallas on Monday rather than playing at Bay Hill. He had been talking for several weeks with Charlie Adams, an old friend and former captain of the college golf team at SMU, about becoming involved in a golf course design project in the Dallas area. Charlie was involved with Jeff Blackard, the developer in Dallas, who held the land on which the prospective golf course might be built. They wanted Payne and representatives from Leader Enterprises to come to Dallas to look over the property.

Payne had been involved in one other golf course design project in California, at Coyote Hills, a 6,700-yard, par-71 course in Anaheim Hills. He had enjoyed the project and hoped to help design more courses, but it wasn't something in which he wanted to become immersed. Jack Nicklaus had confided to Payne that golf course designing took him away from home much more than playing golf on the Tour. That was all that Payne needed to hear. He was delighted to be a consultant on the design work, but he didn't want to be sidetracked from his game. He decided that he could be involved in no more than two golf course designs per year. Payne and Leader Enterprises had been toying with ideas concerning possible courses in Central Florida and Kentucky when the project in Dallas suddenly moved to the forefront.

The developers had wanted Payne and Van Ardan of Leader to make the trip to Dallas for some time. It had just never worked out conveniently with Payne's schedule. But because he was due to play in Houston at the Tour Championship, the Monday visit to Dallas seemed the best chance they'd have to get everyone together. Robert Fraley decided that he would go along on the trip because he wanted to spend some time with Payne.

Payne hated reneging on his commitment to play in the Monday charity tournament. Anyone who knew him could attest that when Payne gave his word, it was golden. You could count on him to follow through with what he said he would do. Payne always said, "Winners make commitments; losers make promises."

Payne called Scott Hoch and spoke to Sally, Scott's wife, and informed her that he would have to withdraw from the pro-am. Sally took the message, and said that Scott would likely want to call him back.

"That's fine," said Payne, "but I really don't have much choice on this one. I've got to go."

When Scott heard that Payne wasn't going to be playing on Monday, he was upset, but he understood. He knew that sometimes schedules changed on the spur of the moment, but he was puzzled nonetheless. It was so uncharacteristic of Payne to back out of a commitment—especially one in which Arnold Palmer was involved. It didn't sit well with Scott. Or with me, for that matter.

Originally, the group planned to take a commercial flight, but both Robert and Payne preferred to fly privately because they felt it was safer. Leader was exploring this speculative project, so Cindy contacted Sunjet, an Orlando aviation company from whom Leader had previously chartered aircraft. Payne had just re-signed a contract with Business Jet Solutions, the company with which he had flown since 1996. Robert was concerned that Leader was taking advantage of Payne's generosity by taking his plane, however, and he knew that Payne would not let him pay for the flight. He didn't want Payne to absorb the expense, so it was settled; they would take a plane chartered by Leader.

On Monday morning, October 25, 1999, we got up early because I had a doctor's appointment and Payne wanted to make the children their breakfast and say good-bye to them before they went to school. Payne made pancakes for Aaron, Chelsea, and me, and then it was time to go. Payne and I hugged and kissed good-bye. "I love you," Payne called after me as the children and I backed out of the garage, around 7:30 a.m. As we waved good-bye, Payne stood on the steps blowing us kisses.

Van Ardan picked up Payne shortly after eight, and together they drove to Orlando International Airport. Dixie dropped off Robert shortly after Van and Payne had arrived. The pilot scheduled for this flight was not the pilot with whom Robert had flown previously. Paul Watkins, the pilot Robert preferred, was unavailable, but Leader was assured by Sunjet that Michael Kling, a former U.S. Air Force pilot, was fully qualified. The copilot for the trip was twenty-seven-year-old Stephanie Bellegarrigue, who had amassed 1,700 flight hours and held a commercial pilot's license.

Bruce Borland, a golf course designer employed by Jack Nicklaus, and known as one of the first course designers to employ the use of high-tech computer graphics in his designs, was also meeting the group at the Orlando airport. Bruce had planned to fly commercially, but simply for convenience, Jeff Blackard had encouraged him to meet the Leader group and travel together aboard the Lear.

Earlier that morning, the plane had flown from the small executive airport in Sanford, outside Orlando, to Orlando International, where the guys had already gathered and were ready to go. They were running about fifteen minutes early. At approximately 8:55 A.M., Van called Cindy and instructed her to inform the people meeting them in Dallas that they were departing early, and the pick-up time should be bumped ahead thirty minutes. At 9:19 A.M., the plane took off from Orlando and streaked toward Ocala, Florida, where, according to its flight plan, the Lear was scheduled to veer westward toward Dallas.

The plane never made the turn. Instead it kept going, higher and higher—nearly nine miles high at one point—and straight ahead. About fourteen minutes into the trip, air traffic controllers lost contact with the jet.

At around 11:15 A.M., Cindy Lisk was preparing to make a sandwich for an early lunch in the Leader Enterprises snack room, when she heard a page on the office intercom system. She returned to her office and picked up the phone. The director of operations of Sunjet Aviation was on the line for her. "We have a problem with the plane," the representative said simply.

Cindy's first thought was that it was a logistical problem. She had spent most of the previous Friday afternoon on the phone with Sunjet, working out the details of the flight. At 5:00 P.M. on Friday, a representative from Sunjet had called and said, "We're sorry, but the plane we had scheduled for you has to go in for routine maintenance." It was improbable, at that late hour, to contact another company, secure credit approvals, and work out all the contract details. Chartering a Learjet is not exactly as simple as renting a car at the airport. "What am I supposed to do now?" Cindy asked the representative from Sunjet. "Do you have another company you can recommend and help us with the arrangements?"

"Let me check and I'll call you back."

Fifteen minutes later, the Sunjet rep had called back. "Don't worry, we found another plane. You're set to go."

Whew! I'm sure glad they worked that out, thought Cindy, as she began sending out the new plane's tail number to Robert and the other passengers.

Naturally, now when the Sunjet director of operations called Cindy on Monday morning and informed her of a problem with the plane, she assumed he meant that they'd had a problem making connections with the flights. Following the day in Dallas, Robert, Van, and Payne were to fly on to Houston, where Payne was to play in the tournament. After spending the night in Houston, Robert was to travel on to Los Angeles to meet with Frank Thomas, and then to Seattle to see Cortez Kennedy, both other Leader clients. Van planned to return to Orlando. With all the logistics, Cindy wasn't surprised that she had encountered another problem.

"What do you mean we have a problem with the plane?" Cindy asked.

"We've lost contact with the plane," the representative said.

Cindy felt a lump leap into her throat. "Has the plane crashed?" Cindy forced herself to ask.

"No, we've just lost radio communication," the Sunjet representative said. The impression he gave Cindy was that it was simply a radio problem. That news comforted Cindy somewhat, allowing her to compose herself and gather her faculties.

"What are you doing about the problem?" Cindy asked bluntly. The manager said that they were continuing to radio the plane, that the Federal Aviation Administration had been notified, and as soon as he knew any more information, he'd call back. As Cindy put the phone down, the thought struck her that in fifteen years of booking Robert's travel, they had never before received a phone call alerting them to a communications problem.

Just then, Cindy heard another page. She picked up her phone again and Leader's loyal receptionist, Rose Marie D'Aiuto, said, "Cindy, Tracey Stewart is on the line for you."

✦ ✦ ✦

I had just returned from an appointment with Kenny Williams, at the property we own at Isleworth, when Gloria Baker, Payne's and my administrative assistant, who worked in our home office, received a call from Dick Christoph, an SMU friend living in Chicago. "What's going on?" Dick wanted to know. "Why are there Air Force F-16s tailing Payne's plane?"

At first, Gloria thought it was a joke. After all, the military loved Payne, raved about his patriotism, and appreciated his many appearances at military bases and his special efforts aboard the aircraft carrier *George Washington*. Ever since Payne's flight in the F-14 fighter jet, he and Commander Carroll had been trying to find an opportunity for Payne to fly with the Blue Angels jet pilots. Gloria knew of Payne's desire and thought, Maybe this is some sort of joke and the military is giving Payne a taste of what it is like to fly together in formation. Maybe there's some sort of colossal prank going on in the sky.

As I walked into the office, carrying a bundle of items from the car, Gloria was still on the phone, and I noticed that she had a look of consternation on her face. I looked at her and she sort of shrugged, so I waited until she put down the phone. "Well, that was a weird call," she said.

"Why, what do you mean?"

"Well . . . it was Dick Christoph, from Chicago . . . saying that, um, some F-16 fighter jets are following Payne's plane."

"That can't be right," I said. "Payne would have been in Dallas over an hour ago." I walked across the room, called Payne's cell phone, and listened while his familiar, whimsical message played through. "Hi! You've reached Payne Stewart's phone. He's not with it right now, . . . but if you leave a message, I'll tell him you called." I left him a message. "Payne, we're hearing some strange things. Call me as soon as you get this message." As I hung up the phone, it rang again. It was Barry Snyder, calling from Pittsburgh, and he was saying the same thing as Dick Christoph. "What's going on?" Barry wanted to know.

"Barry, where are you hearing this?" I asked.

"Well, it's on television right now," Barry said. I turned on the television in our office and started flipping through the channels until I found the newscast that Barry had described. Gloria and I stood in the middle of the room watching as Fox News Network followed the route of Payne's plane across the country. I called Cindy Lisk at Leader. Rose Marie paged her immediately.

By the time Cindy came on the line, I had been watching the eerie reports on the television newscast. "Cindy, tell me what's going on," I said, trying to remain calm and stifle the tears that were already forming in my eyes.

"I wish I could," said Cindy, "but I can't. All I know is that the plane is still in the air."

There was nothing we could do but stand and watch and pray. Gloria and I clung to each other in front of the office television, hanging on every word, scouring every map they put on the screen, hoping for any sign that the plane might have changed course, watching the graphics that were being displayed. We soon learned that two F-16 fighter jets had indeed been deployed in an attempt to make contact with the Lear 35 when it had veered off course about twenty minutes into the flight, some-where above Gainesville, Florida. The report was that the pilots were incapacitated and the F-16s were possibly going to try to tip the wings in an attempt to wake them up.

At first, I felt that everything was going to be OK. After all, Payne had been flying in planes for years and last year had been in the F-14. And even if there were some problem in the cockpit, there were four very intelligent men in the cabin, any one of whom might be able to bring the plane down if adequately coached.

And yet I also realized that if the guys aboard the plane didn't wake up soon, a Lear 35 can only go so far before it runs out of fuel. They had already been flying since around nine that morning. I knew they couldn't go much farther.

By now, Jon Brendle had arrived at the house. I said aloud to Jon, but more to myself, "They're going to run out of fuel." I didn't want to believe this was happening. I was numb and confused. The phones were now ringing incessantly. I went outside, sat down on the steps, where I cried . . . and prayed.

My friends Annalisa Gutierrez, Vivienne Silverton, and Alicia O'Meara came to the house as soon as they heard the news. Their faces said more than words could convey. I knew that hope was gone. Kenny Williams stood by, keeping a silent vigil. Kelly Crofoot and Sally Hoch arrived next. After that, my mind was a blur. Upon hearing the news in Germany, my friend Natasha Woodbridge immediately made plans to return to Orlando to be with me, as did my brother and sisters in Australia.

Although we didn't know it at the time, the U.S. F-16 fighter jets following the plane got within fifty feet of the Lear. They edged closer to the Lear, but couldn't see anyone moving inside the plane. Captain Hamilton said later, "It's a very helpless feeling to pull up alongside another aircraft and realize the people inside that aircraft are potentially unconscious or in some other way incapacitated. And there's nothing I can do physically from my aircraft, even though I'm fifty to one hundred feet away." The F-16s got close, checking on both sides for structural damage to the Sunjet aircraft and finding none. Nor did the Air Force pilots see any broken doors or windows, or cracks that might have caused what experts quickly assumed was a deadly decompression inside the Lear. Despite the close proximity of the F-16, the Lear did not alter its course in any way.

For more than four hours, and fourteen hundred miles, the plane streaked across America with nobody touching the controls. About 1:16 P.M., EST, the $2.5 million, high-performance jet aircraft apparently ran out of fuel and spiraled from the sky at nearly the speed of sound. The Learjet carrying my husband, two of our dearest friends, a trusted business associate, and two pilots, plummeted into a field near Mina, South Dakota. The jet hit the earth at about six hundred miles per hour, blowing a hole in the ground about forty feet wide and ten to fourteen feet deep. My soul

414

mate, my best friend, the father of my children, was gone.

I asked Jon Brendle to go pick up Aaron and Chelsea at school, and then I went upstairs to Payne's and my bedroom and closed the door.

27

A Date in
Heaven

At The First Academy, Aaron and Chelsea were called out of class and taken to the office of Larry Taylor, the middle school headmaster. The school officials wisely decided not to tell the children anything further until I had a chance to talk with them. As they sat waiting out in the hall, they became more and more nervous. Ginger Millsaps, Chris's wife, works at the school, so she accompanied Aaron and Chelsea when Jon Brendle arrived to bring the children home. Together Jon and Ginger tried to explain, "There's been a problem with the plane that your dad is on, and your mom would like to have you home with her."

As Jon drove toward our house, Aaron

wanted to call Payne. "I can get Dad on the phone," Aaron said.

"No, Aaron," Chelsea said quietly.

"Dad always answers his cell phone," Aaron protested.

"Aaron, he won't answer," Chelsea said.

Jon and Ginger looked at each other knowingly. Nobody had told her the full details of what we were facing, but somehow in her heart, Chelsea may have already known that her daddy was gone.

When the children arrived home, I took them upstairs to Payne's and my bedroom, and in the most difficult moment of my life, I told them in simple, straightforward language, "The plane that Daddy, Robert, and Van were on has crashed." The children began screaming and burst into tears as I hugged them tightly to me. For a long while, we just sobbed uncontrollably together. "Daddy is in a better place," I told them. "He is in heaven."

As difficult as it was, I was honest with the children right from the beginning. I didn't want them to hear any grisly details from other kids, so I told them everything I knew about what had happened. I told them that from what we had heard on TV, it was likely that Payne and the others aboard the plane had not suffered long, agonizing deaths, that they had either been unconscious or had perished within seconds from a lack of oxygen after the plane had gone off course. I was equally as frank with the children when we began talking about the funeral arrangements.

At ages thirteen and ten, Chelsea and Aaron grasped the magnitude of the tragedy; but at first, Aaron didn't understand that there wouldn't be a body to bury, that he wouldn't be able to see his father again, not even in a casket in a funeral home. Aaron wanted to dress Payne in one of his favorite T-shirts in the casket.

"Let's dress Dad in his Jimmy Buffett T-shirt," he said. I tried to explain as delicately as possible that there really wouldn't be a body to dress but that we could still put the T-shirt into the gravesite, eventually.

I couldn't decide whether to have a coffin or not. At that point, local and federal investigators were still combing the crash site, and the early reports did not offer much hope of receiving any remains from the horrendously violent crash. I didn't want to give Aaron and Chelsea any false impressions, so to have a casket or not became a tough question for me to deal with.

Finally, I sat down and explained to Aaron and Chelsea, "We are going to have some kind of funeral service for your father, but we won't really have his body, so do you want to have a coffin?" Both Chelsea and Aaron responded, "If we don't have a body, don't have a coffin."

I said, "OK, we'll have a special memorial service for Daddy, and we can display some of our favorite pictures and we'll pick out some special items that he loved." The children actually dealt with it all better than I did, which made the decision easier for me.

The next few days were a blur. Within minutes after the tragedy was confirmed on television, our home began to fill with people—friends from the neighborhood and other PGA Tour players. Pastors Jim Henry and J. B. Collingsworth came and prayed with Chelsea, Aaron, and me, trying to help us find some meaning and consolation in the midst of such an overwhelming, shocking loss.

Knowing that we would be inundated by media and people offering their condolences, Kenny Williams immediately went to the front gate and controlled access to the house. Within an hour, fifteen news trucks, many complete with satellite dishes ready to beam any morsel of news to the world, had pulled in front of the gate. Kenny made them move across the road, allowing room for cars to enter. By nightfall, the number of media trucks lining the narrow lane in front of our home had risen to twenty-five. Kenny stayed at his post until 1:15 A.M. and was back by 5:30 A.M. He checked more than two hundred people through the gate that first afternoon and evening following the crash.

Two people who were absent on Monday afternoon were my mother and father, visiting from Australia. Both in their seventies, Mum and Dad rarely went to any Orlando attractions without Payne and me; but because they were planning to return home soon, they had wanted to go over to Epcot Center. They had spent the entire day at the theme park, and although Gloria Baker had them paged repeatedly, they never heard a word about the accident. On the way home, they stopped to get something to eat, and they bumped into my friend Kelly Crofoot and her family at a Boston Market restaurant. Kelly asked, "Have you been out all day?"

"Why, yes, we've had a lovely day," my mum answered. Kelly realized that they didn't know, so she waited outside until my parents had finished eating, and when she could speak with them privately, she told them the news. Kelly called Alicia O'Meara, who came and drove Mum and Dad home, ostensibly so they wouldn't have to deal with the media, but in reality because she knew they would be so shaken by the news.

Dixie Fraley and her mother, Dorry, were with the children and me upstairs in the bedroom. Although Dixie had lost her husband, Robert, in the accident, she had come to be together with us in our grief. Mum and Dad came in, and we all just clung to one another, bonded by our tears.

D. J. Snell, vice president of Leader, drove Mum, Aaron, Chelsea, and me, while Orel Hershiser and his wife, Jamie, drove Dixie and Dorry, over to see Debbie Ardan, Van's wife, now left to raise their four beautiful children alone. "We'll get by," we kept saying through our tears. "We'll get through this together." In her front yard, we all held hands in the dark, and I prayed for us all.

Over the next few days, J. B. Collingsworth and I discussed the myriad of details regarding the memorial service. PGA Tour Commissioner Tim Finchem came to our home and spent time working out the details with Jon Brendle so those PGA Tour players who wanted to could attend a memorial service planned for Friday. Business Jet Solutions offered to fly anybody we needed flown in from anywhere for the service. "Our entire fleet is at your disposal," they said. Their offer was especially generous in light of the negative publicity the company had received, with many people thinking that it had been Payne's plane that had crashed, rather than the Sunjet Aviation aircraft.

So many people pitched in to help during those days, I will never be able to thank them all. But God knows. Our many friends from school and church literally wrapped us in their love, praying for us constantly, lifting us up, bringing in food all day long, feeding the many people gathered at our home, cleaning up messes, running errands; they were truly a marvelous example of the Christian community in action.

On a fog-shrouded Thursday morning at the Tour Championship in Houston, where Payne was to have been playing, several hundred people gathered around the first tee for a brief ceremony in honor of Payne. The American flag and the Texas flag flew at half-mast, and a blue ribbon was tied around the parking place reserved for Payne in the players' lot.

A lone bagpiper dressed in Scottish apparel marched across the dew-covered grass as he played "Going Home," a traditional Scottish song about a man returning to his homeland. Tom Lehman spoke briefly but eloquently of Payne. With tears streaming down his face, Tom said, "He was a very emotional guy. He loved to laugh, and he was not ashamed to cry. I'm not going to be ashamed of my tears this morning, and neither should you. . . . Payne wore a little bracelet that said, W.W.J.D. on it," Tom reminded the crowd. "What Would Jesus Do? I think a lot has been made of this over the last couple of years; his life seemed very peaceful. I know how he lived his life trying to answer that question. What would Jesus do? And that's what Payne Stewart tried to do. I think we can all learn from that."

The lone bagpiper played "Amazing Grace," then turned and walked off into the fog as he again played "Going Home."

Payne's place in the tournament featuring the top thirty PGA Tour players of the year was not filled. Instead, Duffy Waldorf teed off by himself that morning. In another poignant tribute to Payne, Bob Estes teed off with his putter, purposely hitting the ball only fifteen feet, symbolic of Payne's 15-foot winning putt at Pinehurst. The gesture cost Bob a double-bogey on the hole.

On Thursday night, a number of the players gathered at our home in Orlando. I tried my best to greet everyone and receive their heartfelt expressions of sorrow. I found that it was easier if I kept busy, meeting people, introducing others, but every so often, my emotions got the better of me, and I had to slip away by myself for a while. Looking back, I know I was functioning in somewhat of a fog, running on sheer emotional energy.

At one point, Stuart Appleby asked me if he could possibly wear some of Payne's clothing on Sunday during the tournament. Stuart was quite familiar with grief, having lost his wife, Renay, in a tragic accident fifteen months earlier. Renay and I had been good friends, and I missed her terribly. Knowing that people express grief in various ways, I was touched by Stuart's gesture to honor Payne. Ian Baker Finch helped Stuart pick out an outfit from Payne's closet, including the knickers, hat, kneesocks, and shoes.

The memorial service in Orlando on Friday was incredible, with more than three thousand people attending, including more than one hundred PGA Tour players. On a table in front of the pulpit were family photographs chosen by Aaron and Chelsea, arranged around the words, "We love you, Dad. We will miss you." Also on display were the Wanamaker Trophy (the PGA Championship trophy), the U.S. Open trophy, and the Ryder Cup, on a rare leave from PGA of America headquarters. On one end of the table were Payne's Bible and a W.W.J.D. bracelet; on the other side were a pair of Payne's knickers, a pair of his golf shoes, and, oh yes, the hideous-looking false teeth over which nearly everyone in the church had shared a laugh with Payne at one time or another.

J. B. Collingsworth spoke glowingly of Payne. When Christian recording artist Michael W. Smith sang, "Friends are friends forever," it was almost as though Payne were speaking through the song. Another song, "Hey God," written and performed by Vince Gill, resonated with our hearts as well. Paul Azinger, Chuck Cook, Barry Snyder, and Todd Awe eulogized Payne. All of the guys painted a special picture of Payne, and Paul even managed to make us laugh by donning a tam-o'-shanter cap and rolling up his suit trousers to reveal a pair of argyle socks, imitating a look like Payne's knickers. Paul told funny stories about Payne, but he summed up the heart of the service when he said, "Payne Stewart has finished the race, he has kept the faith, and now the crown of righteousness is his. Payne Stewart loved life and loved people. . . . During this past year, everyone who knew Payne Stewart saw this dramatic change in his life. They saw in Payne what the Bible calls a 'peace which passes all understanding.' Only God can do that because only God can change a heart."

Paul then did one of the most courageous things he could have ever done. In front of his professional peers and millions of people watching on television, Paul said, "It is an honor to stand before you as Payne Stewart's, Robert Fraley's, and Van Ardan's friend. And because I knew them so well, I know what they would have wanted me to say in my closing remarks. Whoever you are, wherever you are, whatever you have done; if you feel the tug of God's Spirit on your heart, do not turn away. If, like Payne, Robert, and Van, you want to know the happiness and peace that only Jesus Christ can bring, I invite you to confess your sins and receive him as your Savior. Regardless of what your life has brought you, his love is enough. And his peace is for real.

"Because I knew these men, my life will never be the same. I am so thankful for their friendship, for their character, and their faith." Nearly overcome with emotion, Paul's voice cracked as he said, "Good-bye, Van . . . good-bye, Robert . . . good-bye, Payne. We love you and we miss you, but we know we will see you again."

Paul sat down, and I gathered my own emotions as I rose to speak to the crowd with my brother, Michael, at my side. I had felt compelled to speak at the memorial service. For eighteen years, I had always been content to stay in the background and let Payne do the talking. I turned down most interview requests and never allowed our children to be exposed to the onslaught of the public life, except for occasional photos in Payne's own publications. Now, however, I knew that I must speak up.

"I feel that I have been blessed by God," I told the crowd, "and I thank him for allowing me to share the last eighteen years of my life with Payne." Somehow, I felt sure that Payne was in heaven listening in, so I said, "I thank you, Payne, for telling me every single day of my life that you loved me. I knew it already, but it sure was good to hear you say it." Memories of our first meeting crossed my mind as I said, "I realize that even after eighteen years of marriage, Payne was still the most beautiful man I'd ever seen. Not because of the way he looked on the outside anymore, but because of what was on the inside.

"We shared laughter, tears, victories, and defeats. I admired your compassion for people and your talent that you were gifted with. You used it well. You were a friend to so many, and I thank you for the joy you brought us." I paused long enough to maintain my own composure, then said, "You will always be my soul mate and my best friend. You are the light of my life and my tower of strength. You'll live in my heart forever. We love you. . . ."

Earlier that day, several people had said that heaven was now a louder place because Payne was there. Payne's friend Terry Anton had quipped, "Payne is now playing on the 'Celestial Tour.'"

I agreed wholeheartedly, so I ended by saying, "Let the party in heaven begin!"

The memorial concluded on a jubilant note. Then came one of the longest walks of my life as the PGA Tour players formed an honor guard on both sides of the aisle for the family and me to walk through as we exited the sanctuary. Each face that I passed held a precious memory of Payne. W.W.J.D. bracelets, provided by Bobby Clampett and Jeff Blackard, were passed out to all in attendance. Many players put the bracelets on and wore them in the tournament the following day.

Back in Houston, the players continued to honor Payne, many of them actually wearing knickers provided by Tom Lehman. Stuart Appleby looked great, because of his resemblance to Payne, but all the guys looked special to my family and to me. We were deeply touched by the players' gestures.

Getting through the next several months was extremely difficult. Every few weeks, we encountered another emotionally charged event. First came our wedding anniversary and Chelsea's birthday in November. Then, of course, going through the first Thanksgiving and Christmas without Payne was stomach wrenching. With each day, however, God has given us strength to make it through. And I often recall Payne's own words of faith and hope.

Several years earlier, when asked in an interview how Paul Azinger's battle with cancer had affected him, Payne replied, "It put a different perspective on my life. All of a sudden, you know, golf isn't everything in my life. I have a beautiful family, a wonderful wife, and two lovely children. If, on the way home, something would happen, and I couldn't play golf again, . . . hey, I've had a wonderful career, but I want to spend the rest of my life with my family and raise them the best that I can and give them all the love that I can, and that's one thing that Paul taught me. Golf isn't everything, and when all of a sudden you have to look at life, and you know, God's going to call you home sometime, and . . . I'm going to a special place when I die, but I want to make sure that my life is special while I'm down here. When I'm done here, then my time's done."

Dixie Fraley, Debbie Ardan, and I drew even closer after the accident. I am continually amazed by their steadfast faith.

One day in early November, I received a phone call from Cindy at Leader. The National Transportation Safety Board had sent several boxes of items they had recovered from the crash site. Dixie, Debbie, and I gathered together in a room at Leader and went through the boxes. The jet had been almost obliterated upon impact, but several items survived the crash intact. Included were Payne's wedding ring; his SMU college ring; a gold pendant (he had worn this on a chain around his neck since the day after we got engaged in Singapore in 1981. I had it fixed and gave it to Aaron as a special gift from his dad for Christmas. Aaron has worn it every day since.); a few articles of his clothing; the face of his Rolex watch, which was part of his winner's prize at the first PGA Tour event he ever won; several mangled golf club heads; two jet fuel–stained golf devotional books given to Payne by Wally Armstrong; Payne's Scripture promise books that he had read the night before; and amazingly, the W.W.J.D. bracelet he was wearing at the time of the crash. It was as though God were saying, "Even in the midst of this tragedy, I will have a witness."

As I leafed through the devotional books, I came to the pages Payne would have read the night before the crash. I was astounded. The message of the Scripture was powerfully appropriate to Payne and what we were about to face:

INTERCESSION
Grant that I may be used to open the eyes of others and to turn them from darkness to light, and from the power of Satan to God, so that they may receive forgiveness of sins, and an inheritance among those who have been sanctified by faith in Jesus.

Acts 26:18

AFFIRMATION
Blessed is the man who perseveres under trial, because when he has been approved, he will receive the crown of life that God has promised to those who love him.

James 1:12

THANKSGIVING
Bless the Lord, O my soul;
And all that is within me, bless His holy
    name.
Bless the Lord, O my soul,
And forget not all His benefits;
Who forgives all your iniquities

And heals all your diseases;
Who redeems your life from the pit
And crowns you with love and compassion;
Who satisfies your desires with good
   things,
So that your youth is renewed like the
   eagle's.

Psalm 103:1–5

CLOSING PRAYER

The Lord is my rock and my fortress and
   my deliverer;
My God is my rock; I will take refuge in
   Him,
My shield and the horn of my salvation,
My stronghold and my refuge—
My Savior, You save me from violence.
I call on the Lord, who is worthy of praise,
And I am saved from my enemies.

2 Samuel 22:2–4

I still have days when I get discouraged.
Sometimes, I get depressed and think, It's not
fair! Millions of people have terrible marriages
and they're still together, and I had a wonderful
husband, whom I loved dearly, and I don't get
to spend the rest of my life with him. On the
other hand, I had eighteen wonderful years with
Payne, and those years were better than some

people experience during their entire lifetime. But it was still too short.

At times, dealing with the "why" questions can be similar to running on a treadmill. Why did Payne go on that Monday trip? Why did the awful tragedy have to happen just as it seemed he was beginning to have a deeper relationship with God, his family, and more of a "peace" in his relationships with competitors and peers? Yet I am aware that God has brought good out of the accident, turning what the enemy meant for evil into an occasion for many people to face their own need for a relationship with God. Inspirational stories abound of people who have been transformed as a result of the accident.

I see the good; I have heard of numerous people who have been won to Christ through our loss, and I'm honored that Payne, Robert, and Van had a part in the salvation of others. But I'd be less than honest if I didn't admit that I wish it wouldn't have cost such a high price.

That helps me understand a little how God must have felt the day his son died.

Most of the time, I recognize that God has done something incredible through this awful accident. I see that best through the lives of our children. For instance, for the past couple of years, Chelsea has been attending the annual

Valentine's Day Father-Daughter, Mother-Son "Date Night" banquet at The First Academy. In past years, when Payne was away on that weekend playing in a tournament, Robert Fraley stood in as her "date." This year, however, neither Payne nor Robert could be Chelsea's date, so our friend Jon Brendle accompanied her.

During the program that night, Larry Taylor, the headmaster of the middle school, said that one of the students' classmates had experienced a very difficult time this year. He introduced Chelsea to say a few words to the crowd of teenagers and parents.

Chelsea stood up, head erect, and walked to the stage and stood in front of the microphone. Chelsea began in a strong voice, "I can't have a date with my dad tonight, but I want to tell you some of the things that characterize my relationship with my father. First, my relationship with my dad was characterized by the love he had for my mother, for my brother, Aaron, and for me. He showed us on a daily basis how much he loved us. He told us he loved us; he played with us; he'd get up and make us pancakes for breakfast; he would drive us to school and other places; and he just carried on and made life fun, and we never for a moment had to wonder how much he loved us.

"Second, he got so involved in participat-

434

ing in our lives. He was interested in everything we were doing. Whenever we asked him to go out and shoot some baskets or to play catch, he dropped everything and came out to play." Chelsea painted a poignant picture of how Payne had played with her and Aaron and made a strong point that even though Payne had to travel a lot, he did not miss out on anything with his children.

Chelsea went on to tell about how Payne had attended her basketball, softball, and volleyball games. And then, looking at the crowd of parents and her peers, Chelsea said with a smile, "And you know how loud he was and how much he loved to scream and holler at the games." Then, almost with a sly look, Chelsea said, "But the best day was a few months ago, when he was asked to be a line judge at one of my volleyball games. For those of you who don't know, the line judge isn't allowed to say anything!"

Chelsea's conclusion blessed my heart more than words can say. Chelsea said, "I may not be able to have a date with my dad here tonight, but there's one thing I know for sure. And that is: I'll have a date with my daddy when I get to heaven."

Me too, Chelsea, me too!

On November 17, 1999, the PGA Tour created the "Payne Stewart Award" to be presented annually to the PGA Tour player who best represents the character, professionalism, community work, ability, generosity, and the ideals that Payne held dearly. The award will be voted upon by a panel selected by the PGA Tour Commissioner's office. The PGA Tour will also create a "First Tee" golf program for Kids Across America at Kamp Kanakuk in Missouri, in Payne's honor.

ABOUT THE AUTHORS

Tracey Stewart was born in Queensland, Australia, where she also attended school. She met Payne Stewart in March of 1980 during the Malaysian Open, in a meeting she describes as love at first sight. After romancing each other around the world, Payne and Tracey were engaged one year later in Singapore and married November 10, 1981, in Southport, on Australia's Gold Coast. As Payne's PGA career took off, the Stewarts moved to Orlando, Florida, where Tracey now lives with their two children, Chelsea and Aaron.

Ken Abraham is the author of over forty books including collaborations with professional golfer Paul Azinger on *Zinger!* and baseball All-Star catcher Gary Carter on *The Gamer*. Abraham currently resides in Franklin, Tennessee.

Walker & Company Large Print books
are available from your local bookstore.
Please ask for them.
If you want to receive a catalog of our titles,
send your name and address to:

Beth Walker
Walker & Company
435 Hudson Street
New York, New York 10014

Look for these latest Large Print titles from
Walker & Company

Boomerang Joy
Barbara Johnson

Enter His Gates
Charles Stanley

Fearfully and Wonderfully Made
Dr. Paul Brand & Philip Yancey

The Great House of God
Max Lucado

Home Town Tales
Philip Gulley

The Lady, Her Lover, and Her Lord
paperback edition
T. D. Jakes

When God Weeps
Joni Eareckson Tada & Steven Estes

Among the many other titles available are:

Abiding in Christ
Cynthia Heald

And the Angels Were Silent
Max Lucado

Apples of Gold
Jo Petty

The Best of Catherine Marshall
edited by Leonard LeSourd

The Bible Cure
Reginald Cherry, M.D.

The Blood
Benny Hinn

A Book of Angels
Sophy Burnham

Breakfast with Billy Graham

Brush of an Angel's Wing
Charlie W. Shedd

Christmas Stories for the Heart
compiled by Alice Gray

Death and the Life After
Billy Graham

Disappointment with God
Philip Yancey

Encourage Me
Charles Swindoll

Eternal Security
Charles Stanley

Experiencing God
Henry T. Blackaby & Claude V. King

Experiencing God Day-By-Day
Henry T. Blackaby & Richard Blackaby

15 Minutes Alone with God
Emilie Barnes

Finding God
Larry Crabb

Finding God in Unexpected Places
Philip Yancey

Footprints
Margaret Fishback Powers

Friends Through Thick & Thin
Gaither, Buchanan, Benson, MacKenzie